OPTIONS
ADVANCED ENGLISH
STUDENTS' BOOK

Michael Hinton and Robert Marsden

Nelson

Thomas Nelson and Sons Ltd
Nelson House   Mayfield Road
Walton-on-Thames   Surrey
KT12 5PL   UK

51 York Place
Edinburgh
EH1 3JD   UK

Thomas Nelson (Hong Kong) Ltd
Toppan Building 10/F
22A Westlands Road
Quarry Bay   Hong Kong

Distributed in Australia by

Thomas Nelson Australia
480 La Trobe Street
Melbourne   Victoria 3000
and in Sydney, Brisbane, Adelaide and Perth

ISBN 0-17-555570-2
NPN 9 8 7 6

Printed in Hong Kong

CONTENTS

INTRODUCTION

Options is a course for students of English at post-Cambridge First Certificate level. It can be used for both examination and non-examination classes alike, since it combines exercises in the Cambridge format with freer, more imaginative activities. The main aims of *Options* can be summed up as follows:

- to expose the student to contemporary written and spoken English in a variety of styles and contexts
- to isolate and practise the language elements that are most vital to the student who is approaching native-speaker competence, including idioms, vocabulary extension, language functions, pronunciation and intonation
- to provide situations in which these elements can and must be used

There are 15 units, each based on a topical theme, and each divided into three main sections, Reading and thinking, Listening and speaking, and Written work or Revision.

Reading and thinking
Reading comprehension

Each unit begins with one or two texts. These have been chosen carefully from a wide variety of sources to provide the student with examples of as many different styles of contemporary English as possible: there are extracts from novels, magazines, travel guides and brochures, advertisements, newspapers, official documents, and a play. Each text is followed by comprehension questions.

Words and structures

The main distinction between the intermediate student and the advanced student lies in the latter's ability to go beyond the bounds of traditional text-book, structure-orientated English, and to understand and use the idioms which form the native speaker's natural mode of expression. So here there are exercises that develop the student's command of idiomatic usage by focusing on the most useful idioms and items of vocabulary in the introductory texts, with excursions into related areas to extend the student's competence. Special emphasis is placed on the use of two-part verbs (grow up, hold up, etc).

The structure sections concentrate on a few important areas that often provide difficulties for students at this level, with emphasis on verbal constructions. It is assumed that the users of this book are fully familiar with the basic areas of English grammar.

Listening and speaking
Discussion and debate

A photograph provides the starting-point for a discussion around the main theme of the unit. This is developed further in group work and roleplay.

Listening comprehension

Realistic conversations, announcements, etc. are used as the basis for developing the student's ability to understand natural spoken English. In addition to answering comprehension questions about specific words and phrases, students are encouraged to make judgements about people's attitudes as expressed by intonation and stress. The conversations also provide examples of the main items practised in the two following sections: Functions and Reading aloud.

Functions

In this section students learn the type of language needed for language functions such as expressing relief, gratitude, excitement, and ignorance, or asking about someone else's attitudes. Conversational formulas and gambits are presented under three headings:

- Informal – phrases that are restricted to usage between friends and relatives
- Formal – phrases that should be used only in formal situations, such as business meetings
- General – phrases that lie somewhere between the two other categories, and are appropriate to the majority of everyday situations

Reading aloud

Here the aim is to improve the student's competence in spoken English, whether reading aloud or taking part in conversation. There are taped exercises in intonation, stress and pronunciation. Several exercises focus on the relationship between spelling and pronunciation.

Activity

Each unit contains one or two open-ended activities designed to

consolidate in a free and realistic context the various elements taught during the unit. Most of them take the form of games or role plays, and many are constructed in several stages involving all the four basic skills, reading, writing, speaking and listening; the activity in Unit 4, for example, requires the students to read a number of theatre reviews, discuss the relative merits of the plays described, write a scene from one of the plays, and act it out. Activities of this type are of special importance to students who live in a country where English is not the native language, and who consequently have little opportunity of using their English in natural surroundings.

Written work and Revision

Each unit has either a Written work section or a Revision section.

Written work

Here the emphasis is on 'connectives', i.e. words and phrases used to connect ideas together in such a way as to indicate the writer's attitude.

Revision

At the end of every second unit there are two or three exercises that revise the vocabulary and idioms presented in the two units. The first exercise is always a 'cloze' test of the type used in the Cambridge examination.

UNIT 1

HOMES

Reading and thinking
Reading comprehension (1)

Setting up home

When Fred Giffin bought his three-storey unconverted Victorian house under the GLC Home-
5 steading scheme, the property market was very different from what it is now.

'There were queues in estate agents' on Saturday mornings,'
10 recalls Fred, 'and competition between buyers was fierce.'

'All I wanted,' sighs Fred, 'was a house in Highbury, North London. As I am a decorator and
15 have got friends in the building trade, the condition of the property was unimportant. I was optimistic that I'd be able to convert almost anything.'
20 What Fred did not realise was the huge amount of money he would have to spend, and the time it would take. He and his wife Mercia and their three children
25 were due to move in six months after buying but they finally moved in eighteen months ago, and the house is still far from finished.
30 The back extension had to be demolished, and the whole house had to be replumbed and rewired, and fitted with new drains. Fred was also keen to restore original
35 features. 'I have seen so many

conversions,' he emphasises, 'where the builders rip out all the good bits – the shutters and pine doors – only to use cheap,
40 modern materials instead.' But knowing what's thrown out with the rubbish can be useful: he said that shutters make very good cupboard doors when cut into
45 three, and he rescued some old iron railings from his garden.

But Fred admits he was very ambitious. 'I was not interested in reselling the house at the time.
50 I was doing it up to keep, so I wanted the work done properly. If I'd been after a "builder's finish" the house would have been completed in half the time.'
55 He hired an architect and, because he is a perfectionist himself, wanted to find the right person for the right job. 'Because I am in the building trade
60 myself,' he explains, 'I am aware of the low standard of work, and I would advise anyone who needs a builder to try and see his work first. If his own house is decent
65 then it follows that his work should be of a similar standard.'

He asked a friend of his to estimate the work. Although it seemed a lot at the time, £25,000
70 was more or less correct. 'It's like

turning on a tap,' says Fred, 'when it comes to doing up old houses. You have no idea how much things are going to cost
75 until you start. I made a series of expensive mistakes – which I now regret.'

'I wanted to do things by the book,' he adds. 'I made sure that
80 all the walls were lined to eliminate dust and dirt. I restored cornices and put back fireplaces. But even now the kitchen still hasn't been decorated, and the
85 utility room hasn't been started.'

Asked about any future plans, Fred expressed a desire to move sometime. Although the house is convenient for public transport,
90 its proximity to Arsenal Stadium means a noisy Saturday after-noon. Given the choice again Fred would like to be in a quieter street, with a bigger garden, and
95 fewer rooms to decorate. With four years' work behind him, Fred is ready for a rest. 'You only learn the hard way,' he says, but his advice to anyone buying old
100 property is to have a healthy bank balance and lots of energy!

Buying and Improving your Home
August 1983

---

1 Which of the following statements are true and which are false? Put ticks (√) by the statements that are true and give reasons for your answers.

a The Giffins moved in six months after buying the house.

b Fred wanted to use cheap, modern materials.

c Fred probably cut up some shutters that had been thrown out.

d Fred always planned to sell the house later.

e It would have been possible to convert the house twice as quickly.

f Fred thinks that building work is usually of poor quality.

g It took four years to complete the conversion.

For questions 2 to 4 choose the phrase which best completes each sentence.

2 The property market has changed in that

a estate agents' now close on Saturday mornings.

b buyers used to fight each other fiercely.

c not so many people are interested in buying houses now.

d not so many people are interested in selling houses now.

3 The £25,000 estimate made by a friend

a was for the cost of the water supply.

b was an expensive mistake.

c made Fred regret his plans.

d was what the conversion actually cost in the end.

4 Fred wanted to do the conversion

a according to the instructions in a book.

b as thoroughly as possible.

c in the same way that a real builder would do it.

d in order to learn how to be a builder.

5 Write a summary explaining what, according to the article, were the advantages and disadvantages of buying this particular house.

Reading comprehension (2)

The Standard 12 August 1983

Here's what's inside a beautiful new home in Park Court, N.W.11.

A superb choice of apartments and maisonettes from £46,500 to £102,500.

You'll find Park Court quietly situated in Wellgarth Road, just off the North End Road, with Golders Green, N.W.11 at one end and Hampstead Heath at the other. Your first impression is of a stylish, modern design bordered by trees and shrubs. Now step inside and you'll find one, two and three bedroom apartments and two and three bedroom maisonettes that all meet the very highest standards of comfort and luxury. Wall to wall carpeting, fitted wardrobes, light airy lounges and dining areas, smart kitchens with panelled units, equipped with cooker, fridge and washing machine, bedrooms and bathrooms pleasantly decorated throughout. All ready and waiting for you to move in and enjoy. There's also a closed circuit TV entryphone security system, peep holes, door chain and private parking space.

Now just look what you'll find outside. Only 500 yards away is the shopping area of Golders Green with its excellent tube and bus connections. Nearby too is the famous shopping centre of Brent Cross. Then there's the whole of Hampstead Heath, Golders Hill Park with its Zoo not to mention all the amenities of Highgate and Hampstead with their golf courses, historic inns, shops and restaurants just a few minutes drive away. You couldn't hope for a finer new home than at Park Court, both inside and out.

And Barratt's generous Open Door Scheme makes the whole move all so easy. With 95% mortgages, subject to status. And by paying the Legal fees, Stamp Duty, Building Society or Bank survey fees and removal costs up to £200. And of course the unique Barratt House Exchange Plan can help you dispose of an existing home simply and economically.

Leases at Park Court are 109 years and prices range from £46,500 for a one bedroom apartment to £102,500 for a three bedroom maisonette.

Come and see the superbly furnished show apartments. They're open 7 days a week from 11 a.m. to 6 p.m. Or ring 01-455 8507 for more details. Once you've seen Park Court, you'll want to move in right away.

Trust Barratt, Britain's leading private housebuilder to help you.

What House HOUSEBUILDER OF THE YEAR Award Winner 1982/83

3 NEW SHOWHOUSES OPEN 7 days a week, 11 am-6 pm or telephone 01-455 8507 for details.

Barratt

*On mortgages, up to £25,000, net of basic rate tax and for houses reserved from 23rd June and subsequently contracted on or before 30th September 1983.

NHBC 10 year Protection

Barratt building houses to make homes in, on over 475 developments throughout Britain.
Barratt Central London Ltd., 1 Wilton Road, London SW1V 1LL. Tel: 01-630 5721.

MORTGAGE RATE HELD AT 10%* FOR 12 MONTHS.

1 What is meant by the following expressions?

  a just off the North End Road (line 2)

  b ... meet the very highest standards of comfort and luxury (line 8)

  c Wall-to-wall carpeting (line 10)

  d dining areas (line 11)

  e closed circuit TV (line 20)

  f peep holes (line 21)

  g excellent tube and·bus connections (line 28)

  h subject to status (line 39)

  i removal costs (line 41)

  j dispose of an existing home (line 44)

  k Leases ... are 109 years (line 47)

  l net of basic rate tax (line 61)

2 What features of the advertised homes make it simple to move in at once?

3 What atmosphere does the advertisement try to create? Look at phrases such as:
  You'll find ... (line 1)
  Your first impression ... (line 4)
  Now step inside (line 6)

  Can you find other phrases that have the same purpose?

What differences can you find between the Giffins' house (in text 1) and the homes in the advertisement (in text 2)?

Words and structures

IDIOMS

■ **Exercise 1**

Explain the meanings of these expressions as they are used in the texts.

Text 1:
a make (line 43)
b cut into three (line 44)
c doing it up (line 50)
d if I'd been after ... (line 52)
e when it comes to (line 72)

Text 2:
a move in (line 18)

b not to mention (line 31)
c right away (line 58)
d houses to make homes in (line 65)

■ **Exercise 2**
House and *home*

Make sure you know the meanings of these expressions. Make sentences to show how they are used.

a feel at home
b make oneself at home
c drive (an argument) home
d bring something home to someone
e to home in on
f home truth
g Home Rule
h home straight
i homecoming
j homeland
k homely
l homesick
m bring the house down
n like a house on fire
o safe as houses
p house-to-house
q on the house
r houseproud
s house-trained *cf potty-trained*
t house-warming
u household
v householder
w housekeeper
x housework

house ≠ building see below

Now choose the most appropriate expressions to fill the gaps in these sentences, making any necessary adjustments to verb forms.

1 I'd never realised how stupid it is to drink and drive until the accident _____.

2 The performance was hilarious, and the final sketch _____.

3 'How much does it cost?'
  'Nothing at all – it's _____.'

4 The party at the Millers' was fairly pleasant, but somehow I didn't really _____ there.

5 This is the last exercise. We're on the _____.

house theatre/jazz for audience

■ Exercise 3

Two-part verbs with *up*

setting up home (headline)
doing up old houses (line 72–3)

Fill each gap with the correct form of one of these verbs, followed by *up*:

break	look
catch	run
draw	set
give	shut
grow	work

Then explain with a word or phrase what each verb + *up* combination means.

Harold keeps *turning up*, like a bad penny. (Explanation: *appearing*)

1 _____ for a moment, will you? I can't hear myself think.

2 The committee's task was to _____ a new five-year plan.

3 There's nothing like physical labour to help you _____ an appetite.

4 I've managed to _____ a meeting between you and the ambassador for tonight.

5 The conference _____ at 2 o'clock this morning.

6 I'm determined to solve this problem; I refuse to _____.

7 He _____ an enormous bill at the Grand Hotel.

8 Falling in love is an essential part of _____.

9 I was ill at the beginning of term, so it may be difficult for me to _____.

10 You'll have to _____ any unusual expressions in the dictionary.

■ Exercise 4

Some combinations of verb + *up*, when hyphenated, are used as nouns. Match these *up* nouns with their definitions.

1 back-up	**a** adult
2 break-up	**b** delay
3 close-up	**c** disintegration
4 grown-up	**d** gramophone needle
5 hold-up	**e** organisation
6 knock-up	**f** parody
7 pick-up	**g** picture showing something in detail
8 send-up	**h** practice before a game of tennis
9 set-up	**i** review
10 shake-up	**j** reorganisation
11 stick-up	**k** robbery
12 write-up	**l** support

Now make a sentence for each *up* noun.

VOCABULARY

■ Exercise 5

Choose the word that best completes each sentence.

1 Now that you've finished school, you should go out and learn a proper _____.
a job **b** task **c** trade **d** work

2 Well done! You've done an excellent _____.
a job **b** task **c** trade **d** work

3 That shirt doesn't fit. You'll have to _____ it.
a alter **b** convert **c** refurbish **d** repair

4 We'll find the answer by a process of _____.
a demolition **b** destruction **c** disposal **d** elimination

5 I intend to _____ my house in London while I'm away.
a hire   **b** lend   **c** let   **d** rent

6 I'm glad I chose this part of town to live in. It's such a pleasant

_____.

a environment   **b** neighbourhood
c proximity   **d** surroundings

7 She was keen to _____ the house to its original condition.
a rebuild   **b** renew   **c** renovate
d restore

8 The Plaza Hotel has excellent _____ for conferences.
a amenities   **b** facilities
c features   **d** provisions

9 And now, I think, a visit to the theatre would provide a _____ climax to a wonderful evening.
a comfortable   **b** convenient
c fitting   **d** suitable

10 Do you prefer photographs with a matt or gloss _____?
a completion   **b** finish   **c** polish
d surface

STRUCTURES

Verbal constructions

One of the greatest problems for advanced students of English is the variety of grammatical constructions that can follow common verbs.

He asked me to go.
*(verb + object + **to** + infinitive)*
He made me go.
(verb + object + infinitive)
He saw me going.
(verb + object + gerund)
He remembered my going.
(verb + possessive adjective + gerund)
He suggested that I should go.
*(verb + **that** + clause)*

For every verb you must learn which constructions are possible.

■ **Exercise 6**

In the following sentences, only one of the four verbs can be used with the given construction. Choose the correct verb, and then make sentences of your own with the other three verbs by altering the construction.

I *like* going to the countryside.
a *hope*   **b** *like*   **c** *plan*   **d** *think*

I hope to go to the countryside.
I plan to go to the countryside.
I think (that) I'll go to the countryside.
I'm thinking of going ...

1 Could I _____ you in joining the Women's Guild?
a advise   **b** interest   **c** persuade
d suggest

2 They _____ the old man sit down.
a allowed   **b** decided   **c** let
d stopped

3 I _____ that I was ill.
a apologised   **b** explained   **c** hated
d wanted

4 We _____ Carolyn to arrive early.
a explained   **b** hoped   **c** promised
d suspected

5 She _____ to hand in the documents.
a believed   **b** considered   **c** failed
d succeeded

Listening and speaking
Discussion and debate

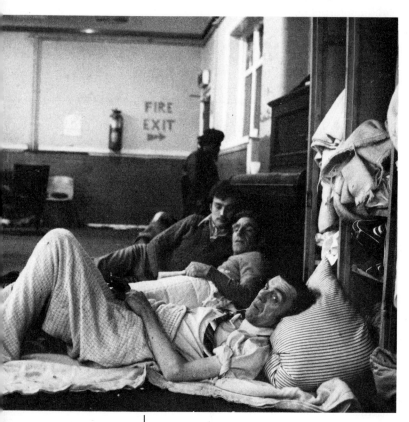

What sort of place do you think this is?
What kind of people are they?
Why are they here?
What would it be like to stay in this place?
What can be done to help people like this?
What sort of home do you live in?
How important is the place you live in?
Would you enjoy converting an old house in the way that Fred Giffin did?

■ Exercise 1

What do you find most important in a home? Rate each of the following features on a scale from 1 to 5, where 1 = absolutely essential and 5 = completely unnecessary. Discuss your answers with the rest of the class, and give your reasons if necessary.

central heating ☐
garage ☐
garden ☐
balcony ☐
fitted carpets ☐
double glazing ☐
running hot water ☐
refrigerator ☐
freezer ☐
smoke detector ☐
burglar alarm ☐
telephone ☐
television ☐
open fireplace ☐
bath ☐
shower ☐
sauna ☐
near shops ☐
near recreation facilities ☐
near countryside ☐
near public transport ☐
swimming-pool ☐
radio ☐
record-player/tape recorder ☐

■ Exercise 2

The following people have been chosen as representatives of various groups within society. They are taking part in a symposium on the future of housing, at the end of which it is hoped that a joint statement can be issued to influence the government in its allocation of resources.

the Minister of the Environment
the manager of a building society
a construction engineer
an architect
an estate agent
a shopkeeper
a farmer
a single parent
a physically handicapped person
a policeman/policewoman
a social worker
a headmaster/headmistress
an old-age pensioner
a student

Divide the roles amongst the members of the class and act out the symposium. One student must act as chairman.

Here are some questions for the symposium to consider. You may, of course, think of other questions to discuss.
- More state-owned housing?
- More high-rise blocks of flats?
- Residential areas separate from shops, offices, industry?
- More government grants for improving old houses?
- Priority for certain parts of the country?

Listening comprehension

You will hear five people talking to each other. The first time you listen to the conversation, write down the first names of all of Peter's guests and make a note of which people they have and haven't met before.

	name	knows	doesn't know
1			
2			
3			
4			

The second and subsequent times you listen to the conversation, fill in as much information as possible in the table and answer questions 1 and 2.

name	lives	job	interests	other information (e.g. family, plans)
Peter				

1 What were the exact words used in the conversation to express the following?
a It's possible that my son will be your pupil.
b They're restoring it now.
c Do you need any help?
d I didn't expect to see you here.
e I think I'll stay for a while.
f Excuse me for interrupting.

2 Describe what you know about Ann and Eileen's relationship. How does it differ from John and Eileen's relationship?

Function: greetings, introductions and leave-takings

The people at this party are greeting each other, introducing themselves and others, and saying goodbye. What exactly do you think they are saying? Fill in the bubbles.

■ **Exercise 1**

Use the tables to help you find suitable replies to these remarks.

1 Hello. I'm Hugh Jenkins.

2 How do you do?

3 How are you?

4 I trust you're keeping well.

5 How's life?

6 Allow me to introduce Mrs Perkins.

■ **Exercise 2**

What would you say in these situations?

1 Your host tries to introduce you to someone you have met before.

2 You're chatting to some friends in your home, when the telephone rings.

3 You're at a party being given by a business colleague you don't know very well. It's time for you to leave, because you have a train to catch.

4 You say goodbye to a fellow student whom you have just arranged to meet the following day.

Introducing yourself

General	
How do you do? My name's Jane. Hello. I'm Jane. Excuse me. I don't think we've met. My name's Jane.	How do you do? I'm Bob Richards. Hello. My name's Bob.
Informal Hi! I'm Jane. Hello! You must be Bob. I'm Jane.	Oh, hello! I'm Bob. Hello! I've heard a lot about you.
Formal *May I/Let me* introduce myself: Jane Higgins. Allow me to introduce myself: Jane Higgins.	How do you do? Pleased to meet you.

Introducing someone else

General		
This is Bob Robertson. Jane, I'd like you to meet Bob Robertson.	How do you do? Pleased to meet you.	How do you do?
Do you two know each other? Bob Robertson – Jane Higgins.	(No,) I don't think so. How do you do? (Yes,) we've already met, actually.	
Informal Bob, meet Jane. You don't know Bob, do you? Bob–Jane, Jane–Bob.	*Hi/Hello*, Bob. Hi, *good/nice* to meet you.	*Hi/Hello*, Jane.
Formal *I'd like to/Let me/Allow me to* introduce Bob Robertson, our new managing director.	(How do you do?) I'm delighted to meet you, Mr Robertson.	How do you do?

UNIT 1
HOMES

Differences formal
complete sentences
would not will
could can
I'm afraid
I regret
at just
Sorry

Greeting someone you have met before	
General *Morning/Afternoon/Evening/Hello, Bob/Mr Robertson*. How are you?	Fine, thanks. And you? Very well, thank you. How are you?
(Very) *good/nice* to see you. You're looking very well.	And you.
Informal Hi (there), Jane. How's life? Hello (there), Jane. How are things (with you)?	(I'm) on top of the world, thanks. *Can't complain./Mustn't grumble.* Not too bad (thanks).
Formal *Good morning/Good afternoon./Good evening./Hello!* I trust you're (keeping) well? NO QUESTION! why?	Yes, I'm extremely well, thank you. I'm in excellent health, thank you (very much).

Taking leave of someone
General Excuse me a *moment/minute*. I'll be back in a minute. I'm afraid I (really) must go now. It's been very *nice/interesting* talking to you. *Goodbye./Goodnight.*
Informal I'll be right back. Hang on a *second/moment*. Well, (I'm afraid) *I must be off/I must dash*, now. Bye (for now)! *Cheerio!/Cheers!* See you (*soon/later/next week*)!
Formal *Will/Would* you excuse me for a moment, please? I'm afraid I *must/shall have to* leave you for a *moment/minute* or two. I'm very glad to have met you. It's been a great pleasure talking to you.

■ **Practice** PW

Act out the situations in Pair work 1a–1f (see Appendix). Situations 1e and 1f in fact require three people: two should take the roles for student A, while the third is student B. Look at your own pair work information only.

Reading aloud: unstressed syllables

The commonest vowel sound in spoken English is /ə/, as in the first vowels of *about* and *perceive* and the final vowels of *curtain* and *over*. Notice where the stress falls on these words:

a<u>bout</u> per<u>ceive</u> <u>cur</u>tain <u>o</u>ver

In fact, /ə/ occurs only in syllables that are not stressed. The unstressed syllables in these words receive full vowel value only in the unlikely event of their being stressed for a special purpose:

I said 'cur<u>tain</u>'/ˈkəːˈtein/, not 'cur<u>tail</u>' /kəˈteil/.

It is essential when you are speaking or reading aloud that you are aware of which syllables are to be stressed and which are not to be stressed, since in many cases this determines pronunciation. This is true of groups of monosyllabic words as well as sounds within words. For example, in the following dialogue, the first *are* is stressed and pronounced /ɑː/, while the second *are* is unstressed and pronounced /ə/.

'I haven't seen you for ages. How are you?'
'I'm fine. How are you?'

■ **Exercise 1**

In each of these words there is one stressed syllable which receives its full vowel sound, and one or more unstressed syllables pronounced /ə/. Underline the stressed syllables and say the words out loud.

table	permission
composer	photographer
conception	standard
perhaps	permanent
mother	banana
parson	traveller
reverent	prevalent
wanderer	

■ **Exercise 2**

Note the way the syllables *con, per, sad, yon, mer* and *ad* vary in sound in the following pairs of words. Mark the stress and say the words aloud.

concert	concerted
yonder	canyon
perfume	perform
merchant	dreamer
saddest	sadistic
additive	malady

■ **Exercise 3**

Make a list of four or five of the words in exercises 1 and 2. Give it to another student. Improvise an oral presentation (descriptive or narrative) that includes all the words on the list you receive, concentrating on the pronunciation of unstressed syllables.

HOMES

Activity: getting to know each other RC

You are the first people to move into a new housing estate, and you are having a party in order to get to know each other. Use item 1 on Role cards 1–12 (see Appendix) to find out who you are, what your interests are, and which of the other guests you already know. Look at your own role card only. During the party you must do two things:

- Behave in a social manner, greeting people, introducing people that you know but that don't know each other, circulating, and saying goodbye.
- Make dates to meet those people whose interests coincide with yours, with a view to organising local sporting or hobby activities. Arrange to meet them all during the coming week, though not more than one per day.

Before you start, choose a first name for yourself that begins with the initial on your role card; write your new name on a piece of paper, in large letters, and fasten it to your clothing, so that everyone can see at a glance who you are. Your host is B. Winfield. Act out the complete party, starting with the arrival of the guests and continuing until everyone has left.

Sunday		
Monday		
Tuesday		
Wednesday		
Thursday		
Friday		
Saturday		

Written work: writing a composition

When you write an article, essay or letter of any kind, there are a number of things you can do to help put your ideas across:

- Choose a topic that you know about, or that you at least are interested in; you are unlikely to be able to interest the reader if you yourself are bored.
- Approach the topic, if possible, from an angle that is unusual and will therefore stimulate the reader in some way.
- Organise your ideas so that your line of thought is easy to follow. It is probably a good idea to make a few notes before you start the actual composition; this will allow you to see at a glance if your ideas really fit into a logical pattern.
- Choose your words carefully to lead the reader from one point to the next. Reading plenty of English literature will help with this, and there are also practical exercises in this book that show you how to link ideas in various ways.

Planning a composition

All compositions can follow this general plan:

- *Introduction*: statement of purpose. Grab hold of the reader's attention with a striking statement that lets him know the purpose of your composition.
- *Middle*: one or more paragraphs that satisfy the curiosity aroused by the opening statement. It may be facts, or arguments for and against, or perhaps a description of objects, people or events, but it will always be relevant to the original statement of purpose. Every new paragraph will add to the effect of the preceding paragraphs.
- *Conclusion*: not a repetition of the introduction, but a concise and definite statement that leaves the reader with a clear impression of the main point of what you have written.

■ Exercise 1

Analyse the article at the beginning of this unit on p. 1 according to the principles described above. Try to answer these questions.

1 What is the topic?

2 What is the angle of approach chosen by the writer?

3 How well has the article been organised? Make notes from it under the headings *Introduction*, *Middle*, and *Conclusion*.

4 Does the introduction 'grab hold of the reader's attention'?

5 Is everything in the middle 'relevant to the original statement of purpose'?

6 Is the conclusion 'concise and definite', leaving you with 'a clear impression of the main point'?

■ Exercise 2

Plan and write a newspaper article based on one of these headlines.

School holidays are too long

Space travel: a waste of resources

CHOOSING THE RIGHT WAY TO TRAVEL

Who'd be a courier?

THE TRIP OF A LIFETIME

UNIT 2

TRAVEL

Reading and thinking
Reading comprehension (1)

The Times 6 August 1983

WARNING: HOLIDAYS CAN DAMAGE YOUR HEALTH

And then, of course, there's the holiday you need to prepare for your holiday. Or
5 the time off you ought to take to organise your time off: to get your pre-travel rest ('at least two good nights' sleep to alleviate the effects of nervous tension and travel fatigue') and ransack the local
10 pharmacy.

Sterile wound dressings? A must. Magnesium sulphate paste, an essential aid to the extraction of sea urchin spines. You may think you are going to the
15 seaside, albeit the foreign seaside, but recent information suggests you are going to war.

Typhoid, rabies, unwholesome water, seafood ('a notorious hazard') and
20 Portuguese men-of-war begin at Calais, according to a helpful booklet I've been reading called *Have a Good Trip!*

There is an old laborious schoolboy joke about 'enjoying the trip' which is
25 sometimes produced when someone falls over. Micropharm Ltd, the publishers of *Have a Good Trip!* seem to have borrowed from its humour, planting instructional banana skins along the
30 routes of all our holiday ambitions. Although representing private enterprise, the inexpensive booklet (50p, 23 passport-sized pages) includes a contribution from the Health Education
35 Council and has their endorsement.

Smokers and drinkers will find this encouraging. *Have a Good Trip!* may signify but a faint flicker of energy diverted from the HEC's attention to
40 their habits, but it's nice to have the no-no's passed around a bit. This catalogue of recreational negatives even tells you when to clock in and out of sunbathing, 'For the first few days, you should not
45 sunbathe in northern Europe between 11.00 a.m. and 3.00 p.m. or in places near the equator between 10.00 a.m. and 4.00 p.m. Never sunbathe between 12.00 and 2.00 p.m. unless you want to be
50 sunburnt.'

I hope it isn't quite medical nonsense to suggest that if you're a regular traveller, then high level of protection can be counter-productive. After years of
55 travelling in Europe it would never occur to me to avoid the local tap-water and this nonchalance, I believe, has now accustomed my system to minor, non-British water-borne bugs.

60 Which brings me to a final complaint about *Have a Good Trip!* Despite the giddy complacency and blithe recklessness of my attitude to holiday health, I was prepared to take advice from the
65 section headed 'Bites, Stings and Creepy Crawly Things' on the subject of my one major phobia about foreign parts.

But Mr B. T. O'Boyle, who put the booklet together, and the Health Educa-
70 tion Council, who blessed it, are singularly unhelpful in this area. They offer only one curt reference: 'The chances of being bitten by a shark are practically nil.'

75 Bitten I can handle. What about eaten?

1 Where might you find an article like this? For what purpose do you think it was written?

For questions 2 to 6 choose the word or phrase which best completes each sentence.

2 You should take time off before your holiday in order to
a avoid getting nervous and tired.
b have plenty of time to take the medicines you need.
c prepare for the journey.
d rest from the previous time you travelled.

3 The writer jokes that 'you are going to war' because
a people think of tourists as an invading army.
b the seaside you are going to is in a foreign country.
c there are diseases and Portuguese men-of-war in Calais.
d you need medical equipment to deal with injuries.

4 *Have a Good Trip!* is _____ by the Health Education Council.
a approved   b financed
c published   d written

5 Smokers and drinkers will be encouraged because
a now the HEC will not be able to criticise their habits.
b now they are not the only people being told by the HEC what not to do.

c the HEC have given their endorsement to smoking and drinking.
d the HEC's contribution does not criticise smoking and drinking.

6 The author thinks that avoiding the local tap-water
a gives a high level of protection.
b makes you immune to the bacteria in the water.
c makes you more susceptible to foreign bacteria.
d is nonchalant.

Now answer these questions.

7 What is meant by 'planting instructional banana skins along the routes of all our holiday ambitions' (lines 28–29)?

8 'giddy complacency and blithe recklessness' (line 62). Describe in your own words the author's attitude to holiday health.

9 What exactly is the writer's 'major phobia about foreign parts (line 67)? And what is the 'final complaint' she has?

10 Describe everything you know about *Have a Good Trip!* and give reasons why you would or would not buy it.

2 DESCRIPTION *SIGNALEMENT*

	Bearer Titulaire	Spouse Epouse
Place of birth Lieu de naissance		
Date of birth Date de naissance		
Height Taille		
Distinctive marks Signes particuliers		

CHILDREN *ENFANTS*

Name Nom	Date of birth Date de naissance	Sex

Usual signature
Signature du ti

Usual signatur
Signature de s

NOTES

1 **Validity**   A passport is valid for ten years, unless otherwise stated. If issued to a child under sixteen years of age it is normally valid for five years in the first instance but may be extended for a further five years without further charge. A passport which is ten years old or has no further space for visas must be replaced by a new one.

5 **2 Citizenship and National Status**   British citizens have the right of abode in the United Kingdom. No right of abode in the United Kingdom derives from the status as British nationals of British Dependent Territories citizens, British Overseas citizens, British protected persons and British subjects.

3 Immigration and Visa Requirements   The possession of a passport does not exempt the

10 holder from compliance with any immigration regulations in force in any territory or from the necessity of obtaining a visa or permit where required. It should be noted in this connection that the majority of British territories overseas have immigration restrictions applicable to British nationals as well as aliens.

4 Family Passports   A family passport which includes the particulars of the holder's

15 spouse can be used by the holder but NOT by the spouse when travelling alone.

5 Children   Children who have reached the age of sixteen years require separate passports.

6 Registration Overseas   British nationals resident overseas who are entitled to the protection of the United Kingdom authorities should contact the nearest British High

20 Commission, Embassy or Consulate to enquire about any arrangements for registration of their names and addresses. Failure to do so may in an emergency result in difficulty or delay in according them assistance and protection.

7 Dual Nationality   British nationals who are also nationals of another country cannot be protected by Her Majesty's Representatives against the authorities of that country. If,

25 under the law of that country, they are liable for any obligations (such as military service), the fact that they are British nationals does not exempt them from it. A person having some connection with a Commonwealth or foreign country (eg by birth, by descent through either parent, by marriage or by residence) may be a national of that country, in addition to being a British national. Acquisition of British nationality or citizenship by a foreigner does

30 not necessarily cause the loss of nationality of origin.

8 Caution   This passport remains the property of Her Majesty's Government in the United Kingdom and may be withdrawn at any time. It should not be tampered with or passed to an unauthorised person. Any case of loss or destruction should be immediately reported to the local police and to the nearest British passport issuing authority (eg

35 Passport Office, London; British Consulate; British High Commission or Colonial authority); only after exhaustive enquiries can a replacement be issued in such circumstances. The passport of a deceased person should be submitted for cancellation to the nearest such passport authority: it will be returned on request.

M/400655/A ★ ★ ★ ★ ★

1 For each of the following four sentences, write a new sentence as similar as possible in meaning to the original, but using the word given.

a The possession of a passport does not exempt the holder from compliance with any immigration regulations in force in any territory or from the necessity of obtaining a visa or permit where required. **must**

b A passport including particulars of the holder's spouse is not available for the spouse's use when he/she is travelling alone. **may**

c Failure to do so may in an emergency result in difficulty or delay in according them assistance and protection. **if**

d Any case of loss or destruction should be immediately reported to the local police. **if**

2 Applying for a passport.
The passport notes are written in a very formal style. See if you can express the same facts in an everyday conversational style.

a Make brief notes from the text. These notes should avoid the exact formulations of the original text wherever possible. For example:

Passport normally valid 10 years–5 years for child under 16, can be renewed for 5 more years–after 10 years, or if full, must be replaced

b Act out the scene at the Passport Office when someone asks for information about passports for the whole family. Use the notes you have made as a basis for your questions and answers. For example:

– *How long is a passport valid?*
– *Well, usually it's valid for ten years, but for children ...*

Words and structures

IDIOMS

■ **Exercise 1**

Explain the meanings of these expressions as they are used in the texts.

Text 1:
a time off (line 5)
b A must (line 11)
c albeit the foreign seaside (line 15)
d private enterprise (line 31)
e but a faint flicker of energy (line 38)
f clock in and out (line 43)
g it would never occur to me (line 56)
h foreign parts (line 67)
i singularly unhelpful (line 71)

Text 2:
a unless otherwise stated (line 1)
b in the first instance (line 2)
c without further charge (line 3)
d in force (line 10)
e Failure to do so (line 21)
f on request (line 38)

■ **Exercise 2**
Time

Make sure you know the meanings of these expressions. Make sentences to show how they are used.

a beat time
b kill time
c take your time
d it's (high) time
e in (the nick of) time
f in (next to) no time
g for the time being
h from time to time
i behind the times
j for old times' sake
k a sign of the times
l at times
m time and again
n on time
o at one time
p timeless
q timely
r time-saving
s time-bomb
t time-lag

TRAVEL

Now choose the most appropriate expressions to fill the gaps in these sentences, making any necessary adjustments to verb forms.

1 Why do you never listen? I've told you _____ to lock the front door when you go out.

2 The paintings of Manet have a certain _____ beauty.

3 The dishwasher is a marvellous _____ device.

4 The teacher _____ on a drum while the children danced.

5 The play didn't start until 9.30, so we decided to _____ by walking round the park.

6 I got to the bank _____, just before they closed.

7 We'll have to accept their offer _____, and hope to get a better deal next year.

Now choose the word that best completes each sentence.

8 Right! Your time is _____. What's the answer?
   a in **b** off **c** out **d** up

9 I plan to take some time _____ from my studies in order to travel.
   a about **b** off **c** out **d** over

10 It's very unusual for trains to run _____ time.
    a by **b** in **c** on **d** with

11 The car broke down, but we managed to get there _____ time for the speeches.
    a by **b** in **c** on **d** with

12 We got there _____ plenty of time to spare.
    a by **b** in **c** on **d** with

■ **Exercise 3**

Two-part verbs with *to*

Make sure you know the meanings of these verbs when used in combination with *to*.

come	see
get	set
keep	stick
hold	take
look	turn

In the following sentences, explain the phrases in italics and replace the words in capitals with one of the above verbs together with *to*.

1 I hope you don't mind my asking you to ARRANGE everything; I've got nobody else to *turn to*.

2 I met John just as the plane REACHED Athens, and I *took to* him immediately.

3 I intend to MAKE SURE THAT YOU KEEP your promise; I'm determined to *stick to* the original plan.

4 I'm EXPECTING you to support me in tomorrow's vote; there's no point in giving an undertaking if you're not going to *keep to* it.

5 The boxers needed no encouragement: as soon as the bell rang, they *set to* with great enthusiasm. One was knocked out, but he REGAINED CONSCIOUSNESS after a few seconds.

VOCABULARY

■ **Exercise 4**

Choose the word that best completes each sentence.

1 They _____ us to get a return ticket.
   a advised **b** asserted **c** offered **d** suggested

2 These rules apply to everyone, without _____.
a exception **b** exemption
c expiry **d** validity

3 His monstrous imagination knows no _____.
a borders **b** boundaries **c** bounds
d frontiers

4 The employment situation has led many Britons to _____ to Australia.
a deport **b** emigrate **c** immigrate
d migrate

5 We had a marvellous _____ down the Rhine.
a route **b** travel **c** trip **d** way

6 The example you gave is hardly _____ to our situation.
a accustomed **b** applicable
c entitled **d** valid

7 There are severe _____ for smuggling.
a charges **b** duties **c** liabilities
d penalties

8 Ice on the roads is one of the most serious _____ of driving in winter.
a accidents **b** hazards
c hindrances **d** obstacles

9 The negotiations _____ in a 2% pay increase.
a arranged **b** handled **c** prepared
d resulted

10 The plane was _____ to Paris because of fog.
a delayed **b** deposed **c** diverted
d rejected

Now write sentences of your own for some of the incorrect answers above to show that you understand how they are used.

STRUCTURES

Verbs and phrases followed by *to* and a noun or gerund

■ **Exercise 5**

For each of the following sentences, write a new sentence as similar as possible in meaning to the original but using the word given as well as *to* followed by a gerund.

The witness said that he had seen Jones outside the bank. **testified**
The witness testified to having seen Jones outside the bank.

1 The evidence suggests that she is innocent. **points**

2 Harriet would never do anything so undignified as talk to me. **stoop**

3 I refuse to be interrogated by you. **submit**

4 It's unacceptable that I have to tidy up after you. **object**

5 'All right!' said Chapman. 'I stole the jewels.' **confessed**

■ **Exercise 6**

The following expressions are also followed by *to*. Write sentences of your own for some of them, including the expression followed by *to* plus a gerund.

to react	to be used
to refer	to be opposed
to resort	to be conducive
to swear	to be tantamount
to limit oneself	in addition to
to devote oneself	thanks to
to adapt (oneself)	it is due to
to confine oneself	owing to
to resign oneself	as to
to be accustomed	

n.b. these verbs also take to before a noun

reflexive verbs to also before noun. Non-reflexive + first verb without to i.e. ordinary accusative

TRAVEL

Listening and speaking
Discussion and debate

What sort of place do you think this is?

What are the tubes for? Describe what your impressions would be if you used one.

Is this an example of what buildings and transport will be like in the future?

What sort of holiday do you like best?

What's your main reason for going on holiday?

Which country would you go to if given a free choice? Why?

What is your opinion of package holidays?

■ **Exercise 1**

These people are all members of a travel club who are meeting in order to plan their annual holiday.

1 a geography student
2 a retired bus driver
3 a professor of classical languages
4 a coal-miner
5 a writer of detective stories
6 an actor
7 a journalist
8 a musician
9 a travel agent
10 an aeroplane pilot
11 a psychologist
12 a spy
13 a politician
14 a keen amateur sportsman

Choose one of these roles and, first of all, decide for yourself what sort of holiday you would like. Make notes. Then act out the discussion. Eventually you must all agree on one trip; try to persuade the others that your suggestions are the best, but be prepared to compromise.

possible destination(s)	itinerary	cost	length of trip	activities	transport

■ Exercise 2

Imagine that you have just completed the trip that you agreed on. Write a letter to a friend describing where you went and what you did.

■ Exercise 3

Prepare and give a short talk on one of these themes.

- Holidays can damage your health.
- There's no place like home.
- Transport and travel in the future.
- All public transport should be free.

Listening comprehension

You will hear a conversation about holidays. The first time you listen to it:
- identify the situation
- find out how many people take part in the conversation, and who they are
- fill in as many details as possible in the table below.

The second and subsequent times you listen to the conversation, complete the advertisement and answer questions 1 to 4.

1 What do you think is the family's final order of preference? Put '1' by their first choice, '2' by their second choice, and so on. If your fellow students disagree with you, give reasons for your answers.

2 Which word best describes the travel agent's manner?
a Arrogant   **b** Formal   **c** Informal
d Servile
Explain how you reach your answer.

3 The parents' manner towards the child is
a aggressive.   **b** distant.   **c** irritated.
d protective.

4 What did the parents agree and disagree on during the course of the conversation?

place	type of accommodation	price	dates	facilities/other information
CORFU				
SARDINIA				
FRENCH RIVIERA				
COPENHAGEN				

Function: permission and requests

What do you think they are saying? Fill in the bubbles.

■ Exercise 1

Use the tables to help you find suitable replies to these remarks.

1 Any chance of borrowing your car this afternoon?

2 Would you be so kind as to let me do the talking, for a change?

3 Is there any objection to my bringing up the subject of foreign business?

4 Sorry to trouble you, but would you mind holding my baby for a moment?

■ Exercise 2

What would you say in these situations?

1 You want to buy an expensive item of clothing, but have no cash with you. Ask the assistant if you can pay by cheque.

2 You're carrying a heavy load, so you ask a stranger to open a door for you.

3 Your teacher has given you a lot of homework. However, you are very busy and would like to hand it in the following week instead.

4 You've just negotiated an important business deal and wish to know if the person you have been negotiating with agrees to your making a statement to the press.

5 You ring up a client in order to postpone a meeting.

Asking for permission	Granting permission	Refusing permission
General *Can/May/Could* I ...? Is it all right if I ...? Would it be possible to ...?	Yes, *certainly/of course.* That's *fine/all right.* By all means.	(No,) I'm afraid not.
		I'm sorry. I'm afraid *it's/that's* not possible.
Do you mind if I ...?	*Not at all./Of course not.*	(I'm afraid) it's out of the question.
Informal Any chance of -ing ...? Mind if I ...? *OK/All right* if I ...?	*Sure./Go ahead./Why not?* That's *OK/fine/all right* (by me). Feel free (to ...).	(Sorry,) that's not on. No way.
Formal *Do you have/Is there* any objection if I ...? *Do you have/Is there* any objection to *me/my* -ing .?	That seems to be *perfectly/quite* acceptable. That's *quite/perfectly* in order.	(I'm afraid) no one is *allowed/permitted* to ...

Making a request	Granting a request	Refusing a request
General *Could/Would/Will* you ..., please? Do you think you could ..., please? Excuse me, ... Sorry to trouble you, but ...	Yes, *of course/certainly.* I'd be happy to.	I'm afraid not.
		I'd prefer not to. I'm sorry, *I can't/it's not possible.* I'd rather not, actually.
Do/Would you mind ..., please?	No, of course not.	
Informal You couldn't ..., could you? Any chance of ...? Do me a favour and ..., please.	*Sure./OK.* Right you are. No problem.	(Sorry,) I'm not too keen on ... I don't (really) fancy ... Only wish I could, but ... *Not likely!/No way!*
Formal I wonder if you'd mind -ing ...? Could you possibly ...? Do you think it would be possible to ...? Would you be so kind as to ...?	By all means. Not at all. I should be delighted. I see no objection (to ...).	(Well,) to be *honest/frank*, I don't think ... I'm rather reluctant to .. I'm sorry to say it's quite impossible.

23

TRAVEL

■ **Practice** PW

Act out the situations in Pair work 2a and 2b.

Reading aloud: word stress

Most English words have a fixed stress pattern with which they are always associated, no matter what the emotional, situational or grammatical context.

visit
It's time to visit my aunt.
I'll pay her a visit tomorrow.
What on earth do you mean 'a visit'?

Here *vis-* carries a strong main stress, while *-it* is much weaker, or unstressed.

■ **Exercise 1**

Read the following words aloud. Exaggerate the strength of the stressed syllables and the weakness of the unstressed syllables. Then improvise sentences of various types for each of the words, as in the example with *visit*, being careful to keep the stress pattern constant.

interest	correct
programme	demand
mistake	gamble
wonder	button
feature	order
attempt	sentence

■ **Exercise 2**

There is a fairly large group of words where grammatical function determines the stress.

Make pairs of sentences for the words below to practise saying them aloud as nouns and verbs.

accent
Jack has a strong Australian accent.
If you use 'convict' as a verb, you have to accent the second syllable.

noun	verb	noun	verb	noun	verb
accent	accent	desert	desert	present	present
addict	addict	dictate	dictate	produce	produce
attribute	attribute	discount	discount	progress	progress
combine	combine	escort	escort	prospect	prospect
conduct	conduct	exploit	exploit	rebel	rebel
conflict	conflict	export	export	record	record
conscript	conscript	extract	extract	refuse	refuse
console	console	import	import	reject	reject
contest	contest	incense	incense	subject	subject
contract	contract	increase	increase	survey	survey
converse	converse	insult	insult	suspect	suspect
convert	convert	object	object	transfer	transfer
convict	convict	overflow	overflow	transport	transport
decrease	decrease	permit	permit	upset	upset

■ Exercise 3

Make a list of five or six words taken from the words in exercises 1 and 2 and pass it to another member of the class. Use the list you receive as the basis for an improvised oral presentation (story, description, etc.), in which you use each word at least once.

■ Exercise 4

Look at the conversation on pp. 205–6. Go through everything said by the agent and mark the main stress in all words of two syllables or more. Practise saying these words aloud, and then read the complete conversation.

Activity: the Globe Travel Agency

Study these extracts from a travel brochure: notice what information is included and how it is presented.

Canberra A Great Ship For a Great Holiday

A cruise on P&O's famous flagship *Canberra* is truly one of the world's great holiday experiences. Come with us for a moment. Imagine that you've decided to sail on *Canberra*. The day you've been waiting for for months–or even years–is finally here. Already you're impressed by the sparkling elegance, the wide open spaces of your floating home. And now, you stand high up on the Promenade Deck. On the quay below you, a uniformed band launches into 'A Life On The Ocean Wave'. Thousands of bright streamers flutter down from the ship to the cheering crowds. The last rope is cast off and *Canberra* begins to slip effortlessly away from the dock. You're off, on the most wonderful holiday of your life.

Canberra – your world afloat

The great 45,000 ton flagship of the P&O fleet. Stabilised and air-conditioned with ten passenger decks, three swimming pools, a paddling pool, two restaurants, three shops, a kiosk, hairdressing and beauty salons, children's playroom, table-tennis room, cinema, dance floors, discotheque, nine bars, fifteen public rooms including a card room, reading room and library, plus deck space galore.

Top value for money

As well as all your main meals and accommodation your cruise fare includes much, much more:–
*Continental breakfast in bed, or early morning tea, coffee or fruit juice *Mid-morning coffee and ice-cream *Afternoon tea *Late night coffee or tea with sandwiches in the Restaurant *Deck chairs *All your entertainment from deck sports to cabaret, bands and cinema *Special interest talks and classes on subjects like bridge, flower arranging, keep fit and dancing *A good library *Insurance covering cancellation, medical expenses, personal accident, baggage and cash.

P & O Cruises

406 – 16 nights **Jun 29–Jul 15**
Southampton
Fri 29 Jun evening sailing
Gibraltar
Mon 2 Jul arr 0830 stay 5½ hrs
Haifa *(for Jerusalem)*
Fri 6 Jul arr 0730 stay 14 hrs
Izmir
Sun 8 Jul arr 0730 stay 11 hrs
Athens
Mon 9 Jul arr 0730 stay 11½ hrs
Cagliari *(Sardinia)*
Wed 11 Jul arr 0730 stay 10½ hrs
Southampton
Sun 15 Jul arr early morning

407 – 14 nights **Jul 15–29**
Southampton
Sun 15 Jul evening sailing
Gibraltar
Wed 18 Jul arr 0830 stay 9½ hrs
Palermo
Fri 20 Jul arr 1300 stay 6 hrs
Loutraki *(for Athens)*
Sun 22 Jul arr 0700 stay 13 hrs
Corfu
Mon 23 Jul arr 0730 stay 11 hrs
Malaga
Thu 26 Jul arr 0800 stay 11 hrs
Southampton
Sun 29 Jul arr early morning

'Standby' Supersaver scheme

'Standby' fares offer big savings but you must 'take a chance' on the cruise departure date, duration and type of cabin. You may list your preferences but the final choice will be made by P&O depending on availability. You will be given not less than one month's notice. **'Standby' accommodation is limited so early application is essential.**

Cabins & Standby Fares

per adult	13/14	16
	nights	nights
Type of cabin	£	£
4 berth	470	560
2 or 3* berth	670	790
2 or 3 berth *with shower/WC*	750	890
1 or 2 bedded *with shower/WC*	880	1050
*4 berth cabin let for 3		

TRAVEL

Write an information sheet or small brochure that advertises ten to twelve different types of holidays:

- Decide on a format for the information.
- In groups, write the holiday descriptions. If you can find travel brochures in English, you can use these as a starting-point; otherwise, use your imagination.
- Put all your descriptions together and devise a booking form.

Act out the situation at the Globe Travel Agency when would-be holiday-makers come to book holidays advertised in your brochure.

Two assistants:
You have direct contact with customers; you must fill in booking forms and always check with the co-ordinator about which trips are already booked. You work on commission, so no one must leave without booking a holiday!

One co-ordinator:
You are the agency's 'computer'; you keep a list of the trips which are available or already booked. You have no direct contact with customers. You should decide initially how many of each of the holidays are available (1–4 of each).

Customers:
Work in pairs or small groups; before you talk to an assistant, decide together what sort of holiday you'll be looking for.

Revision: units 1 and 2

■ Exercise 1

Fill each gap with one word; it need not be the actual word used in the original text, but it must be appropriate to the context.

_____(1)_____ Fred did not realise _____(2)_____ the huge amount of money he would have to spend, and the time it would take. He _____(3)_____ his wife Mercia and their three children were _____(4)_____ to move in six months after _____(5)_____ but they _____(6)_____ moved in eighteen months _____(7)_____, and the house is still _____(8)_____ from finished.

The back extension had to be demolished, and the whole house had to be replumbed and rewired, and _____(9)_____ with new drains. Fred was also _____(10)_____ to restore original features. But knowing what's thrown _____(11)_____ with the rubbish can be useful: he said that shutters _____(12)_____ very good cupboard doors when cut _____(13)_____ three, and he rescued some old iron railings from his garden.

But Fred admits he was very ambitious. 'I was not interested in _____(14)_____ the house at the time. I was doing it _____(15)_____ to keep, so I wanted the _____(16)_____ done properly. If I'd been _____(17)_____ a "builder's finish" the house would have been completed _____(18)_____ half the time.'

■ Exercise 2

Write definitions for any five of the expressions below, and pass them to someone else in the class. This person should then try to guess what the original expressions were and make up a story or description that includes all five of them.

alien
alleviate
a must
behind the times
clock in
come to
complacency
divert
dressings
endorsement
entitle
equator
exempt
exhaustive
expire
hazard
in force
in the first instance
in the nick of time
kill time
look to
nonchalance
notorious
on request
overseas
particulars
phobia
ransack
see to
stoop
submit
take to
tamper
time and again
time off
time-saving
timely
turn to
unwholesome
validity

UNIT 2
TRAVEL

UNIT 3

HEALTH AND FITNESS

Reading and thinking
Reading comprehension (1)

Fitter... But not much thinner (Yet)

Remember all those glowing plans last month? Massive tyres about to roll from the old flabby frame, etc., etc... well, pressure of work and shortage of time have restricted my visits to the excellent Grimsby Squash Rackets Club's Health Studio. One thing you do *not* do is leave the exercise alone for a fortnight as yours truly did; the effort back in the gym seems double the initial dose, but one thing still proves the value of exercise, and that's the immediate mental well-being after a session. It's nothing really to do with the club's sauna, jacuzzi and steam room, which are really the cream on a very rich cake (ah food again . . .); even a quick hot shower still leaves your body singing after an hour on the simple equipment in the Health Studio.

So is my shape altering? No one has noticed yet, but because I've taken up running each day to fill in the time between visits to the club, I have lost five pounds, bringing my weight down from a grisly 13st. 9lbs. to 13st. 4lbs.

But to really enter into the almost evangelistic spirit of rejuvenation and complete health you must get down to serious exercise at least twice a week.

Apparently, it really is, after all, only exercise which keeps you thin, as every diet fails in the end because you lose not only fat, but muscle. Apparently, when the weight is put back on (as it always is, I can assure you . . .) that lost muscle is usually replaced with fat, and so the vicious circle goes on with miserable diet after miserable diet.

What exercise does, that is vigorous aerobic exercise, is replace that muscle and harden what you already have; your weight will go down, as I am finding through these determined weeks, even though I've been scoffing ravenously between sessions. Right. Back on the exercise cycle!

The Humberside & South Yorkshire Executive July 1983

1 What associations do the following words and phrases conjure up? Explain the author's purpose in using them.
a glowing (line 1)
b Massive tyres about to roll from the old flabby frame (line 2)
c seems double the initial dose (line 11)
d the cream on a very rich cake (line 17)
e singing (line 20)
f evangelistic (line 30)
g vicious circle (line 41)
h determined weeks (line 48)
i scoffing ravenously (line 49)

2 What, according to the text, is the factor that lies behind all increases in weight?

3 What is the passage really about? Summarise the important information as briefly as possible.

Reading comprehension (2)

What do 100 kcal/day (400 kJ) correspond to?

It's easy to feed 100 kcal (400 kJ) to the body but difficult to burn them, as the drawings illustrate.

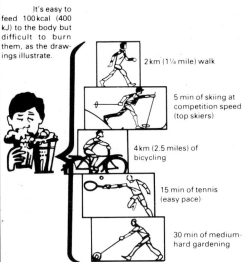

- 2 km (1¼ mile) walk
- 5 min of skiing at competition speed (top skiers)
- 4 km (2.5 miles) of bicycling
- 15 min of tennis (easy pace)
- 30 min of medium-hard gardening

The energy contents of some food items	*kcal	*kJ
4 cubes of sugar (12 grams or 0.4 oz)	50	200
1 piece of pastry or cake	250	1,000
1 roll	150	600
6 grams (0.2 oz) of butter or margarine	50	200
1 slice of buttered bread	100	400
65 grams (2 ¼ oz) of chocolate	350	1,500
100 grams (3 ½ oz) of boiled potato	90	380
1 bottle of beer	135	570
0.04 liter (1.4 fl. oz) of brandy	120	500
0.2 liter (6.8 fl. oz) of milk	120	500
0.2 liter (6.8 fl. oz) of skimmed milk	75	340

*kcal = kilocalorie (normally called simply 'calorie'); kJ = kiloJoule. These are two different ways of measuring energy.

1 How far must you walk in order to burn up the energy contained in a piece of cake and a slice of buttered bread?

2 What advice for the person who is growing obese is contained in the paragraph 'If a person ...'?

3 Which of the exercises are designed for which parts of the body? Tick the relevant boxes.

	stretching	lunges	sit-ups
arms	✓		
legs	✓	✓	
stomach	✓		✓

1 If a person takes in 50 kcal/day (210 kJ) more than he needs, his annual surplus will be 18,000 kcal (75 MJ), corresponding to nearly 3 kg (7 lbs) of fat. This could lead to a 30 kg (70 lbs) weight increase in 10 **5** years. If you should one day decide to eliminate your routine mile-walk each day but maintain your eating habits, statistically you will gain 100 pounds in 10 years! It's not surprising that obesity's approach is stealthy as life becomes more sedate, **10** thanks to the automobile, more sedentary jobs and less time devoted to exercise. In this context, the period between 25–30 years is rather critical.

Stretching
- Stretch arms up and out slowly in various directions.
- Use the legs and trunk as well, to make it a total-body stretch (like a cat!).

Lunges
(for toning calf and thigh muscles).
- Lunge forward with left leg, knee bent, and right leg held straight behind (count 1–2–3).
- Jump up brightly on count of 4, to bring feet together.
- Repeat, alternating legs.

Sit-ups
(for abdominal muscles).
- Lie on back, knees and feet flat on the floor.
- Lift head, shoulders, and upper trunk, and stretch hands to knees (count 1–2).
- Slowly uncurl (keeping head forward) back to starting position, arms on the floor (count 3–4).
- Squeeze abdominal muscles, through counts 1–2–3 and relax on 4.

From *Health and Fitness* by Professor Åstrand

4 Cover up the instructions that accompany the training exercises. Now describe the movements by referring to the pictures alone.

Is the first text written in the same style as the paragraph in text 2 beginning 'If a person ...'? Give reasons for your answer, together with examples.

29

HEALTH AND FITNESS

Words and structures

IDIOMS

■ Exercise 1

Explain the meanings of these expressions as they are used in the texts.

Text 1:
a yours truly (lines 9–10)
b It's nothing really to do with (lines 14–15)
c taken up running (lines 23–4)
d fill in the time (line 24)
e after all (line 34)
f put back on (lines 38–9)

Text 2:
a takes in (line 1)
b lead to (line 4)
c thanks to the automobile (line 10)
d devoted to exercise (line 11)

■ Exercise 2

Body language

Make sure you know the meanings of these expressions. Make sentences to show how they are used.

a on foot
b by heart
c at heart
d behind someone's back
e in cold blood
f at hand
g on one's toes *auf Zacke sein*
h in one's bones
i in the flesh *in Person*
j in hand
k on the tip of one's tongue
l by the skin of one's teeth

Now choose the most appropriate expressions to fill the gaps in these sentences. You may have to change the pronouns.

1 I can't quite remember his name, but it's _____.

2 Don't worry! The army have the situation _____.

3 He's a very kind man _____, despite his forbidding appearance.

4 I've seen the Queen on television, but never _____.

5 The enemy could appear at any moment, so stay _____.

■ Exercise 3

Two-part verbs with *down*

get down to (line 31)
go down (line 47)

Fill each gap with the correct form of one of these verbs, followed by *down*:
break   *lose self-control*
cut   *reduce*
lay   *state firmly*
pin   *restrict*
shout   *silence by shouting*
Then explain with a word or phrase what each verb + *down* combination means.

I *turned down* their offer because I wanted more money. (Explanation: *refused*)

1 If you want to get slimmer, you'll have to _____ your calorie intake.

2 After two days of torture the prisoner _____ and confessed.

3 It's impossible to make a definite appointment with Jim; he hates being _____ in advance.

4 Alan loves being in charge. He's always _____ the law.

5 When the Prime Minister rose to speak, she was _____ by the opposition and was unable to make herself heard.

■ Exercise 4

Some combinations of verb + *down* are used as nouns. Match the following *down* nouns and their definitions. Then make a sentence for each *down* noun.

1 breakdown ᵇ	**a** anticlimax
2 close-down ᵈ	**b** collapse
3 count-down ᵍ	**c** demonstration or strike where people refuse to move
4 let-down ᵃ	
5 showdown ᶠ	
6 shut-down ʰ	**d** end of a broadcast
7 sit-down ᶜ	**e** landing of an aircraft
8 touchdown ᵉ	**f** open trial of strength
	g sequence of numbers in reverse order
	h stoppage of work

VOCABULARY

■ Exercise 5

Fill each gap in the following passage with one word. Below the passage is a list of words which may help you; you will not need all of these, while some may be used more than once. Only basic root words are given, and in some cases you will have to find other forms of these words, e.g. *coach—coaching*.

I'm one of the ____(1)____ for the local hockey club: my job is to ____(2)____ the under-16 team. When we meet on Thursday evenings, we start with some warm-up ____(3)____ in the gym. One of the ____(4)____ we often do is like skiing: you hop on the spot with your feet together, twisting your hips so that your knees are turned first to the right and then to the left; this sequence has to be ____(5)____ twenty times. It's very tiring, but excellent ____(6)____ for the calf and thigh muscles; and you'll never be fit if you don't ____(7)____ yourself from time to time. Then we relax with brief ____(8)____ of the theory ____(9)____ the previous week, followed by some new item such as attacking through the centre. Finally we go outside to put the theory into ____(10)____;

spelling!

and if an important match is coming up, we have a sort of dress ____(11)____ where we ____(12)____ our tactics at corners, free hits and the like. Some people complain that my ____(13)____ methods are too hard and monotonous, but ____(14)____ makes perfect, that's what I say! *spelling!*

coach	*rehearse*
drill	*repeat*
exert	*revise*
exercise	*teach*
learn	*train*
practise vb.	

■ Exercise 6

Choose the word that best completes each sentence.

1 It's important to keep your body in good ____ᵈ____.
   a contour   **b** figure   **c** form   **d** shape

2 Alcoholic drinks have a ____ᵇ____ effect on many people.
   a sedate   **b** sedative — to make you sleep
   c sedentary   **d** sedimentary

3 At the end of last year the club's books showed a large ____ᵇ____ ...
   a deficiency   **b** deficit   **c** scarcity
   d shortage

4 ... but we're hoping to show a considerable ____ᵈ____ in the near future.
   a bonus   **b** excess   **c** surfeit
   d surplus

UNIT 3
HEALTH AND FITNESS

X N.B verb to sedate
to make you sleep
to give a sedative
to keep under sedation

HEALTH AND FITNESS

■ **Exercise 7**

Parts of the body

Write the correct numbers in the boxes.

appendix	23	ligament	17	☐
artery	10	liver	9	☐
bone	19	lung	6	☐
brain	2	muscle	15	☐
disc	11	nerve	16	☐
heart	7	pelvis	12	☐
joint	20	rib	5	☐
kidney	13	skin	18	☐
large intestine	24	skull	1	☐
larynx	3	small intestine	22	☐
		spine	8	☐
		stomach	21	☐
		vein	14	☐
		windpipe	4	☐

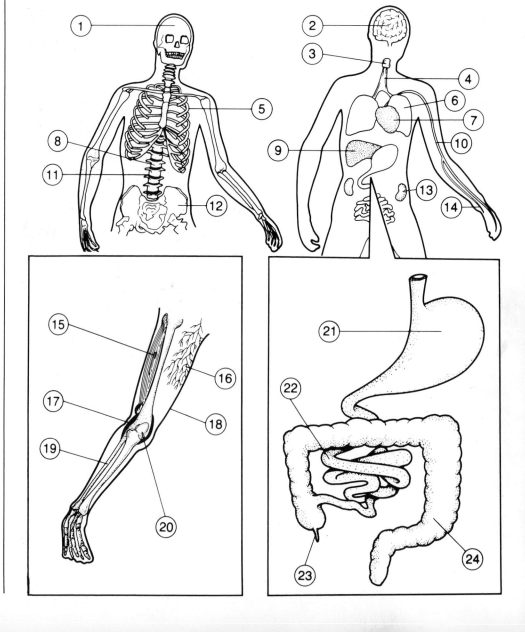

STRUCTURES

Verbs followed by either infinitive or gerund

■ Exercise 8

Some verbs have completely different meanings depending on whether they are followed by an infinitive or a gerund. In the following pairs of sentences, explain the differences in meaning between the underlined expressions.

1 I <u>forgot having met</u> her at your party.
  I <u>forgot to meet</u> her at the station.

2 She was <u>afraid to jump</u>. *— consequences of jumping*
  She was <u>afraid of hurting</u> herself. *she might hurt herself*

3 He <u>stopped combing</u> his hair.
  He <u>stopped to comb</u> his hair.

4 That boy <u>wants talking to</u>, the silly fool. *needs*
  That boy <u>wants to talk</u> to us.

Now make pairs of sentences of your own with the following verbs, and then explain the differences in meaning:
remember
try
go on
need

afraid to — *rational worked out consequences dangerous result could be unpleasant deliberate*

A subjective emotional what may happen.

go on
Teacher was talking about the Amazon river. After break he went on talking about it (same topic)
he went on to talk about other rivers — North America, s.th. different

Listening and speaking
Discussion and debate

Describe the scene.
What are these people doing?
What is the purpose of their activities?
Why are they dressed like this?
Why are they so fat?
What would it feel like to be in their situation?
What sort of exercise do you enjoy?
How important is keeping fit, and being slim? Have you ever been on a diet?

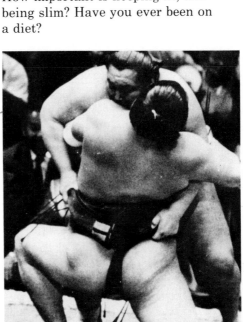

HEALTH AND FITNESS

■ Exercise 1

Imagine that you are going to spend two days in the middle of a desert as part of a training programme. You will be allowed to take with you some of the food items listed on p. 29, but not all of them; you will not be allowed any other food or drink.

1 Individually, without any discussion, rank these food items in order of importance by putting '1' by the one that you consider to have the highest survival value, down to '11' for the least important item.

2 Meet in groups of 2–4 students to compare your lists and produce a compromise order that all members of the group can agree to. Try to persuade the others in your group that your order is best, without being stubborn.

3 Meet as a whole class, and compare the decisions reached by the groups. See if you can reach agreement on one final order, though it's important now that you should support the compromise list produced in the small groups, rather than your own original list.

■ Exercise 2

Homework

Hold a debate on one of these topics.

■ You are what you eat.
■ An apple a day keeps the doctor away.
■ Inside every fat man there's a thin man struggling to get out.
■ Without physical fitness there can be no mental fitness.
■ The world's food resources should be divided equally amongst all nations.
■ Drinking alcohol is immoral and should be banned.

■ Exercise 3

Write a well-balanced essay on one of the topics in exercise 2.

Listening comprehension

You will hear a salesman advertising a new product in a department store. Listen to what he says and fill in the product specification form with as much information as possible; you will not be able to fill it all in.
Then listen again and answer questions 1 to 5.

Name of product ———————

Model ———————

Purpose ———————

Manufactured by ———————

Made of ———————

Components ———————

Weight ———————

Dimensions ———————

Normal retail price ———————

Introductory price ———————

Introductory offers ———————

Guarantee period ———————

Service requirements ———————

Other features ———————

1 Describe how to operate the product being advertised.

2 What would be the advantages of having this device at home?

3 Explain what the salesman meant when he used these expressions.
   a keep your wits about you in these days of equality
   b you name it
   c this must cost the earth
   d we're giving them away
   e beat that if you can
   f have a go

4 What were the exact words used by the salesman when he

 a offered to help one of the customers?

 b offered the mashed banana to someone?

 c replied to the woman who thanked him after eating some banana?

5 Was he a good salesman? Did he leave out any important information? Would you be persuaded to buy this product?

Function: giving, thanking, offering and inviting

What do you think they are saying? Fill in the bubbles.

■ Exercise 1 PW

p.183

Look at the expressions in Pair work 3a. Student B must find the most p.188 appropriate responses to what student A says.

■ Exercise 2

DO TABLES FIRST!
Homework

Use the tables to help you find suitable remarks in these situations.

1 The presentation of the first prize after a sporting event.

2 Helping an old person to cross the road.

3 Coming to the end of a two-week stay with a family in a foreign country.

4 Someone wants help with their homework.

5 Giving a present to a member of the family.

HEALTH AND FITNESS

Giving	Thanking
General Here's *a/the/your* . . . This is for you. Here are *the/your/some* . . . *Can I/I'd like to* give you . . . *Here/There* you are. Scot. There ya go!	Thank you (*very much/very much indeed*). Many thanks. Thank you (*very much*) for . . .
Informal Here.	Thanks (*very much/a lot*). *Cheers!/Great!*
Formal Please accept . . . I have great pleasure in giving you . . . Allow me to present you with . . .	*That's/How* (extremely) *kind/thoughtful* of you. I (do) appreciate . . . I'm *extremely/immensely* grateful . . . I really can't thank you enough (for . . .).

N.B.
a SMILE
as response
no bitte – danke

Responding to thanks	Offering something
General Not at all. *It's a/My* pleasure. (Please) don't mention it.	**General** Would you like . . . ? Can I offer you . . . ? What can I get you . . . ? *Why don't/Won't* you have . . . ?
Informal That's *OK/all right*. Any time.	**Informal** Like *a/some* . . . ? Have *a/some* . . . What'll you have?
Formal (I'm) *glad/delighted* to have been of (some) *help/assistance/service*. It was the least I could do.	**Formal** *Could I/Allow me to/I wonder if I might give/pass/get* you . . . Do have *a/some* . . .

Inviting

General
Would you like to ...?
(Please) do ...
You will ..., won't you?

Informal
What/How about ...?
Do you fancy ...?
Why don't you ...?
Like to ...?

Formal
We/I should be delighted/very pleased
if you could/were able to ...

Offering help

General
Can I help?
Is there anything I can do (to help)?
Let me help you (with ...).
Can I/Let me give you a hand (with
...)?
What can I do to help?
Would you like any help?

Informal
Want a hand (with ...)?
Need *some/any* help?
Can I help out?

Formal
May I be of (any) assistance?
Perhaps I *could/might* help in some
way?

Accepting an offer or invitation

General
Thank you (very much).
That *sounds/would be* very nice.
That's very kind of you.
Yes, please!

Informal
Great!
Lovely!
Cheers!
You bet!

Formal
That'd be delightful.
Thank you so much.
You are most kind.

Declining an offer or invitation

General
No, thank you (very much).
(Well,) that's very kind of you, but ...

Informal
Thanks all the same, but ...
I wish I could, but ...
I won't, if it's all the same to you.
No, it's *all right/OK*, thanks.

Formal
I'm afraid it won't be possible, but
thank you very much anyway.
It's very good of you to offer, but ...

■ **Practice** PW

Act out the situations in Pair work
3b–3h.

bet - wager

*- course of action your best bet
would be to*

*- opinion view my bet is that
he will change his mind*

UNIT **3**
HEALTH
AND
FITNESS

37

HEALTH AND FITNESS

Reading aloud: word stress in long words

Words of Latin or Greek origin

The stress varies depending on what is added to the beginning or end of the root syllable.

compete   potent
competitor   potential
competence   impotent
competition   omnipotent

Although there are many exceptions, there is a tendency for words of three or more syllables, of classical origin, to carry stress on the third syllable from the end (antepenultimate stress); the examples above show this clearly, especially if endings such as -tion and -ial are seen as consisting of two syllables—they were in fact pronounced as two syllables not so very long ago.

- Words with the following endings nearly always have antepenultimate stress (that is, immediately before the ending): -cient, -eous, -ety, -ial, -ian, -ical, -ion, -ious, -itant, -itive, -itous, -itude, -ity, -ual, -uous
- Verbs only, of three or more syllables and with the following endings, have antepenultimate stress: -ate, -fy, -ise/-ize
  Exceptions: recent formations such as capitalise, characterise, conceptualise
- Words ending with -ic have the stress on the preceding syllable: patriotic, economic
  Important exceptions: Arabic, arithmetic, catholic, heretic, lunatic, politic, rhetoric
- the adverb ending -ly does not change the position of the stress: mathematical—mathematically

Exercise 1

Write down at least one word with each of the endings given above. Underline the stressed syllables and say the words aloud.

Words of Germanic origin

The stress usually remains on the root syllable whatever is added to the beginning or end.

place replace irreplaceable
stand understand misunderstanding

Important exceptions: some nouns and adjectives beginning with fore and up, such as

foremost, foreman, uproar, upright

Exercise 2

Look at the texts on pp. 28–9 and make a list of all the words of three or more syllables. Mark the stress and say the words out loud. How many of them are stressed in accordance with the principles outlined above? Finally, read the first text out loud, making sure you stress all the words correctly.

Activity: health packages

1 You work for an advertising agency that has been given the task of promoting a new diet package. Split up into small groups and plan the campaign.
   - Decide the contents of the package.
   - Who is it for? (age-group, social group, etc.)
   - Which media are you going to use? Suggestions: health/food magazines, general interest magazines, newspapers, posters in public places (e.g. public transport), TV, cinema, radio.
   - Are you going to use any special gimmicks, such as special offers, free gifts, competitions, etc.?
   - Compose advertising copy for the various media being used.

For the final part of the activity, two groups should come together: one group represents the manufacturer of the diet package, while the other represents the agency. The agency should present the whole campaign to the manufacturers, and they in turn should comment and criticise.

2 Imagine that you run a health farm. Plan menus and timetables of activities for two-day visits by any of the following groups of people.

- Old-age pensioners.
- Professional sportsmen/women.
- 6 to 7-year-old children.
- Teenagers.
- Overweight business executives.

Written work: connecting ideas (1)

Addition and concession

In a recent survey into the effectiveness of five commercial health programmes, five hundred people were put on controlled diets and training schedules under strict laboratory conditions; they had to follow the manufacturers' or promoters' instructions to the letter for the time specified in each programme. The table shows the results of the survey, including, in the final three columns, the participants' subjective impressions on a scale of 0 (worst case) to 100 (best possible result).

Name of programme	Price	No. of days	Physical exercise hours/day	kcal intake per day	total kg. weight lost	ease of use/ motivation	variety	overall satisfaction
A	£50	3	5	1000	0.3	47	12	12
B	£75	4	3	800	0.5	28	19	10
C	£80	7	2.5	1600	1.5	83	38	25
D	£180	7	4	1800	2.2	68	75	92
E	£200	14	2	1500	3.0	51	47	36

■ Exercise 1

Combining two ideas

Make pairs of sentences or clauses about the health programmes, and combine them with expressions taken from this list.

and
(and) also/too/as well
not only ... but ... also/too/as well
In addition
Furthermore
Moreover
In addition to -ing
As well as -ing
Apart from -ing
both ... and
neither ... nor

'A' was both the cheapest and the shortest programme.
In addition to being one of the most expensive programmes, 'E' was also the most effective.

■ Exercise 2

Contrasting two ideas

Do the same as in exercise 1 but with these expressions.

but
although
despite
in spite of
yet
nevertheless
however
notwithstanding

Despite being the easiest programme to use, 'C' did not give the greatest overall satisfaction.

■ Exercise 3

Write a brief report for a health magazine recommending one of the programmes.

UNIT 4

THEATRE

Reading and thinking
Reading comprehension

The Real Thing by Tom Stoppard
Henry, Charlotte, Max and Annie are in the sitting-room of Henry and Charlotte's flat. They are talking about Private Brodie, a soldier who has been imprisoned after an incident during a demonstration against the use of nuclear weapons.

HENRY: I say, Annie, what's this Brodie Committee all about?
5 Charlotte was asking.
MAX: You know, Private Brodie . . . It was quite remarkable. Brodie was on his way to the demonstration, just like Annie. So they got to talking.
HENRY: *Really?*
ANNIE: Yes.
10 HENRY: How did you know he was going to the demonstration? Was he wearing a 'Missiles Out' badge on his uniform?
ANNIE: He wasn't in uniform.
MAX: Imagine it. The guts of it, the sheer moral courage. An ordinary soldier using his weekend pass to demonstrate against their bloody missiles.
15 HENRY: *Their?* I thought they were ours.
MAX: No, they're American.
HENRY: Oh, yes—*their* . . .
MAX: Pure moral conscience, you see—I mean, he didn't have our motivation.
HENRY: *Our?*
20 MAX: Mine and Annie's.
(HENRY *appears not to understand.*)
Owning property in Little Barmouth.
HENRY: Yes, of course. Brodie didn't own a cottage there, you mean.
MAX: No, he's a Scots lad. He was stationed at the camp down the road. He was
25 practically guarding the base where these rockets are making Little Barmouth into a sitting duck for the Russian counter-attack, should it ever come to that.
HENRY: (*To* ANNIE) I see what you mean.
ANNIE: Do you?
HENRY: Well, yes. Little Barmouth isn't going to declare war on Russia, so why
30 should Little Barmouth be wiped out in a war not of Little Barmouth's making?
MAX: Quite.
CHARLOTTE: Shut up, Henry.
MAX: Is he being like that?
35 CHARLOTTE: Yes, he's being like that.
MAX: I don't see what he's got to be like that about. We were never consulted about being a target for the Russians. Let their rockets fall somewhere else.
HENRY: (*Capitulating enthusiastically*) Absolutely! So you got to talking. You met Brodie on the train, and he was going to your demo, and you got to talking.

40 ANNIE: Yes.

MAX: (*To* ANNIE) How *did* you know?

ANNIE: What?

MAX: How did you get talking?

(*Small pause.*)

45 HENRY: Annie was wearing the badge. And Brodie said, 'I see you're going to the demo down Whitehall.' Right?

ANNIE: No. He recognized me from the serial. Very flattering. I've hardly been on the box for five years, but he asked for my autograph. He watched me when he was a kid.

50 MAX: How *about* that? It seems like the day before yesterday Annie was doing *Rosie of the Royal Infirmary*. He's *still* a kid.

ANNIE: Yes. Twenty-one.

MAX: He's a child.

HENRY: He kicked two policemen inside out, didn't he? The ones who arrested

55 him?

MAX: Don't be so naïve. They're now both up for perjury on a previous case.

HENRY: Sorry, sorry. I suppose it is logically contingent that perjurors never tell the truth, is it?

MAX: I don't condone vandalism, however idealistic. But the authorities over-

60 reacted badly.

HENRY: Yes, well, as acts of vandalism go, starting a fire on the Cenotaph using the wreath to the Unknown Soldier as kindling scores very low on discretion. I assumed he was trying to be provocative,

MAX: Of course he was, you idiot. But he got hammered by an emotional

65 backlash.

HENRY: No, no, you *can't*—

MAX: Yes, he bloody was!

HENRY: I mean 'hammer' and 'backlash'. You can't *do it!*

MAX: Oh, for Christ's sake.

70 HENRY: And anyway, if you'd got Brodie to plead drunkenness and grovel a bit instead of being cocky and putting the judge's back up, he would probably have got the three months which you are all now agitating to get him, if you follow me.

MAX: (*Pompous under pressure*) This is your house, and I'm drinking your wine,

75 but if you don't mind me saying so, Henry—

HENRY: *My* saying, Max.

MAX: Right.

(*He puts down his glass definitively and stands up.*)

Come on, Annie.

80 (*To* HENRY) There's something wrong with you. You've got something missing. You may have all the answers, but having all the answers is not what life's about.

HENRY: I'm sorry, but it actually *hurts*.

MAX: Brodie may be no intellectual, and I'm not saying he's a saint either, but

85 he did march for a cause, and now he's got six years for a stupid piece of bravado and a punch-up, and he'd have been forgotten in a week if it wasn't for Annie. That's what life's about—messy bits of good and bad luck, and people caring and not necessarily having all the answers. Who the hell are you to patronise Annie? She's worth ten of you.

90 HENRY: I know that.

MAX: I'm sorry, Charlotte.

(MAX *leaves towards the front door.* CHARLOTTE, *with a glance at* HENRY, *rolling her eyes in rebuke, follows him out of room.*)

UNIT 4
THEATRE

homework

1 True or false? Put ticks (√) by the statements that are true.
  a When Annie met Brodie, she was going to a demonstration in London. ☐
  b They were going to demonstrate against the Russians. ☐
  c Annie's reason for demonstrating was that she owned a cottage in Little Barmouth. ☐
  d Brodie had seen Annie on television. ☐
  e Brodie was wearing a badge. ☐
  f They had met previously in an Infirmary. ☐
  g Max thinks that the policemen who arrested Brodie were liars. ☐
  h Brodie was imprisoned for three months. ☐

2 'Is he being like that?'—'Yes, he's being like that.' (lines 34 and 35). What do these lines tell us about Henry's character?

3 How do Max's and Henry's attitudes to Brodie differ?

4 The passage contains two illustrations of Henry's attitude to the use of language. What is his attitude? What is it that 'hurts' (line 83)?

5 Explain what the words 'their' (line 17) and 'our' (line 19) mean to Max and Henry.

6 Describe the relationship between Annie, Charlotte, Henry and Max.

7 Describe in your own words what you know about Annie's past.

8 Imagine that you are Brodie. Describe what happened on the day of the demonstration, and why; what was the result of your actions?

9 What do you think the Brodie Committee is, and what has it got to do with the people in this text?

Words and structures

IDIOMS

■ Exercise 1

Explain the meanings of these expressions as they are used in the text.
  a they got to talking (line 7)
  b The guts of it (line 13)
  c a sitting duck (line 26)
  d should it ever come to that (line 26)
  e wiped out (line 30)
  f a war not of Little Barmouth's making (line 30)
  g How *about* that? (line 50)
  h They're now both up for perjury (line 56)
  i as acts of vandalism go (line 61)
  j putting the judge's back up (line 71)
  k if you follow me (lines 72–3)
  l You've got something missing (line 81)
  m march for a cause (line 85)
  n a punch-up (line 86)
  o if it wasn't for Annie (line 86)

■ Exercise 2

More two-part verbs with *up* and *down*

Fill each gap with the correct form of one of these verbs, followed by *up* or *down*:

back	do
blow	keep
bring	pull
close	talk
die	wear

Then explain with a word or phrase what each verb + *up/down* combination means.

1 Audiences have been so small that the theatre will be forced to _____ very soon.

2 Don't _____ to me, you patronising old goat!

3 I was virtually _____ on the stage: I made my first appearance at the age of two.

4 Jones's tactics were to _____ the opposition by talking incessantly.

5 That policeman's signalling to us— you'd better _____.

6 _____ the good work! We're proud of you!

7 The guerillas have _____ the Kiang-tung bridge.

8 When the fuss has_____, we'll find that a lot of good has come of it.

9 Wilson was forced to_____ when nobody supported him.

10 _____ your coat buttons, dear. It's cold outside.

VOCABULARY

■ Exercise 3

Find the words in the text that are defined here.

1 Absolute, complete.
2 Be condescending towards.
3 Conceited.
4 Humble oneself.
5 Innocent, simple.
6 Overlook, forgive.
7 Permit.
8 Prudence, good judgement.
9 Self-important.
10 Story divided into instalments.
11 Surrendering.

■ Exercise 4

Look at the illustration below and write the correct numbers in the boxes.

acrobat	☐	director	☐
actor	☐	footlights	☐
actress	☐	gallery	☐
aisle	☐	juggler	☐
box	☐	magician	☐
circle	☐	spotlight	☐
clown	☐	stage	☐
comedian	☐	stalls	☐
compère	☐	usher	☐
conductor	☐	wings	☐
curtain	☐		

the gods

STRUCTURES

Verbs and phrases followed by a gerund with no preposition

if you don't mind my saying so (lines 75–6)

- Use the object form (*me*, *them*, *John*, etc.) when these are the object of the main verb.

  I saw him doing it.
  (What did you see? Him.)
  They heard a noise coming from the corner.
  (What did they hear? A noise.)

- Use a possessive adjective (*my*, *your*, etc.) or genitive (*John's*, *Mary's*) when the action itself is the object of the main verb and its meaning is to be limited to a particular person or thing.

  I don't mind your leaving.
  (What don't you mind? Your leaving.)
  I will not tolerate their hitting me.
  (What won't you tolerate? Their hitting.)

- Note that in colloquial usage the object forms (*me*, *them*, etc.) are very often substituted for possessive forms. Expressions such as *if you don't mind me saying* are widespread; examination candidates should, however, avoid them in their written work.

■ Exercise 5

For each of the following sentences, write a new sentence as similar as possible in meaning to the original, but using the word given followed by a gerund with a possessive or object where necessary.

She was annoyed that Peter had gone away. **resented**
She resented Peter's having gone away.

1 They hoped that they wouldn't meet me. **avoid**

2 There's no point. They shouldn't try to convince him. **good**

3 You should certainly go and see the Taj Mahal. **worth**

4 It gives me pleasure to see my old friends. **enjoy**

5 It'll mean that Peter must buy a car. **involve**

6 The police arrived while I was stealing the money. **caught**

7 This will mean that you will have to give up everything. **necessitate**

8 It's very unpleasant to have to wait. **stand**

9 I'm grateful that Mr Mattson came so promptly. **appreciate**

10 I wish I had asked her to marry me. **regret**

Listening and speaking
Discussion and debate

Describe what is happening in the photograph.
Why is the boy doing this? Is he suffering at all?
Do you think the audience is enjoying the show?
Why do people find activities of this sort fascinating?
Are there any forms of entertainment that you find repulsive, or that you think should be restricted?

■ **Exercise 1**

Study this table of statistics, and then discuss the questions.

Leisure activities by sex, 1977 Great Britain	In full-time employment		Other	
	Men	Women	Men	Women
Proportion in each category doing selected activity at least once in previous 4 weeks	%	%	%	%
Home-based activities				
Television	98	98	95	97
Radio	88	90	85	86
Gardening	50	30	46	37
Hobbies	13	3	8	3
Do-it-yourself	57	25	35	20
Sporting activities				
Total active outdoor sports	52	39	35	30
Total active indoor sports	38	22	12	10
Spectator sports	15	10	13	9
Other leisure activities				
Visits to countryside	9	10	8	9
Visits to seaside	16	16	12	17
Going out for a meal/drink	78	74	53	51
Going to bingo	5	11	5	11
Going to cinema/theatre	21	29	14	18
Total number of activities engaged in at least once in previous 4 weeks (annual average)	8.9	8.4	7.1	7.3

from *Facts in Focus* Penguin Books in association with HMSO

1 Which activities are the most/least popular?

2 Which activities show the greatest difference in popularity between
   a women and men?
   b fully employed and others?

3 What do you think are the reasons for the differences in popularity?

4 If statistics about leisure activities in your home country were compiled, do you think the results would be very different from those shown here?

■ **Exercise 2**

How many of the activities in the table have you done in the past month? Are there any activities that you like doing and that have been left out of the survey?

■ **Exercise 3**

Devise a questionnaire that will allow you to find out the leisure interests of students in your class or school. Then carry out interviews and compare the results with those above.

UNIT 4
THEATRE

■ **Exercise 4**

Imagine that you are retiring after a long career as one of the following:

a clown
a magician
a trapeze artist
a comedian
a singer
an actor/actress
a disc jockey
a playwright
a critic
a costume designer
a set designer
a ballet dancer
a choreographer
a composer
a conductor
a musician
a doorman
a stage manager

Give a short speech at a party held in your honour: explain why the job has been important to you and, if possible, recount an anecdote or two.

■ **Exercise 5**

Write a newspaper report on one of the speeches.

Listening comprehension

You will hear a short conversation followed by a longer one. The first time you listen, identify the situation and make a note of the words and occurrences that give you this information. On the second and subsequent hearings, answer questions 1 to 4.

1 Complete the information in the table.

2 Put ticks by the plays that the man and woman have both seen.
Bats ☐
The Revolving Staircase ☐
The Diplomat ☐
Molotov and the Spare Part ☐
Three's Company ☐

3 What does the way the man and woman speak tell you about their age, their social standing, their attitudes to the play and the actors, and their relationship?

4 What were the exact words used to express the following?
a Likes and approval.
b Dislikes and disapproval.
c Preference.

actor's name	John Hodsworth	Martin Muller	Julia Donaldson
age			
role			
acting ability (good, bad, average)			
plays previously acted in			

Function: likes, approval and preference

What do you think they are saying? Fill in the bubbles.

■ **Exercise 1** [PW]

Look at the expressions in Pair work 4a. Student B must find the most appropriate responses to what student A says.

■ **Exercise 2**

Use the tables to help you find suitable remarks in these situations.

1 Two friends, Bill and Belle, talk about:
   Bill's new haircut/Belle's new shoes.
   whether or not Belle is suitably dressed for a wedding.
   two new films or plays.

2 A restaurant manager comes up to one of his customers to ask if everything is satisfactory.

3 A reporter is carrying out a street survey into things that people approve or disapprove of:
   corporal punishment.
   nuclear weapons.
   compulsory military service.
   any other topic that people feel strongly about.

Asking about likes and approval

General
Do/Don't you *like/enjoy* ...?
...is *nice/pleasant*, isn't it?
... are *nice/pleasant*, aren't they?
Is/Are ... *all right/a good idea*(, do you think)?
Do you think ... is *all right/a good idea*?
Do you think ... are *all right/a good idea*?

Informal
Isn't/aren't ... *great/fantastic*?
Don't you love ...?
Is *this/that OK/all right*?

Formal
What *are your feelings/do you feel* about ...?
Don't you find ... (very) *exciting/fascinating*?
Do you approve (of ...)?
Is/Are ... *acceptable/satisfactory*?

THEATRE

Expressing likes and approval

General
I (really) *like/enjoy/love/adore* ...
I'm (very) keen on ...
There's nothing I *like/enjoy* more
(than ...).
... *is/are very nice/good/excellent/an
excellent idea.*

Informal
You can't beat ...
... *is/are* (really) *great/fantastic/
terrific.*
That's a *great/fantastic* idea!
OK!/Great!/Fantastic!/Just the job!

Formal
What I *particularly/especially* enjoy
is ...
I'm (really) very *fond of/keen on* ...
I *find/think* ... (*most/quite*)
acceptable/satisfactory
I can thoroughly recommend ...

Expressing dislikes and disapproval

General
(I'm afraid) I *hate/don't like/am not
very keen on* ...
There's nothing I *like/enjoy* less
(than ...).
I don't think ... *is/are very
good/interesting.*
I (really) *don't/can't* approve of ...
How *awful/dreadful/appalling!*

Informal
I can't *bear/stand/put up* with ...
I don't think much of ...
Oh, no!
I'm (dead) against ...

Formal
(*I have to admit/I must say*) *I rather
dislike/I'm not too fond of* ...
... *doesn't/don't* appeal to me very
much.
I *disapprove of/am opposed to/cannot
support* ...
I find ... (*completely/quite*)
unacceptable/unsatisfactory.

Asking about preference

General
Do/Would you prefer ... or ...?
Would you rather ... (or ...)?
Which *seems better/would you prefer*?
Do you like ... *better/more* (*than* ...)?

Informal
What's it to be/What do you say?
... or ...?

Formal
Do you find/Is ... or ... more
enjoyable/interesting/appealing?
Which appeals to you more? ... or
...?

Expressing preference

General
(*On the whole/As far as I'm
concerned*) I *like/enjoy* ...
more/better (than ...).
I'd *rather/prefer* ...

Informal
Give me ... *any/every* time.
I'd *go for/plump for* ...
I'll *go for/plump for* ...

Formal
I (*much/really*) prefer ...
I (really) have a strong preference
for ...
... appeals to me more than ...
... is much more *satisfactory/
interesting* than ...

■ **Practice** PW

Act out the situations in Pair work 4b–4d.

Reading aloud: sentence stress 〔▭〕

To decide which words in a sentence are to be stressed, it is necessary to distinguish between *content words*, which carry the meaning of the sentence, and *form words*, which define grammatical structure but are less important to meaning.

content words/usually stressed
nouns: **theatre**, **behaviour**, etc. interrogative pronouns: **who**, **what**, etc. demonstratives: **this**, **that**, etc. adjectives: **unacceptable**, **bad**, etc. adverbs: **quite**, **only**, etc. verbs (except auxiliaries): **find**, **go**, etc.

form words/usually unstressed
prepositions: **to**, **for**, etc. auxiliaries: **have**, **can**, **is**, **are**, etc. conjunctions: **and**, **but**, etc. pronouns: **he**, **her**, **them**, etc.

Note: The lists are intended to provide only a rough guide. Often words in the right-hand column are used as content words, and are therefore stressed.

I _have_ been there, I promise!
I confess. _But_! In my defence, I should like to say . . .
I gave it to _her_, not _him_.

Similarly, words in the left-hand column may carry no important meaning, in which case they are unstressed; this category includes words like *one*, *things*, etc. used to stand for something that has already been mentioned or implied.

I _want_ to _talk_ things _over_ with you.
I prefer the _striped_ ones, _actually_.

■ Exercise 1

The following sentences are taken from the conversation at the theatre. Underline the content words, and then listen to the conversation again to see if these words were stressed. Then say the sentences out loud.

1 What is the meaning of this?

2 We can get some coffee in the next interval.

3 I can't stand the man.

4 But you really can't beat him when it comes to acting.

5 She always seems to be a housekeeper.

■ Exercise 2

Go through the listening comprehension dialogue on pp. 207–8 underlining the content words. Then read the conversation aloud.

THEATRE

Activity: critics choice

1 Read the *Critics' Choice* and, in small groups, discuss which plays you prefer. Talk about these questions:
- Which play would you prefer to see?
- Which play would be most suitable for staging by your class?
- Which play would be most likely to be a commercial success?

2 Choose one of the plays and invent a synopsis of its story: this should contain one or two paragraphs about each scene or act, but should not contain any dialogue. Write a list of the characters, too, with a brief description of their roles.

3 Write the dialogue for one of the scenes in the play, and act it out.

Critics' choice

ARDEN OF FAVERSHAM
The Pit (628 8795)
Mon-Fri at 7.30pm; matinée Thurs at 2pm. In repertory with Lear by Edward Bond (today at 7.30pm)
Terry Hands's gripping and perceptive production of the anonymous Elizabethan murder drama, now transferred from Stratford, reveals it as a fascinating, enigmatic classic. Jenny Agutter and Robert O'Mahoney play the adulterous couple whose attempts to kill her stolid husband (Christoper Benjamin) combine pathos with agreeably black humour.

CHARLEY'S AUNT
Aldwych (836 6404)
Until Sept 24, Mon-Fri at 7.30 pm, Sat at 5pm and 8.30pm; matinée Wed at 2.30pm
Griff Rhys Jones makes one of the best "aunts" ever in a joyous production with an excellent supporting cast.

HAPPY FAMILY
Duke of York's (836 5122)
Mon-Thurs at 8pm, Fri and Sat at 5.45pm and 8.30pm
Giles Cooper's clever, disturbing 1960s comedy about three grown-up siblings imprisoned in childhood ritual is still theatrically gripping and full of psychological and political nuance. Excellent direction by Maria Aitken of an impressive cast led by Ian Ogilvy and Angela Thorne.

NOISES OFF
Savoy (836 8888)
Mon-Fri at 7.45pm. Sat at 5pm and 8.30pm; matinée Wed at 3pm
The funniest farce for years. Michael Frayn's brilliantly contrived complex of on-stage disasters and backstage dramas is still keeping houses full and audiences helpless with laughter after its first cast change. Phyllida Law, Benjamin Whitrow and the rest of Michael Blakemore's crack company give it the best of both worlds – the commercial hit and the connoisseur's classic.

YOU CAN'T TAKE IT WITH YOU
Lyttelton (928 2252)
Today at 3pm and 7.45pm; Mon, Thurs and Fri at 7.45pm. In repertory with Inner Voices by Eduardo de Filippo Tues and Wed at 7.45pm; matinée Wed at 3pm
Once again the National strikes gold in America, this time with Kaufman and Hart's endearing 1936 comedy about a family of happy eccentrics. Jimmy Jewell as the genial, drop-out grandpa, Geraldine McEwan as dotty, authoress mother, Gaye Brown as alcoholic actress and Margaret Courtenay as a Russian grandee turned waltress combine in a gloriously funny, subversive hymn to independence.

The Times 27 August 1983

Revision: units 3 and 4

■ Exercise 1

Fill each gap with one word: it need not be the actual word used in the original text, but it must be appropriate to the context.

Apparently, it really is, _____(1)_____ all, only exercise which keeps you thin, as every diet fails in the _____(2)_____ because you lose _____(3)_____ only fat, but muscle. Apparently, when the weight is put _____(4)_____ on (as it always is, I can assure you ...) that lost muscle is usually replaced with fat, and so the _____(5)_____ circle goes on with miserable diet _____(6)_____ miserable diet.

What _____(7)_____ does, _____(8)_____ is vigorous aerobic exercise, is replace that muscle and harden what you already have; your _____(9)_____ will go _____(10)_____, as I am finding through these determined weeks, even though I've been scoffing ravenously between sessions. Right. Back on the exercise cycle!

If a person _____(11)_____ in 50 kcal/day more than he needs, his annual _____(12)_____ will be 18,000 kcal, _____(13)_____ to nearly 3 kg of fat. This could lead to a 30 kg weight increase in 10 years. If you should _____(14)_____ day decide to _____(15)_____ your routine mile walk each day but maintain your eating habits, statistically you will _____(16)_____ 100 pounds in 10 years! It's not _____(17)_____ that obesity's approach is stealthy as life becomes more sedate, _____(18)_____ to the automobile, more _____(19)_____ jobs and less time _____(20)_____ to exercise.

■ Exercise 2

Write definitions for three of the following words or phrases and see if your classmates can guess the right words from your definitions. Alternatively, you might like to do a mime for some of the words.

aisle
(to) blow up
capitulate
cocky
condone
conductor
demonstration
footlights
grovel
guts

juggler
magician
patronise
plead
pompous
(a) punch-up
sheer
serial
sitting duck
wipe out

UNIT 5

GAMES

Reading and thinking
Reading comprehension (1)

PRACTICAL COMPUTING APRIL 1980

TV GAMES

PROGRAMMABLE £29.50 + VAT.
COLOUR CARTRIDGE TV GAME

1 The TV game can be compared to an audio cassette deck and is programmed to play a multitude of different games in COLOUR, using various plug-in cartridges. At long last a TV game is available which will keep
5 pace with improving technology by allowing you to extend your library of games with the purchase of additional cartridges as new games are developed. Each cartridge contains up to ten different action games and the first cartridge containing ten sports
10 games is included free with the console. Other cartridges are currently available to enable you to play such games as Grand Prix Motor Racing, Super Wipeout and Stunt Rider. Further cartridges are to be released, including Tank Battle, Hunt the Sub and
15 Target. The console comes complete with two removable joystick player controls to enable you to move in all four directions (up/down/left/right) and built into these joystick controls are ball serve and target fire

buttons. Other features include several difficulty option
20 switches, automatic on-screen digital scoring and colour coding on scores and balls. Lifelike sounds are transmitted through the TV's speaker, simulating the actual game being played.
Manufactured by Waddington's Videomaster and
25 guaranteed for one year

EXTRA CARTRIDGES

ROAD RACE – £8.87 + VAT. Grand Prix motor racing with gear changes, crash noises

SUPER WIPEOUT – £9.17 + VAT. 10 different games
30 of blasting obstacles off the screen

STUNT RIDER – £12.16 + VAT.
Motorcycle speed trials, jumping obstacles, leaping various rows of up to 24 buses etc.

NON-PROGRAMMABLE TV GAMES
35 **6 Game – COLOURSCOPE II – £13.50 + VAT.**
10 Game – COLOUR SPORTSWORLD £22.50 + VAT.

---

1 Complete the table by putting ticks (√) in the correct boxes.

	included	can be bought now	cannot be bought yet
Super Wipeout	☐	☑	☐
Hunt the Sub	☐	☐	☑
10 Sports Games	☑	☐	☐
Grand Prix Motor Racing	☐	☑	☐
Stunt Rider	☐	☑	☐
Tank Battle	☐	☐	☑
Target	☐	☐	☑

For questions 2 and 3 choose the phrase which best completes each sentence.

2 The TV game is similar to an audio cassette deck in that it
√ **a** can use various plug-in cartridges.
b is programmed.
c uses improved technology.
d can play various programs.

3 The TV game will 'keep pace with improving technology' because
a there is an extensive library of games available.
√ **b** the same equipment can be used for new games in the future.
c the cartridges contain technically advanced action games.
d it is the result of technological developments.

4 Which of the following features are included?
√ **a** numbers displaying the score
√ **b** buttons to shoot at targets
c real sound recordings
d a ball-shaped control for serving
√ **e** different levels of difficulty

5 Which aspects of the colour cartridge TV game are *not* described in the advertisement?

Reading comprehension (2)

SPORTING BEHAVIOUR

The biology of sport—a modern hunting ritual

Sporting activites are essentially modified forms of hunting behaviour. Viewed biologically, the modern footballer is revealed as a member of a disguised hunting pack. His killing weapon has turned into a harmless football and his prey into a goal-mouth. If his aim is accurate and he scores a goal, he enjoys the hunter's triumph of killing his prey.

5 To understand how this transformation has taken place we must briefly look back at our ancient ancestors. They spent over a million years evolving as co-operative hunters. Their very survival depended on success in the hunting-field. Under this pressure their whole way of life, even their bodies, became radically changed. They became chasers, runners, jumpers, aimers, throwers and prey-killers. They co-operated as skilful male-group attackers.

10 Then, about ten thousand years ago, after this immensely long formative period of hunting their food, they became farmers. Their improved intelligence, so vital to their old hunting life, was put to a new use—that of penning, controlling and domesticating their prey. The hunt became suddenly obsolete. The food was there on the farms, awaiting their needs. The risks and uncertainties of the hunt were no longer essential for survival.

15 The hunting skills and the hunting urges remained, however, and demanded new outlets. Hunting for sport replaced hunting for necessity. This new activity involved all the original hunting sequences, but the aim of the operation was no longer to avoid starvation. Instead the sportsmen set off to test their skill against prey that were no longer essential to their well-being. To be sure, the kill may have been eaten, but there were other, much simpler ways of 20 obtaining a meaty meal. The chase became exposed as an end in itself. The logical extension of this trend was the big-game hunter who never ate his kill, but merely hung its stuffed head on his wall, and the fox-hunter who has to breed foxes in order to release them to hunt them down. Here there is no longer even any pretence that the chasing and killing are a means to an end. They are openly accepted as their own reward.

25 An alternative solution was to transform the activities of the hunting pack into other patterns of behaviour. Superficially these new activities did not look like hunting, but beneath the surface all the basic elements were there. The key to the transformation lies in the fact that there was no longer any need to eat the prey. This being so, then why bother to kill an edible animal? Why indeed kill any animal at all? A symbolic killing is all that is needed, 30 providing the thrill of the chase can be retained. The Greek solution was athletics—field-sports involving chasing (track-running), jumping, and throwing (discus and javelin). The athletes experienced the vigorous physical activity so typical of the hunting scene, and the patterns they performed were all elements of the ancient hunting sequence, but their triumph was now transformed from the actual kill to a symbolic one of 'winning'.

35 In other parts of the world, ancient ball-games were making a small beginning: a form of polo in ancient Persia, bowls and hockey in ancient Egypt, football in ancient China. Here the element of the primeval hunting sequence to be retained and amplified was the all-important hunter's action of aiming. Whatever the rules of the game, the physical act of aiming was the essence of the operation. This more than any other has come to dominate 40 the world of modern sport. There are more aiming sports today than all other forms of sport put together. One could almost define field-sports now as competitive aiming behaviour.

From *Manwatching* by Desmond Morris

GAMES

1 What aspects of hunting are the original equivalents of these elements of modern football?
   a The team.
   b The ball.
   c The goal-mouth.
   d Scoring a goal.

2 What change took place about ten thousand years ago, and what effect did it have on man?

3 Why did 'hunting for sport' replace 'hunting for necessity'?

4 Which statements are true and which are false, according to the writer?
   a Foxes are hunted to be eaten.
   b The fox-hunter only pretends to hunt and kill the fox.
   c Foxes are bred in order to be hunted and killed.
   d The fox-hunter receives a reward for killing the fox.

5 What are the similarities and differences between athletics and hunting for food?

6 What was the reason for the development of ball-games?

7 Trace the development in man's behaviour that led from hunting for food to modern competitive sports. Use your own words as far as possible.

8 Explain how a game that you know well can be seen as a 'modified form of hunting behaviour'.

How do you think the passage on sporting behaviour relates to the TV games described above?

Words and structures

IDIOMS

■ **Exercise 1**

Explain the meanings of these expressions as they are used in the texts.

Text 1:
a plug-in (line 3)
b At long last (line 4)
c on-screen digital scoring (line 20)
d colour coding (line 20)
e rows of *up to* 24 buses (line 33)

Text 2:
a Their *very* survival (line 6)
b To be sure (line 19)
c an end in itself (line 20)
d The logical extension of this trend (line 20)
e a means to an end (line 23)
f beneath the surface (line 24)
g making a small beginning (line 35)
h amplified (line 37)
i put together (line 41)

■ **Exercise 2**

Play

1 play a trick (on someone)	a be fair and honest
2 play ball	b behave stupidly or frivolously
3 play havoc (with …)	c cheat
4 play into someone's hands	d co-operate
5 play it by ear	e destroy
6 play second fiddle (to …)	f do something dangerous
7 play the fool	g give (an opponent) an advantage
8 play the game	h improvise
9 play truant	i stay away from school
10 play with fire	j take a less important part (than …)

Match up the expressions and definitions. Then write ten sentences of your own that include the expressions on the left.

Now choose the most appropriate expressions from the above list to fill the gaps in these sentences, making any necessary adjustments to verb forms.

1 The weather _____ with our plans for last summer.

2 I'm tired of _____ to my boss; I'm sure I could do his job much better than he does it.

3 We needed Joe desperately, but he refused to _____ .

4 You'll be _____ if you go to the police; that's exactly what he wants you to do.

5 I've never been in a situation like this before, so I'll have to _____ .

■ **Exercise 3**

Two-part verbs with *play*
Choose the word that best completes each sentence.

1 The Senator tried to play _____ the importance of his youthful amorous adventures.
a down **b** off **c** out **d** with

2 Even though it was very late, they decided to play _____ until a clear winner emerged.
a in **b** on **c** out **d** up

3 To stay in power, a leader must be able to play _____ his opponents against each other.
a along **b** off **c** on **d** out

4 I'm afraid I'm not fit for tomorrow's game—my knee has been playing _____ for the last couple of days.
a about **b** back **c** down **d** up

5 You're not really interested in politics, you're just playing _____ it.
a at **b** for **c** in **d** on

VOCABULARY

■ **Exercise 4**

Fill each gap with the most appropriate word from the lists below.

David Moorcroft is the _____(1)_____ holder of the world 5,000 metres record. But there is no _____(2)_____ that he will win in the Olympic Games. I think he has a good chance, however, since he is one of the most _____(3)_____ athletes in the world. He says that his next _____(4)_____ is to _____(5)_____ the 13-minute barrier for 5,000 metres.

1 **a** actual **b** contemporary
 c current **d** topical

2 **a** guarantee **b** necessity
 c obligation **d** promise

3 **a** reliable **b** reliant
 c trusting **d** trustworthy

4 **a** aim **b** goal **c** mark **d** purpose

5 **a** beat **b** break **c** strike **d** win

■ **Exercise 5**

Fill each gap in the following passage with one word. Below the passage is a list of words which may help you; you will not need all of these, while some may be used more than once. Only basic root words are given, and in some cases you will have to find other forms of these words, e.g. *compete-competition*.

Chess is a fascinating _____(1)_____, though sometimes what happens off the _____(2)_____ is more interesting than what happens on it. The World _____(3)_____ of 1972 had been preceded by a long series of _____(4)_____ throughout the world to determine which _____(5)_____ would have the right to _____(6)_____ Boris Spassky, the current _____(7)_____. Bobby Fischer of the United States _____(8)_____ as the winner of these preliminary _____(9)_____, and his _____(10)_____ with Spassky began on July 11th. It turned into a _____(11)_____ of nerves, with the _____(12)_____ making more and more extravagant accusations about each other. At one stage the

Russians alleged that the American was using 'electronic devices and a chemical substance' to undermine his _____(13)_____'s playing ability. The _____(14)_____ system was simple: the winner of each game received one _____(15)_____, while the _____(16)_____ got zero. If a game resulted in a _____(17)_____, both received half. The first _____(18)_____ to reach twelve and a half would be the _____(19)_____. Eventually Fischer won the _____(20)_____, and the final _____(21)_____ was: Fischer $12\frac{1}{2}$, Spassky $8\frac{1}{2}$. Fischer had seven _____(22)_____ and three _____(23)_____, while eleven games were _____(24)_____.

battle	*mark*
beat	*match*
board	*meet*
challenge	*oppose*
champion	*play*
compete	*point*
contest	*race*
draw	*score*
emerge	*sport*
gain	*war*
game	*win*
lose	*tournament*

Now do the exercise again, this time so that no word is used more than once.

STRUCTURES

Verbs and phrases followed by *in* and a noun or gerund

■ **Exercise 6**

For each of the following sentences, write a new sentence as similar as possible in meaning to the original sentence, but using the words given, as well as *in* followed by a gerund.

Smoking a few cigarettes each day is not harmful. **harm**
There is no harm in smoking a few cigarettes each day.

1 Your interfering in my affairs was not justified. **you**

2 Watching the television took all my attention. **engrossed**

3 He won't stop pestering me. **persists**

4 It was a mistake to think I could trust him. **mistaken**

5 It was easy for me to find the way. **difficulty**

6 It would be pointless to start now. **there**

7 It's important for me to stand up for what is right. **believe**

8 At last she managed to break the record. **succeeded**

9 Will you defend our country with us? **join**

10 The headmaster greatly enjoyed punishing us. **pleasure**

The passive
the modern footballer is revealed ... (line 2)

■ Use: To show that the person or thing that performs an action is not as important as the action itself. In the example in the heading here, it is of no importance *who* it is that reveals the facts about the modern footballer; it is the action—the 'revealing'—that the author is interested in.

■ Formation: Part of the verb *to be* followed by the past participle. All verb forms, including the infinitive and the gerund, have a passive form.

They were afraid of being beaten. (gerund)
He could not be persuaded to leave. (infinitive)

■ **Exercise 7**

Go through the two texts at the beginning of this unit and make a note of all the uses of passive verb forms. If possible, convert them into active forms.

The TV game can be compared to an audio cassette deck.
You can compare the TV game ...
It is possible to compare ...

Discuss why some of them cannot be converted without changing the meaning or emphasis.

■ Exercise 8

Fill the gaps in the following passage with suitable verbs in the passive form.

'Welcome to Wembley for the second half of the cup final between Liverpool and West Ham. In the first half the West Ham defence ____(1)____ continually by the Liverpool forwards, but as yet no goals ____(2)____. This programme ____(3)____ in five different countries and it ____(4)____ that the match ____(5)____ by 20 million people. First of all, a word or two about the rules of the competition: if this match ____(6)____, a replay ____(7)____ next week; if that match also ends in a draw, the game ____(8)____ by penalty kicks. Liverpool's record in the cup is outstanding: if they ____(9)____ (not) by Birmingham last year, the cup ____(10)____ back to Liverpool for the third successive year. Unfortunately Johnson cannot play today as a result of ____(11)____ in last week's game. Anyway, the match is due ____(12)____, and the second-half commentary ____(13)____ by Joe Lamb.'

Active sentences such as *They gave me the blue car* can be expressed in the passive in two ways:

I was given the blue car. (normal usage)
The blue car was given to me. (special emphasis, either on <u>blue</u> or on <u>me</u>)

■ Exercise 9

Rewrite the following sentences in the passive, beginning with the words given.

1 They offered Jane a job. (**Jane** ...)

2 Someone has sent me an anonymous letter. (**I** ...)

3 They're telling us a pack of lies. (**We** ...)

4 We paid John the money, not Harry. (**The money** ...)

5 Someone will have to find a better solution. (**A better** ...)

Listening and speaking
Discussion and debate

Describe the people in the photograph.
What are they doing?
Are they enjoying themselves?
Why do they do it?
Would you enjoy doing it?

UNIT 5
GAMES

■ **Exercise 1**

Why do people play games? Complete the table below by putting crosses to show which needs are best satisfied by which sports and games. Add more games and needs if you wish to.

Then compare your answers with those of the rest of the class. If your fellow students disagree with you, try to convince them that you are right.

	meeting people	physical skill	mental skill	using up excess energy	keeping fit	slimming	outlet for aggression	competitiveness	physical contact	financial gain	taking risks			
poker														
table tennis														
soccer														
American football														
bridge														
squash														
tennis														
ice hockey														
chess														
golf														
bingo														
horse-racing														
basketball														
swimming														
jogging														
boxing														
weight-lifting														
orienteering														
skiing														
cycling														
athletics														
gymnastics														

■ **Exercise 2**

Some of the following people are taking part in a radio discussion programme on the subject of games and sport.

a professional footballer
a non-sportsman married to a world-class athlete
a sports journalist
a retired boxing champion
an official of the International Amateur Athletics Federation
a promising young chess player
a relative of someone killed while taking part in a sport (e.g. motor-racing)
a politician
a school teacher
a police officer
a doctor

Decide which questions the panel is going to discuss. Here are some suggestions:
■ Should blood sports be banned?
■ In what ways is money involved in sport?
■ Is amateurism desirable?
■ Which games or toys are unsuitable for children?
■ What is the best way to deal with hooliganism amongst spectators?
■ What are the rights and wrongs of using sport as a political tool?
■ What do you think of sports that require physical violence?

Divide the roles amongst the members of the class. One student should act as chairman, deciding when to move from one topic to the next, and ensuring that everyone gets a chance to participate. Spend some time preparing your roles, and jotting down some ideas on the questions you are going to discuss. Then hold the discussion.

■ **Exercise 3**

Write a well-balanced essay on one of the topics discussed.

Listening comprehension

You will hear the end of a radio commentary at a sporting event, followed by interviews with the participants. The first time you listen, try to decide what the event is, and make a list of the words and phrases that give you this information. Then listen to the commentary again and answer questions 1 to 8.

1 Complete the table of results.

Quarter-finals	Semi-finals	Final	Winner
JONES CARTER	CARTER		
DEBENHAM			
BROWN			

For questions 2 to 4 choose the word or phrase that best completes each sentence.

2 The commentator's reaction to the result is _____.
   a bewilderment   **b** disbelief
   c relief   **d** surprise

3 Carter thinks he won because he was _____.
   a confident   **b** in the mood
   c lucky   **d** on form

4 Carter thinks that John Fairlight can be beaten _____.
   a every day   **b** never
   c on most days
   d only when he isn't on form

5 Which word best describes the interviewer's attitude to Smith?
   a Aggressive.   **b** Critical.
   c Neutral.   **d** Sympathetic.

6 Compare the two players' thoughts about the tournament officials.

7 Did the interviewer do a good job? Summarise the information he obtained from the players.

8 What were the exact words used in the interview to express the following?
   a Praise.
   b Sympathy.
   c Criticism.

Function: praise, commiseration and criticism

What do you think they are saying? Fill in the bubbles.

■ **Exercise 1**

Match up the comments on the left with the most appropriate responses on the right.

1 Bad luck!	**a** I thought it was quite good.
2 Well done!	**b** It can't be helped.
3 Well, I didn't succeed.	**c** It was nothing really.
4 What a dreadful performance!	**d** Never mind.

■ **Exercise 2**

Use the tables to help you find suitable remarks in these situations.

1 After the opening night of a new play, you congratulate one of the actors—a close friend of yours.

2 You are a teacher; one of your pupils has just handed in a short, untidy and unimaginative essay.

3 You go to a friend's house for the first time; you want to say how much you like the house and the way it is furnished and decorated.

4 You and a friend have just been beaten in a tennis doubles match; you think your partner played badly.

5 You have just heard that a close relative of a colleague at work has died; what do you say to your colleague?

Giving praise	Accepting praise
General What a *good/great/wonderful* match! Congratulations on . . . Well done!	Thank you. (It's) (very) nice of you to say so. I'm glad you *like/liked/enjoyed* it.
Informal What (a) *terrific/fantastic* . . . (You were) *great/fantastic*.	
Formal *Let me/May I/I must* congratulate you on . . . My compliments on . . .	

Commiseration	Criticism
General (What) bad luck! (Oh dear,) I **am** sorry (about . . .). What a *pity/shame* (you *couldn't/didn't* . . .).	**General** What a *terrible/dreadful* match! What a disappointment! You were *awful/terrible*.
Informal Never mind. There'll be plenty of other opportunities. Poor (old) *you/John*. I know how it feels.	**Informal** (You) (stupid) *idiot/fool!* Rubbish! Can't you do better than that?
Formal I am/was most *upset/distressed* to *hear/learn* that . . . I (do) sympathise (with you).	**Formal** (I'm afraid) I found your performance disappointing. (I'm afraid) I'm disappointed (*in you/by your . . .*).

■ **Practice** ⬚PW⬚

Act out the situations in Pair work
5a–5c. 5a and 5b can be done several
times, using different situations.

Reading aloud: intonation

The most important factor in intonation is whether the voice rises or falls from the last significant stress in the sentence.

Tune 1—falling intonation

When did you last watch ⬊television?
I watched it ⬊yesterday.
Turn the ⬊radio off! It sounds ⬊awful.

The last important stress in these sentences is on <u>tele</u>vision, <u>yes</u>terday, <u>radio</u> off, and <u>aw</u>ful. The voice starts to fall on the stressed syllable and continues to fall until the end of the sentence.
■ Use: Tune 1 expresses definiteness or a sense of completion. It is therefore very often used in orders, definite statements, as well as questions that begin with a question word (What? Where? Who? etc.).

Tune 2—rising intonation

Did you watch ⬈television yesterday?
Are you the ⬈vicar?
May I borrow your ⬈newspaper, please?

The last important stress in these sentences is on <u>tele</u>vision, <u>vic</u>ar and <u>news</u>paper. The voice starts to rise on the stressed syllable and continues upwards until the end of the sentence.
■ Use: Tune 2 expresses doubt or incompleteness. It is used in questions that have no question word, or statements in which the speaker is unsure of himself or is inviting comment from the listener. It often makes statements sound softer or questions more polite and friendly.
For example, a routine question such as:

How ⬊are you?

is normally spoken as indicated, with a falling intonation. But the speaker can express greater concern with a rising intonation:

How ⬈are you?

Lists

A good example of the connection between tunes 1 and 2 and the idea of completeness is the intonation pattern normally used for counting or listing objects:

⬈One, ⬈two, ⬈three, ⬈four, ⬈five,
⬈six, ⬈seven, ⬈eight, ⬈eight, ⬈nine,
⬊ten.
The ⬈red one, the ⬈green one, the
⬈blue one, and the ⬊yellow one.
Here the rises indicate incompletion—there is more to come—while the falls show that the last item has been reached.

■ Exercise 1

Underline the final significant stress in each sentence. Then mark each underlined syllable with an arrow, to show whether it falls or rises.

1 How do you do?

2 Let me take your coat.

3 Do you know each other?

4 Nice to see you.

5 Can I read my comic?

6 Sir, would you like to have a go?

7 Beat that if you can.

8 Anyone else like to try it out?

9 Have you seen it before?

10 He should find something better to do with himself.

■ Exercise 2

Go through the interviews on p. 208 and mark the final stresses in all the sentences. Then listen closely to the interviews again to check that you found the correct answers. Finally, read the dialogue aloud.

Activity: word games

1 Ghost

- Ghost is a game for three or more players. First of all a player announces the first letter of any word that contains at least three letters. Within thirty seconds the person on his left must then add a letter, such that the two together could form the beginning of a word. Then the third player adds a letter, and so on until the letters form a complete word.

- The object of the game is to avoid being the person who completes a word. Eventually someone will be forced to say the last letter of a word (or will be unable to think of a suitable continuation), and this person loses a life. Anyone who loses three lives is a 'ghost' and has to drop out.

- Words that are not in the dictionary, or that are designated as slang, proper names, or foreign words, are considered illegal. If a player, when it is his turn, thinks that the letters given so far cannot form a legal word, he may challenge the player who said the last letter. If the player thus challenged cannot say a legal word consistent with the letters, he loses a life; otherwise the challenger loses a life.

- Play 'Ghost' a few times. When you have mastered it, you can try 'Superghost': the only difference is that a letter may be added at either end of an incomplete word.

Examples:

		Game 1	Game 2
Player	1	B	P
	2	A (thinking of BANK)	L (thinking of PLAN)
	3	S (thinking of BASS)	O (thinking of PLOT)
	4	I (thinking of BASIC)	M (bluffing—he can't think of a letter that doesn't end a word)
	5	L (thinking of BASILISK) Player 5 loses a life, because he has inadvertently made the word BASIL (a type of herb)	Player 5 challenges, and player 4 loses a life, since there is no word he knows that begins PLOM-

2 Categories

Peter and Paul are playing the game of 'Categories'. So are Ann and Judy. Read their two conversations carefully and formulate the rules for the game. Then play it, either in pairs or as a team game.

Peter: Flying saucer. Paul: Is it 'things in space'? Peter: No. Er ... football. Paul: Is it 'toys'? Peter: No, it isn't. Mm ... plate. Paul: 'Round things'? Peter: Yes, that's right.	Ann: Bomb. Judy: Is it 'weapons'? Ann: No. Hush Judy: Ah! It must be 'noises'. Ann: No. Plump. Judy: Is it 'words that begin and end with the same letter'? Ann: Yes, it is.

Written work: connecting ideas (2)

Processes

The following are some of the more common expressions that are used to show the order in which the various stages of a process are carried out.

firstly first of all to begin with the first step is the first stage is the first stage begins with	secondly next then later subsequently after this the next step is	eventually finally the last step/stage is and so on

■ Exercise 1

Look back at the rules of 'Ghost' and see which of the above expressions were used there.

■ Exercise 2

Expand the following notes into a complete set of instructions, and use expressions from the list above where appropriate.

2 players—each draws a square containing 16 smaller squares (4 × 4) —one person says a letter—both put it in one of their squares—other player says a letter—both put it in an empty square—continue alternately until all squares are filled—no letter may be erased or moved—object: to get as many 4-letter words as possible, vertically, horizontally or diagonally (but only left-to-right and top-to-bottom)—legal words as in 'Ghost'— winner has most 4-letter words.

■ Exercise 3

Invent a set of instructions for one of the TV games on p. 52.

UNIT **6**

CRIME

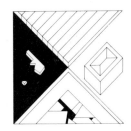

Reading and thinking

Reading comprehension

THE GREAT TRAIN ROBBERS TELL THEIR STORY

1 On Thursday August 8, 1963, fifteen masked men stopped the night train from Glasgow to London and robbed it of £2,500,000. It was called the crime of
5 the century, and the thieves were relentlessly pursued by Scotland Yard until half the gang were behind bars serving huge prison terms. But the story did not end there. First one, then another
10 escaped in thrilling style and fled abroad, catching the world's imagination and making the Train Robbers into folk heroes.

Thirteen years later the gang combined
15 to tell their story, and Piers Paul Read, author of the bestselling ALIVE, agreed to write it. Here in his brilliant hands is the complete and exclusive story of the century's most audacious crime and its
20 even more sensational aftermath.

CORONET BOOKS/HODDER AND STOUGHTON

Non-fiction: General

UNITED KINGDOM	£1.25
AUSTRALIA	$3.75*
NEW ZEALAND	$3.95
REP. OF IRELAND	£1.27½

ISBN 0 340 23779 1

*recommended but not obligatory

. . . If we analyse more closely the Train Robbers and their milieu we may find that even this apparently evil act (the coshing of train-driver Mills) does not necessarily prove that they are wicked men. First there is their background, by which I do not mean only the context of their infancy and adolescence, but the
25 whole sub-society of working-class South London. There is no doubt that there was and still is endemic poverty juxtaposed to conspicuous consumption north of the river. It is not difficult to imagine the young Bruce Reynolds, for example, bicycling across the Thames to London's West End where the houses were large, light and elegantly proportioned; where the shops and department stores of Bond Street and
30 Knightsbridge displayed every variety of diverse and luxurious merchandise; nor hard to guess his feelings as he returned to the meagre tenement where his father struggled to feed his family on the wages of unskilled labour.

The Train Robbers were all determined to change this inequality of condition but only for themselves. None was a Robin Hood. Even Bruce, the son of a Socialist
35 and Trades Unionist, was consistently selfish in his drive to escape from the slums of Battersea.

Yet even where a thief does not act as a Robin Hood, he may still be seen as one. As E. J. Hobsbawm says of rural bandits, 'there is no doubt that the bandit is considered an agent of Justice, indeed a restorer of morality, and often considers
40 himself as such'. The same might be said of those urban bandits, the Train Robbers, who were and still are regarded with considerable sympathy, and were given much tacit support in their own circles. A small army of auxiliaries brought them information, ran errands and hid their money – not just because they hoped for some of the money itself. Even total strangers brought them information, not for a
45 whack or a drink, but because they enjoyed the discomfiture of the rich and powerful.

Certainly there would be an insignificant amount of crime if large numbers of ordinary people did not feel themselves to be the friends of thieves – or at any rate the enemies of the police, who they see as oppressive, hypocritical and cruel. The
50 picture of the Metropolitan Police, particularly of the Flying Squad in the early 1960s, which emerges from the Train Robbers' story – some of them taking bribes to alter evidence or drop charges, and others fabricating evidence to secure convictions – may well be exaggerated, but because so many Metropolitan police officers have been convicted of corruption or dismissed from the force since the
55 Train Robbery took place, it cannot be regarded as totally false.

The Train Robbers showed total repugnance for the rules and formalities of the modern state – licences, permits, taxes, National Insurance Stamps. This anarchism explains their appeal to the poor. I myself, who have everything to gain from literate values and everything to lose from savagery, find something seductive in the
60 life and values of the Train Robbers. They seem the last traces of an age which drew upon fundamental human qualities of courage and loyalty. Their lives as well as their liberty could stand or fall on the strength of friendship: love could mean the sharing of great luxury and great suffering. Poor youths like Buster, Bruce, Tommy and Charlie took to crime to escape not so much from the poverty of their condition
65 as the emasculation of menial, repetitious labour for a paltry wage.

from *The Train Robbers* by Piers Paul Read

1 Two areas of London (the West End including Bond Street and Knightsbridge, and South London including Battersea) were mentioned in the passage. What was the point of mentioning them?

2 Does the author approve of the train robbers? What are his reasons?

3 What is the significance of the remarks about Robin Hood?

4 If people changed their attitude to the police, what would be the effect on crime? Explain this.

5 Now read lines 1–20 again. This is the publisher's "blurb", printed on the outside cover to persuade potential buyers that this book is worth reading. Note the type of language used: *thrilling, catching the world's imagination,* etc.
Can you find any other expressions whose purpose is obviously to advertise rather than to inform? Make a note of these, and then try to find expressions of your own to replace them. Discuss the relative merits of your version and the original.

6 Look closely at lines 21–32 (*If we analyse ... unskilled labour*). Make a list of the descriptive adjectives and compare them with those used in the blurb. What are the differences, and what are the reasons for the differences?

7 Do not look at the original text, but use the lists you have made in questions 5 and 6 as a basis for reconstructing the story and argument.

Words and structures

IDIOMS

■ Exercise 1

Explain the meanings of these expressions as they are used in the texts.

a catching the world's imagination (line 11)
b in his brilliant hands (line 17)
c unskilled labour (line 32)
d in his drive to escape (line 35)
e in their own circles (line 42)
f ran errands (line 43)
g at any rate (line 48)
h drop charges (line 52)
i could stand or fall (line 62)

■ Exercise 2

Two-part verbs with *take*
take to (line 64) *take place* (line 55)

Match up the expressions and definitions.

1 take after	a adopt as profession or hobby
2 take down	b apply for and obtain
3 take in	c write (from dictation)
4 take off	d begin on a course of conduct, get to like
5 take on	e engage (employees)
6 take out	f resemble (by inheritance)
7 take over	g assume responsibility
8 take to	h assume control
9 take up	i leave the ground
10 take (it) upon oneself	j understand

CRIME

Now fill each gap with an appropriate form of *take*, followed by a preposition, from the list.

1 Before you get married , you have to _____ a marriage licence.

2 John's very musical: he _____ his mother.

3 If business continues to boom, we'll have to _____ more staff.

4 I'm thinking of _____ photography.

5 Now I'm going to speak very slowly so that you can _____ everything I say.

■ **Exercise 3**

Choose the most appropriate word or expression to fill each gap, and explain its meaning.

1 I hope you won't take it _____ if I don't wear the pullover you gave me.
   a amiss **b** easy
   c for granted **d** seriously

2 Twelve people were there, but only six took _____ in the discussion.
   a seriously **b** hold
   c part **d** place

3 Your work has improved, Jones; you seem to have taken my criticism _____.
   a for granted **b** into your head
   c to heart **d** upon yourself

4 We're in no hurry, so take _____.
   a a back seat **b** notice
   c to your heels **d** your time

5 You can't afford to let the situation get worse. You must take _____ to put it right.
   a directions **b** sides
   c steps **d** turns

VOCABULARY

■ **Exercise 4**

Fill each gap in the following passage with one word. Below the passage is a list of basic root words for you to use; in some cases you will have to find other forms of these words. Some of them may be used more than once.

Bert made a mess of ____(1)____ the bank: two ____(2)____ were waiting outside for him. 'Come along', they said. 'You're under ____(3)____.'

At the ____(4)____, Bert's ____(5)____ couldn't think of a good ____(6)____, so it all went very quickly. 'You have been found ____(7)____ of ____(8)____,' said the ____(9)____. 'You know very well that it is an ____(10)____ to ____(11)____ money from other people. In fact it is a very serious ____(12)____, and I ____(13)____ you to two years' ____(14)____.'

arrest	*prison*
defend	*rob*
guilt	*sentence*
judge	*steal*
law	*thief*
offend	*try*
police	

■ **Exercise 5**

Choose the word that best completes each sentence.

1 It's easier to understand new words when they are used in their proper _____.
   a background **b** context
   c environment **d** milieu

2 I'd like you to read pages 18 to 20 _____.
   a excluded **b** exclusive
   c included **d** inclusive

3 Because of fog, traffic was _____ away from the city centre.
   a divergent **b** diverse
   c diverted **d** diverting

4 _____ representation is the fairest form of democracy.
  a Proportional   **b** Proportionate
  c Proportioned   **d** Proportioning

5 The controls on this instrument are very _____, so you don't need a lot of strength.
  a sensational   **b** sensible
  c sensitive   **d** sensual

STRUCTURES

Verbs and phrases followed by *of* and a noun or gerund

■ **Exercise 6**

For each of the following sentences, write a new sentence as similar as possible in meaning to the original sentence but using the word given as well as *of* followed by a gerund.

If it costs too much, we'll have to reconsider.   **event**
In the event of it costing too much, we'll have to reconsider.

1 The policeman told John he was a thief.   **accused**

2 They thought you murdered the old lady.   **suspected**

3 The judge decided that I had been driving dangerously.   **guilty**

4 Mary used to drop in without warning.   **habit**

5 I should like to keep things as they are.   **favour**

6 He pretended to leave, but in fact hid behind the door.   **pretence**

7 He said he had too much work to do.   **complain**

8 It's not a good thing to let children stay out at night.   **disapprove**

9 I intend to retire soon.   **thinking**

10 I do not intend to give you any money.   **intention**

Deductions, possibility and impossibility
Who do you think was the killer?

Well, it can't have been Tom, because he was at home with his wife. I suppose Dick might have done it; he certainly hasn't got a very good alibi. Harry could have done it, too, because we know he was there at the time. Yes, he had a very strong motive as well, so it must have been him.

Notice the way we make deductions and express possibilities:
he can't have done it = it is completely impossible that he did it
he might have done it = it is possible that he did it
he could have done it = he had the opportunity to do it
he must have done it = it is certain that he did it

■ **Exercise 7** PW

Yesterday afternoon, six acts of terrorism were committed in Europe. The police suspect four men, code-named the Rat, the Mole, the Viper, and the Spider. With the help of the information in Pair work 6a, make statements about who *might/can't/could/must have* committed the crimes. Student A has the list of crimes, with places and times, while student B has information about the times at which the police observed the suspects at various places.

Listening and speaking
Discussion and debate

Describe the scene.
What do you think has caused this situation?
How would you feel if you returned home to a scene like this?
What can be done to protect property against criminals?
How can the victims of crime be compensated?
What would you do if you found a thief in your home?

■ Exercise 1

Which crimes deserve which punishments? Read the article and discuss whether or not the death sentence is the right punishment for murderers, rapists and car thieves. Then look at the list of crimes and fill in the table with the minimum and maximum punishments that you think should be given to people found guilty of them. Then discuss your suggestions with the rest of the class.

	min.	max.
accepting bribes		
armed robbery		
arson		
assault		
bigamy		
burglary		
counterfeiting bank notes		
driving without a licence		
drunken driving		
espionage		
fraud		
helping criminals escape		
hijacking an aeroplane		
kidnapping		
manslaughter		
murder		
offering bribes		
parking in the wrong place		
receiving stolen property		
shoplifting		
smuggling		
tax evasion		
treason		
trespass		

The Times August 24, 1983

Thousands cheer death sentences

Peking (AFP, AP) – Thirty criminals were sentenced to death at a mass rally attended by thousands of cheering spectators yesterday and later executed.

The executions were part of a law-and-order campaign launched about 10 days ago. It was the largest group to be executed in Peking for several years.

A notice posted at the Peking intermediate court, which imposed the death sentences, said that the 30 executed criminals included 19 accused of murder, 10 rapists and one car thief. One woman was among those executed. None was older than 35.

■ Exercise 2

Hold a debate on one of these topics.

- The purpose of the law is to protect people from themselves.
- Censorship is a necessary evil.
- Don't blame the criminal, blame his background.
- The existence of armed security guards working for privately owned companies is a threat to democracy.

■ Exercise 3

Write a short newspaper report on the debate.

Listening comprehension

You will hear a conversation about what happened after a bank robbery. The first time you listen to it, look at the list of places below the map, and mark the order in which the thieves visited or passed them; put '1' by the place they went to first, '2' by the place they went to second, and so on. The second and subsequent times you listen to the conversation, answer questions 1 to 3.

1 Mark the places listed on the map by writing their initial letters in the correct places. Then make notes about what happened at each place; one of them has been done for you.

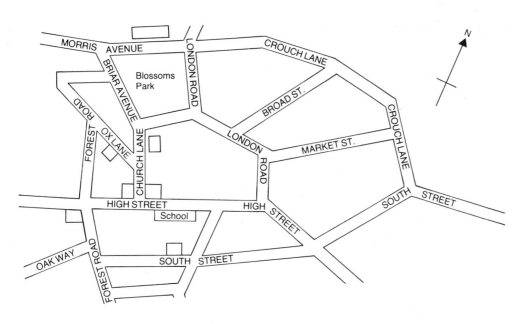

order	place	notes
1	Bank	
	Garage	
	Railway station	
	Police station	
	Library	
	Church	
	Traffic lights	*car stalled – got out and pushed*

2 Imagine that you are a police officer giving evidence at the gang's trial. Describe their journey from the bank.

3 What were the exact words used to
a accept responsibility?
b deny responsibility? **c** apologise?
d blame others?

Function: blame and apology

What do you think they are saying? Fill in the bubbles.

■ **Exercise 1** PW

Look at the expressions in Pair work 6b. Student B must find the most appropriate responses to what student A says.

■ **Exercise 2**

Use the tables to help you find suitable remarks in these situations.

1 By mistake, a man treads on a woman's toes.

2 A football team have just lost 10–0. Their manager accuses some of the players of not trying hard enough; some deny responsibility, while others accept it and apologise.

3 A customer realizes that a shop assistant has given too little change.

4 The Chief of Police asks three police officers about their failure to catch a gang of criminals; they all try to put the blame on someone else.

5 An applicant for a job arrives ten minutes late for an interview.

Blaming

General
It *is/was my/your fault/responsibility*.
I *am/was responsible/to blame*
(for . . .).
You *are/were responsible/to blame*
(for . . .).
There's no point in denying it.

Informal
I/You did it.
It was *my/your/his* fault (for . . .).

Formal
The *fault/blame* is entirely
yours/mine/his.
If it hadn't been for *your/my*
carelessness/bad judgement (, this
would never have happened).

Denying responsibility

General

It *isn't/wasn't* my *fault/responsibility*.
I'*m not/wasn't responsible/to blame*.

Informal

It wasn't me.
I didn't do it.
I had nothing to do with it.
It *had/was* nothing to do with me.

Formal

I refuse to accept responsibility.

Apologising

General

I'*m/I (really) am (so/very/terribly/
awfully)* sorry (*for/about* ...).
It/*That* was (entirely) my fault.

Informal

Sorry (*for/about* ...).
How *silly/stupid/clumsy* of me.

Formal

I (really) *do/must* apologise
(*for/about* ...).
Please accept my apologies (for ...).
Please forgive me (for ...).

Accepting an apology

General

That's (quite) all right.
It (really) doesn't matter (at all).
Please don't worry.

Informal

That's OK.
Forget it.
Not to worry.

Formal

It's/*That's* perfectly all right.
There's no *need/reason* to apologise
(for ...).

■ **Practice** PW

Act out the situations in Pair work
6c–6f.

Reading aloud: spelling and pronunciation

1 hop—hopping   2 hope—hoping
3 bid—bidding   4 bide—biding
5 tap—tapping   6 tape—taping
7 run—running   8 tune—tuning
9 let—letting   10 delete—deleting

■ **Exercise 1**

What spelling/pronunciation principles
can you deduce from the above groups
of words?

■ **Exercise 2**

Which of the underlined syllables follow
the principles illustrated above? Which
are exceptions to them? Make lists
numbered 1 to 10: in each list put those
words which follow the above principles
and whose underlined syllables have the
same vowel sounds as the numbered
words above. Make a separate list of the
exceptions.

appalling	expose	police
beginning	game	programming
buses	improving	regret
chatting	inclusive	plotting
coding	living	plug
come	multitude	runner
competing	obsolete	scoring
completion	pace	simulating
console	permitting	surviving
crepe	plug	using
		vetting

■ **Exercise 3**

Read the words in your lists aloud.

■ **Exercise 4**

Look at the script of the conversation
on pp. 208–9. Practise reading it aloud,
remembering everything you have
learnt about stress and intonation in
previous units.

CRIME

Activity: deduction

1 Who killed Mrs Cooper? RC

Read this report of what happened in central London recently, and then use the information in your role cards to answer the questions below; each student is given one item of extra information which may be communicated orally to the others but not shown to them in written form. Writing and note-taking are allowed.

> Last Friday at 3 a.m., a passer-by heard a scream coming from a five-storey building, and then saw a woman stagger out of the front door and fall dead on the pavement. No one else left the building, and it was later confirmed by the police that there was no other possible way out of it.
>
> Detectives arriving on the scene were able to identify the woman as Australian millionairess Mrs Audrey Cooper; she had been brutally stabbed to death.
>
> When they investigated the building, which contained just one flat on each floor, the detectives discovered some remarkable facts: in each flat there was one man; no two men had the same name, age or nationality; all had different motives for wanting to kill Mrs Cooper, and they each had just one weapon with which they might have killed her.

- Use information 6a in Role cards 1, 3, 5, 7, 9 and 11 to answer the question:
  Which floor was Greg on?
- When you have found the answer, use information 6b in Role cards 2, 4, 6, 8, 10 and 12 to answer this question:
  Who killed Mrs Cooper?

2 Spy Conference RC

You are taking part in an International Spy Conference. Role card 6c gives you three passwords, a set of code letters, and the name of the country you are spying for.

- Move around the room making small talk with all the delegates; by introducing your passwords unobtrusively into your conversation and listening to the replies you get, you should be able to identify one other spy from your country. You must not, of course, reveal your passwords or the name of the country you are working for to anyone else, since this might jeopardise your position as a spy.
- When you have found your colleague, you should be able to combine your sets of code letters to make one of the following expressions connected with spying; if you can't, then you have probably got the wrong person!
  DOUBLE AGENT
  ESPIONAGE
  INTELLIGENCE
  JAMES BOND
  TOP SECRET
  UNDERCOVER

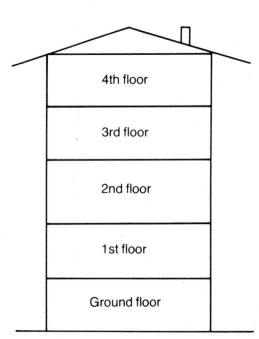

Revision: units 5 and 6

■ Exercise 1

Fill each gap with one word; it need not be the actual word used in the original text, but it must be appropriate to the context.

____(1)____ activities are essentially modified forms of hunting behaviour. ____(2)____ biologically, the modern footballer is revealed ____(3)____ a member of a disguised hunting pack. His killing weapon has turned into a harmless football and his prey ____(4)____ a goal-mouth. If his aim is accurate and he ____(5)____ a goal, he enjoys the hunter's ____(6)____ of killing his prey.

To understand how this transformation has taken place we must briefly look ____(7)____ at our ancient ancestors. They spent over a million years ____(8)____ as co-operative hunters. Their ____(9)____ survival depended on success ____(10)____ the hunting-field. Under this pressure their whole ____(11)____ of life, ____(12)____ their bodies, became radically changed. They became chasers, runners, jumpers, aimers, throwers and prey-killers. They co-operated as skilful male-group attackers.

____(13)____, about ten thousand years ago, ____(14)____ this immensely long, formative period ____(15)____ hunting their food, they became farmers. Their improved intelligence, so ____(16)____ to their old hunting life, was ____(17)____ to a new use—____(18)____ of penning, controlling and domesticating their prey. The hunt became suddenly obsolete. The food was there on the farms, ____(19)____ their needs. The risks and uncertainties of the hunt were no longer ____(20)____ for survival.

■ Exercise 2

Twenty questions

Choose one of the words or phrases listed here. The rest of the class must find out which one you have chosen by asking you questions to which you can answer 'yes' or 'no'.

Is it the name of a crime?—No.
Is it a type of criminal?—Yes.
Is it someone who steals things?—Yes.

offence	burglar
alibi	unskilled labour
blurb	arson
sentence	take up
imprisonment	judge
thief	Robin Hood
espionage	smuggling
take for granted	take off
milieu	lawyer
errand	slums
fraud	burglary
take after	take place

UNIT 7

THE SENSES

Reading and thinking
Reading comprehension

The 'Five Senses' and a Few More

The world is known to us through many senses, not just hearing, smell, vision, and at close range, touch and taste.

Our skins let us know whether the air is humid or dry, whether surfaces are wet without being sticky or slippery. From the uniformity of slight pressure, we can be aware how deeply
5 a finger is thrust into water at body temperature, even if the finger is encased in a rubber glove that keeps the skin completely dry. Many other animals, with highly sensitive skins, appear able to learn still more about their environment. Often they do so without employing any of the five senses Aristotle knew.

By observing the capabilities of other members of the animal kingdom, we come to realise
10 that a human being has far more possibilities than are utilised. We neglect ever so many of our senses in concentrating on the five most conspicuous ones. At the same time, a comparison between animals and man draws attention to the limitations of each sense. The part of the spectrum seen by colour-conscious man as red is non-existent for owls and honey-bees. But a bee or a butterfly can see far more in flowers than we, because the ultra-violet to
15 which our eyes are blind is a stimulating part of the insect's spectrum, and, for honey-bees at least, constitutes a separate colour.

Differences in the importance of various senses to the many kinds of animals must alter their understanding of the world about them. The dog's world is one full of intriguing odours, the bat's a place of meaningful echoes, the hawk's a mosaic of finely seen details
20 among which some features of movement betray a mouse or a grasshopper for dinner.

The first sense to be measured quantitatively was none of the famous five. A century ago Ernst Weber tested his own ability, and then that of others, to tell which was the heavier of two weights held one in each hand. He discovered that this sensitivity is relative and not absolute.
25 Most people can judge that an object weighing 82 grams (2.89 ounces) is heavier than one weighing 80 grams (2.82 ounces), or that 4.1 pounds is more than 4.0 pounds, or 41 pounds more than 40 pounds. Any lesser difference is beyond the limits of our sense of weight. For all senses tested since Weber's time, the 'just discriminable difference' has this ratio form. Differences of two per cent are about as fine as the nervous system will appreciate.
30 Sometimes we describe ourselves as being 'a bit under the weather', without realising that this may be true. In Europe recently, factory workers were found to show slower mental activity, more mistakes, and a higher accident rate when the barometer was falling and a storm on its way, than under a rising barometer and clearing skies. So far no one has discovered where the sensitivity to weather resides in the body. The man who claimed he
35 could predict rain because his amputated leg ached before the clouds gathered may have been telling the truth.

From *The Senses of Animals and Men* by Lorus and Margery Milne

1 Which are 'the five senses Aristotle knew'?

2 The text mentions five other senses that humans have. What are they?

3 In what ways does man's sight differ from that of honey-bees?

4 How does our understanding of the world differ from that of a dog, a bat and a hawk?

5 According to the text, would you be able to judge that an object weighing 1,010 grams was heavier than one weighing 1,000 grams?

6 What does the author suggest happens when you feel 'a bit under the weather', and what causes this feeling?

7 What is the point of the final sentence (The man who . . . the truth)?

Words and structures

IDIOMS

■ Exercise 1

Explain the meanings of these words and phrases as they are used in the text.

a at close range (lines 1–2)
b we come to realise (line 9)
c draws attention to (line 12)
d mosaic (line 19)
e on its way (line 33)

■ Exercise 2

Sight

Match up the expressions and definitions. Then write six sentences of your own that include the expressions on the left.

1 far-sighted	a able to see distant objects more clearly than near ones
2 long-sighted	b beyond the range of vision
3 out of sight	c blind
4 sightless	d of unpleasant appearance
5 unsighted	e prudent, able to foresee consequences in the distant future
6 unsightly	f with one's view obscured

What do these words mean?
foresight, hindsight, insight, oversight, second sight
First fill in the gaps in the sentences below with the correct words, then write your own definitions for them, and finally read out your definitions to the rest of the class, to see if they can guess which words they refer to.

1 He must have some sort of _____; he always seems to know what's going to happen next.

2 I'm very sorry, but due to an unfortunate _____ your claim has not been dealt with.

3 In stating that Chamberlain should never have made an agreement with Hitler, we have of course the benefit of _____.

4 Our aim is to give you a deeper _____ into the complexities of human behaviour.

5 With a bit more _____ you'd never have got into this mess.

■ Exercise 3

Two-part verbs with *on*

Choose the word that best completes each sentence.

1 _____ on a minute, and I'll see if she's at home.
 a Call b Hang c Keep d Let

2 The spy _____ on the message to his contact in Washington.
a held **b** laid **c** passed **d** put

3 You've got to be there on time. I'm _____ on you.
a counting **b** hanging
c holding **d** sitting

4 There were many obstacles, but we _____ on regardless.
a passed **b** pressed
c put **d** set

5 I like that pullover. Can I _____ it on, please?
a catch **b** set **c** take **d** try

6 You've never been to Hong Kong! You're _____ me on.
a catching **b** having
c laying **d** playing

7 I think it was the bad weather that _____ on the attack of pneumonia.
a brought **b** put
c set **d** took

8 Several hundred people _____ on while the two men fought.
a let **b** looked **c** passed **d** sat

9 Your son is _____ on very well. He'll be out of hospital soon.
a coming **b** going
c keeping **d** taking

10 Leave him alone, you bully. _____ on someone your own size.
a Catch **b** Hold **c** Lay **d** Pick

VOCABULARY

■ Exercise 4

Sense and *sensitivity*

Fill each gap with a word which has *sense* as its root, e.g. *sense, sensible, sensitive, nonsense.*

1 Come on, now, be _____! That plan will never succeed.

2 Be careful what you say to Kim— he's a very _____ person.

3 I've just heard the most _____ news. The government has resigned.

4 I think John's suggestion makes _____, so let's hear a few more details.

5 'I saw a flying saucer and three green men.'—'Oh, don't talk _____.'

6 Our ears are _____ to very fine differences of pitch and timbre.

7 Paul could never be a doctor; he's completely _____ to other people's needs and problems.

8 The purpose of this course is to increase the participants' _____ to their surroundings.

9 I have terribly _____ skin. Anything except pure cotton makes it itch.

10 A gourmet is always looking for new taste _____.

11 I don't like newspapers that go in for _____. They're more interested in their sales figures than in the truth.

12 Hokito's designs caused a _____ in Paris last summer.

13 The stone struck Grant on the back of the head, and he fell _____ to the ground.

14 We get all our information about our environment through our _____ organs.

15 I find listening to Debussy's music a very _____ experience—I don't think my intellect is involved at all.

■ Exercise 5

Read the passage and fill in the missing words in the diagram. Then cover up the text and give your own description of how you see.

From *Your Body*
by David Scott Daniell

The eye is such a delicate organ that it is particularly well protected. It is set in a strong, bone eye-socket in the skull, well lined with soft fat. Eyelids protect the front, with lashes to keep out dust, eyebrows to keep out sweat and rain, and a supply of a liquid, tears, to keep the round eyeball washed clean.

The eye is protected at the front by a transparent layer called the *cornea*. Looking at the eye from the front, the coloured part is the *iris*, and the black circle is the *pupil*. This is a hole into the interior of the eyeball, and looks black because the interior of the eyeball is dark. The pupil widens or closes according to the amount of light falling on the eye; it is widest at night and smallest in bright light.

Behind the iris is suspended the lens through which the rays of light pass on to the *retina*, which is the light-sensitive inner layer shown in the diagram. On the retina, the rays of light form a small image (upside down) of what you see, and this is passed along the *optic nerve* to the brain, where it is turned the right way up. In the same way, a camera lens inverts an image on to a film. Your eye collects the message, your brain interprets it—and you see.

1 ....

2 ....

3 LIGAMENTS ....

4 ....

5 ....

6 ....

7 ....

8 ....

9 FLUID ....

10 ....

11 ....

12 MUSCLE ....

13 FLUID ....

STRUCTURES

Order of adjectives

He was a nice cheerful old man. They've just bought a shiny new oil-fired central heating system.

When several adjectives describe the same noun, it is important that they are written in the correct order.

numbers quantifiers determiners	general	age	colour	participle	nationality origin	material noun	defining	main noun	phrase clause
Some	cheap		brown			leather		shoes	with no laces.
The most	beautiful			haunting			love	song	I've ever heard.
A	nice	young			French		social	worker.	
Three	shiny	new		computerised			milking	machines.	

- Closest to the main noun is the 'defining' adjective, which answers the question *what sort?*; for example, *an interesting political debate, a difficult moral problem*. These adjectives are essential to the meanings of the nouns. As we go further left, away from the noun, the adjectives become less defining and more subjective and vague.
- Within the category 'general', adjectives can also be ordered according to the rule 'vague on the left, defining on the right'. Size usually comes before shape; and, within size, height comes before width (e.g. *a tall fat man*). Words with very little meaning, such as *nice*, come before all other general adjectives.

■ Exercise 6

Put the words in the best order. The main noun appears last in each case.

1 the/summer/first/quiet/evening

2 the/china/beautiful/butter/Dresden/antique/dish

3 their/sleeping/rather/daytime/unusual/habits

4 my/tailor-made/dinner/expensive/new/cotton/black/jacket

5 some/old/Swedish/funny/very/horror/films

6 the/elephant/Victorian/most/old-fashioned/gun

7 a/wooden/walking/well-used/stick

8 the/complete/war/only/Viking/ship

■ Exercise 7

Describe the following using at least three adjectives each time.

1 A person.
2 A building.
3 A town.
4 A film.
5 Something you are wearing.

■ Exercise 8
Words and phrases followed by *on* and a noun or gerund

For each of the following sentences, write a new sentence as similar as possible in meaning to the original sentence, but using the word given, as well as *on* followed by a gerund.

She loves to play tennis.   **keen**
She's very keen on playing tennis.

1 She is very pleased that she's a good driver.   **prides**

2 He said it was essential for me to be there.   **insisted**

3 She is determined to move to the seaside. **heart**

4 June said, 'Well done, Harry! You won the race.' **congratulated**

5 If we strive to improve our productivity, our other problems will be solved automatically. **concentrate**

6 It was so important for her to get there on time that she forgot to bring her husband with her. **intent**

7 'What a pretty colour you've painted the hall!' he told her. **complimented**

8 It's a risk, but we're hoping that they'll arrive on time. **gambling**

Listening and speaking
Discussion and debate

Describe the scene and the two people. Put yourself in their situation and describe your sensations.
What difficulties do blind people have to face?
What about people with a poor sense of hearing, taste, smell or touch?
What can be done to improve their situation?

Is it possible that we have senses that science cannot as yet explain, and that we ourselves are not even aware of? How would you set about testing whether or not you had telepathic powers?

■ Exercise 1

Imagine that you have been banished for ever to a desert island. You can take with you the five objects that you think will best please your five senses: sight, hearing, touch, taste and smell. In small groups, see if you can agree on which five objects to take.

■ Exercise 2

Read the description of experiments in telepathy.

> **March, 1967.** Karl Nikolaiev sits in a Leningrad laboratory harnessed to several devices for measuring physiological changes. He is under the supervision of Drs Lutsia Pavlova and Genady Sergeyev, physiologists at Leningrad University. Hundreds of miles away in Moscow, biophysicist Yuri Kamensky, also wired up to numerous machines, is given the signal to start telepathic transmission. Abruptly, three seconds later, Nikolaiev's brain-wave pattern changes 'drastically'.
>
> Dr Pavlova reported: 'We detected activation of the brain within 1 to 5 seconds after the beginning of telepathic transmission.'
>
> Karl Nikolaiev claimed that he trained himself to be 'psychic', and that with a little effort anyone can develop the talent. 'I worked hard to realise a potential most people don't even think about,' he explains. 'I started out the only way I knew—by trying. I had friends think orders to me. They'd think "light a cigarette, change your mind and crush it out," and I did.'

From *An Index of Possibilities—Energy & Power*

■ Exercise 3

All art forms are very closely related to our senses: painting is related to sight, music to hearing, and so on.
What other art forms can you think of, and which senses are they most closely related to?
Are there any senses that have no art forms connected with them?
What do you think the reasons for this might be?
Can you imagine an art form that would appeal to all of the senses?

UNIT 7
THE SENSES

■ Exercise 4

Hold a debate on one of these topics.

- Seeing is believing.
- In the country of the blind, the one-eyed man is king.
- The purpose of all art is to entertain.
- Art that is controlled by commercial interests is no longer art.

■ Exercise 5

Write an article for a newspaper on the topic you have just debated, basing it on some of the arguments that were put forward.

Listening comprehension

You will hear interviews with three people. The first time you hear them, try to identify the situation: who are these people? why and by whom are they being interviewed? Then listen again, and answer questions 1 to 3.

1 Fill in the missing information about the objects described by the interviewees. Write as briefly as possible.

2 Write a brief newspaper report (100–150 words) on the phenomenon which the interviewees claim to have witnessed. Give your opinion, with reasons, on the truth of their statements.

3 What were the exact words used to
   a ask for information?
   b express certainty and uncertainty?
   c express lack of knowledge?

	man	woman	child
shape			
colour			
size			
movements			
sounds			
surface texture			

Function: asking for information and replying

What do you think they are saying? Fill in the bubbles.

■ **Exercise 1**

Use the tables to help you make up
short conversations for these situations.

1 Ask a stranger what the time is—but
his watch isn't working properly.

2 Ask a porter when the train to
London leaves—he doesn't know, but
suggests asking at the booking office.

3 Ask at the Tourist Information Office
about sports and entertainment
facilities in the town you are in.

4 Ask a teacher for information about
Great Britain—population,
industries, customs, and so on.

5 In a library, someone asks for a book
called *How Things Work*—the
librarian asks who wrote it, who
published it, and what it's about, but
the customer doesn't know; the
librarian suggests where it might be
found.

Asking for information
General (Excuse me,) do you (happen to) know ... (, please)? (Excuse me,) *can/could* you tell me ... (, please)? (Excuse me,) I'd like to know ... (, please).
Informal Know (anything about) ...? (Got) any idea (*if/about*) ...?
Formal (Excuse me,) I wonder if *you/someone* could tell me ...? I hope you don't mind my asking, but ...? *Can/Could* you give me any information *on/about* ... (, please)?

Saying you are certain
General (Oh yes,) I'm (*quite/absolutely/fairly*) *sure/certain* (...). I know ... *I've/There's* no doubt (*about/that* ...).
Informal Sure. Absolutely *certain/positive*.
Formal There can't be any doubt (*about/that* ...). I don't think there can be any doubt (*about/that* ...). I'm *quite/completely* convinced (*that/of* ...).

THE SENSES

Saying you are uncertain

General

(*Sorry*/*I'm afraid*,) I'm not (*really*/*quite*) sure (about . . .).
It's hard to *say*/*tell* (. . .).
I don't think . . .

Informal

(I) *can't*/*couldn't* say for *certain*/*sure*.
I'm not/*I wouldn't* be too sure (about . . .).

Formal

(I'm afraid) I can't be certain (about . . .).
There's (*still*) some doubt (about . . .).
I'm not at all convinced (*of*/*about*/*that* . . .)

Saying you don't know

General

(I'm *sorry*/*afraid*) I (really) don't know (*anything*/*very much* about . . .).
(I'm afraid) *I can't help you*/*I've no idea.*

Informal

(Sorry,) (I) *don't know*/*haven't (got) a clue.*
No idea.
Don't ask me.
I wish I knew.

Formal

I'm sorry to say that I *know very little*/*don't know very much* about . . .
I *must*/*have to* admit that I don't know very much about . . .

■ Practice PW

1 Ask and answer questions about the map in Pair work 7. Each student has symbols on his map to show where various shops and other amenities are. You will find that you haven't got enough information to answer all the questions you are asked.

2 Imagine that you are on holiday in the town in Pair work 7. Ask for directions to various places in the town. You are standing outside the railway station.

—*Excuse me, can you tell me how to get to the theatre, please?*
—*Yes, of course. You cross over here, go straight along Mountfield Road and take the second turning on the left. The theatre is on the left, just opposite the bus station.*
—*Thank you very much.*

Reading aloud: *hair* or *here*? *bear* or *beer*?

- /ɛə/ is usually spelt **-are** or **-air**, as in **care** and **fair**
- /iə/ is usually spelt **-eer** or **-ere**, as in **beer** and **here**
- **-ear** is used for both sounds, e.g. **bear** and **hear**, as well as the sound /ɔ:/ in **learn**
- There are a few words in **-ere** pronounced /ɛə/, e.g. **where**, **there**, **compère**

■ Exercise 1

Sort the following words into two groups: those with the sound /ɛə/, and those with the sound /iə/.

aeroplane	imperious	sphere
beard	interfere	stair
beware	Mary	stare
bier	mayor	their
cereal	near	they're
dare	pair	various
deer	pear	wear
ear	pier	weir
fear	really	we're
heir	series	where
here	serious	year

■ Exercise 2

Practise saying the words in the list in exercise 1. One student says a word: the others call out 'one' if it has the sound /ɛə/, and 'two' if it has the sound /iə/.

■ Exercise 3

Look through the passage called *The 'Five Senses' and a Few More* on p. 76, and see how many words you can find that contain the sounds /ɛə/ and /iə/.

■ Exercise 4

Improvise sentences that contain some of the words in the list in exercise 1.

Mary dared to interfere with the mayor's beard.

Activity: games

1 What does it feel like?

- Find two objects that are small enough to fit into your hand. Do not show them to anyone else. Make a list of the adjectives and phrases you would use to describe them.
- Work in groups of three. Student A puts his hands behind his back, and student B puts an object into them, making sure that student A doesn't see it. Student A must then describe its physical characteristics (shape, size, texture, materials, etc.) without making any reference to what it might be used for. Student C may ask questions and must try to guess what the object is. Student B makes a note of the descriptive words used.
- The group compares the prepared list of descriptive words with the description that was actually given. What were the differences? Which words did the 'guesser' actually find most useful?
- Repeat with all the group's objects.

2 Tongue-twisters RC

The whole class sits in a ring. Look at your Role card 7a and whisper the statement there to the person on your left, who must then whisper it to the person on his left, and so on until it gets back to you.
This can be made more complicated if several different statements circulate simultaneously, some clockwise and some anticlockwise.

3 What does it look like? RC

Look at the picture in Role card 7b. Describe it to the rest of the class, but do not show it to anyone. See if you can match up your picture with the descriptions given by some of the other students: the twelve pictures you have can be combined to make three larger pictures.

Written work: connecting ideas (3)

Attitudes

■ Exercise 1

Read the letter carefully, and then fill each gap with the most appropriate of the alternatives given below.

1 **a** naturally **b** really
 c technically

2 **a** In theory **b** Unfortunately
 c With respect

3 **a** Apparently **b** Eventually
 c Practically

4 **a** evidently **b** to be honest
 c to be precise

5 **a** literally **b** officially
 c personally

6 **a** roughly speaking
 b strictly speaking
 c to my surprise

7 **a** Clearly
 b If I may say so
 c To tell you the truth

8 **a** Generally speaking
 b Ideally
 c Understandably

■ Exercise 2

Write a letter to a friend describing something you have seen or heard that has made a strong impression on you. Use expressions from the exercise above to show your attitude.

37A Park Street
Cheltenham,
Glos, GL54 4DF
24th November 1983

Dear Pamela,
 There's something I very much need to talk to you about. You've not going to believe this, but the day before yesterday I actually saw a spaceship and a group of little green men in the field behind my house. I went straight to the police, and (1) _____ they made a show of ridiculing me. But there was one nice man who took the trouble to talk to me about UFOs. (2) _____, he said, there may be life on other planets, but the chances of our being visited by aliens are practically nil. (3) _____ it would take several centuries to get here from the nearest planet that might conceivably support some form of life.
 The police weren't surprised by what I said, you know; (4) _____ they've had other reports too, and (5) _____ I think that they are hiding something. In fact, they told me there'd be trouble if the press got to know my story, so (6) _____ I shouldn't be telling you any of this.
 But I must talk to someone about it. (7) _____ I'm beginning to doubt my memory and my sanity. I really want to talk to you. (8) _____ you should come and spend the weekend here, though I suppose there will be practical problems. Why don't you ring me anyway, as soon as you get this letter?
 With love from
 Janet

UNIT 8

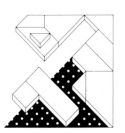

LEARNING

Reading and thinking
Reading comprehension

The headmaster sighed and crossed to the window. His was a most expensive prep school. 'The fact of the matter is, and you must appreciate that I have had some thirty years in the teaching profession, that Peregrine is an unusual boy. A most unusual boy.'

'I know that,' said Mr Clyde-Browne, 'And I also know that every report I've had says his
5 behaviour is impeccable and that he tries hard. Now I can face facts as well as the next man. Are you suggesting he's stupid?'

The headmaster turned his back to the desk with a deprecatory gesture. 'I wouldn't go as far as to say that,' he murmured.

'Then how far would you go?'
10 'Perhaps "late developer" would be more accurate. The fact of the matter is that Peregrine has difficulty conceptualizing.'

'So do I, come to that,' said Mr Clyde-Browne. 'What on earth does it mean?'

'Well, as a matter of fact . . .'

'That's the third time you've prefaced a matter of no fact whatsoever by using that phrase,'
15 said Mr Clyde-Browne in his nastiest courtroom manner. 'Now I want the truth.'

'In short, he takes everything he's told as Gospel.'

'As Gospel?'

'Literally. Absolutely literally.'

'He takes the Gospel literally?' said Mr Clyde-Browne, hoping for a chance to vent his
20 feelings about Religious Education in a rational world.

'Not just the Gospel. Everything,' said the headmaster, who was finding the interview almost as harassing as trying to teach Peregrine. 'He seems incapable of distinguishing between a general instruction and the particular. Take the time, for instance.'

'What time?' asked Mr Clyde-Browne, with a glazed look in his eyes.
25 'Just time. Now if one of the teachers sets the class some work to do and adds, "Take your own time," Peregrine invariably says "Eleven o'clock".'

'Invariably says "Eleven o'clock"?'

'Or whatever the time happens to be. It could be half past nine or quarter to ten.'

'In that case he can't invariably say "Eleven o'clock",' said Mr Clyde-Browne, resorting to
30 cross-examination to fight his way out of the confusion.

'Well, not invariably eleven o'clock,' conceded the headmaster, 'but invariably some time or other. Whatever his watch happens to tell him. That's what I mean about him taking everything literally. It makes teaching him a distinctly unnerving experience. Only the other day I told his class they'd got to pull their socks up, and Peregrine promptly did. It was
35 exactly the same in Bible Studies. The Reverend Wilkinson said that everyone ought to turn over a new leaf. During the break Peregrine went to work on the camellias. My wife was deeply upset.'

Mr Clyde-Browne followed his glance out of the window and surveyed the stripped bushes. 'Isn't there some way of explaining the difference between metaphorical or colloquial
40 expressions and factual ones?' he asked plaintively.

'Only at the expense of a great deal of time and effort. Besides we have the other children to consider. The English language is not easily adapted to pure logic. We must just hope that Peregrine will develop quite suddenly and learn not to do exactly what he's told.'

From *Vintage Stuff* by Tom Sharpe

1 Tick (√) the statements that describe correctly Peregrine and his behaviour.

a He behaves very well. ☐

b He is not as bright as other boys of his age. ☐

c He reads the Bible. ☐

d He is always saying what the time is. ☐

e He always does exactly what he is told to do. ☐

f He often misunderstands his teachers. ☐

g He destroyed some flowers. ☐

2 What did the teachers in fact mean when they told their pupils to do the following?

a take their own time (line 25)

b pull their socks up (line 34)

c turn over a new leaf (line 35)

3 What is the relationship between Mr Clyde-Browne and Peregrine? How do you know?

4 What expressions can you find that give an indication of Mr Clyde-Browne's profession?

5 What do you think Mr Clyde-Browne felt about 'Religious Education in a rational world' (line 20)?

6 Why is teaching Peregrine 'a distinctly unnerving experience' (line 33)?

7 Why is the interview 'almost as harassing as trying to teach Peregrine' (line 22)?

8 Make brief notes on the information we are given about the school—what type of school it is, its teachers, subjects taught, etc.

Words and structures

IDIOMS

■ Exercise 1

Explain the meanings of these expressions as they are used in the text.

a face facts (line 5)

b as well as the next man (line 5)

c I wouldn't go as far as (line 7)

d come to that (line 12)

e What on earth (line 12)

f takes everything . . . as Gospel (line 16)

g fight his way out (line 30)

h went to work on (line 36)

i at the expense of (line 41)

■ Exercise 2

Clothes

pull their socks up (line 34)

Read these sentences carefully, and then choose the definition that matches each of the underlined expressions.

1 Don't believe him! He's <u>talking through his hat.</u>

2 I decided to <u>give him a dressing-down</u> when he was late for the tenth time.

3 I <u>take my hat off</u> to you. You handled that extremely well.

4 I wouldn't like to <u>be in your shoes</u> when Betty finds out.

5 Jenny's retiring, so I think we should <u>pass the hat round</u> for her.

6 Jessica <u>wears the trousers</u> in this house.

7 Let's <u>dress up</u> this evening.

8 Pete has lost, unless he <u>has something up his sleeve.</u>

9 She'll <u>get the boot</u> if she asks for a rise.

10 They should have waited until after the party; there was no need for them to <u>wash their dirty linen in public.</u>

   a be in another person's position

   b collect money

   c congratulate

   d discuss private or family problems in the presence of other people

   e have a secret plan

   f lose one's job

   g make all the decisions

   h put on special clothes

   i reprimand

   j talk about things one knows nothing about

a bee in her bonnet.

VOCABULARY

■ **Exercise 3**

Classroom

Write the correct numbers in the boxes.

adaptor	12	loudspeaker	13
ballpoint pen	9	microphone	15
board duster	22	overhead projector	1
bulb	6	paperclip	27
chalk	17	pencil	26
drawing pin	14	pencil sharpener	4
exercise book	21	plug	2
felt-tip pen	11	pocket calculator	23
file	20	rubber	19
fountain pen	24	ruler	5
hole puncher	16	scissors	18
		screen	10
		socket	7
		stapler	8
		tape recorder	25
		typewriter	3

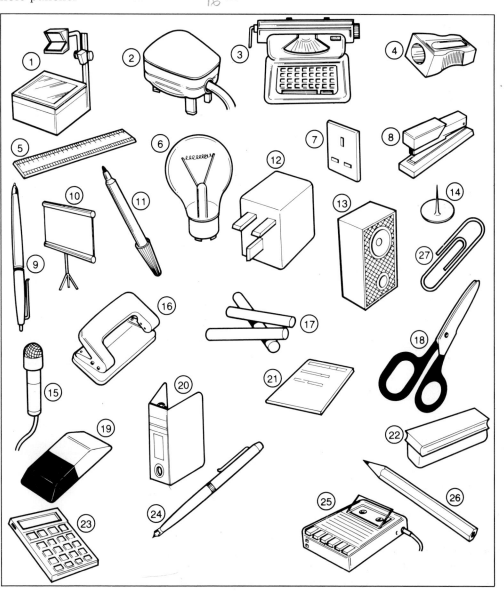

■ Exercise 4

Synonyms *homework*

Find words in the text on p. 87 that mean the same as the following.

1 Admitted.
2 At once.
3 Close questioning.
4 Examined.
5 Express.
6 Expressionless, like glass.
7 Faultless.
8 Introduced, begun.
9 Muddle, mix-up.
10 Realise.
11 Sorrowfully, sadly.
12 Without exception, always.

■ Exercise 5

Choose the word that best completes each sentence.

1 James is the _____ critic of the *Daily News*.
  a lettered   **b** literal
  c literary   **d** literate

2 You've been getting into bad _____ recently. It's time to pull your socks up.
  a behaviour   **b** customs
  c habits   **d** manners

3 It's completely _____ to expect me to do all the work.
  a irrational   **b** rational
  c reasonable   **d** unreasonable

4 'Take your own time' is a/an _____ expression.
  a colloquial   **b** idiomatic
  c literal   **d** metaphorical

5 This seat is reserved for _____ persons.
  a disabled   **b** incapable
  c ineffectual   **d** unable

Make sure you know the meanings of the incorrect alternatives in exercise 5. Use five of them in sentences of your own, to show their meanings.

STRUCTURES

Reported speech

Reported	Direct
Only the other day I told his class they'd got to pull their socks up.	'You've got to pull your socks up!'
The Reverend Wilkinson said that everyone ought to turn over a new leaf. *had to*	'Everyone ought to turn over a new leaf.' **or** 'You must all turn over a new leaf.'

■ Exercise 6

Here are some extracts from the conversation on p. 87 in reported form. Compare them with the original, and make a note of the changes that have been made: think particularly about verb tenses (which have been altered and which haven't); personal pronouns such as *he*, *you*, etc.; phrases that express aspects of time (*yesterday*, *now*, etc.); and the addition of introductory verbs (*said*, *asked*, etc).

(line 1)
The headmaster said that Peregrine was a most unusual boy. Mr Clyde-Browne agreed, and added that every report he had had said that Peregrine's behaviour was impeccable and that he tried hard. He assured the headmaster that he could face facts as well as the next man, and wondered if the headmaster was suggesting that Peregrine was stupid.

(line 32)
The headmaster said that it made teaching Peregrine a distinctly unnerving experience. Only a few days before, he had told his class that they'd got to pull their socks up, and Peregrine promptly had. It had been exactly the same in Bible Studies. The Reverend Wilkinson had said that everyone ought to turn over a new leaf.

■ Exercise 7

Write a new version in reported form of the conversation from line 6 to line 16 (Are you suggesting—he's told as Gospel).

■ Exercise 8

Without looking back at the passage on p. 87, write in direct speech form the conversations reported in exercise 6.

■ Exercise 9

Write a dialogue of 5 or 6 lines, in direct speech form, between a teacher and a parent of one of the pupils. Then exchange dialogues with another student and write a report on the one you receive.

Listening and speaking
Discussion and debate

Describe the scene.
Why are the people in the photograph dressed like this?
What can you guess about the type of school they go to, by looking at their appearance and the way they are standing?

What is the value of school uniforms?
What are the differences between state schools and privately run schools?
Do single-sex schools have any advantages over mixed schools?

LEARNING

■ **Exercise 1**

Discipline in schools
These headlines and reports have all appeared in British newspapers in the last few years.
How do you react to them?
Do schools in your country have problems with discipline?

Hold a debate on the theme:
■ Discipline is the key to learning.

The Observer 28 August 1983

Drink, drugs, sex and burglary —all at one private school

THE headmaster of an expensive private school has sent an extraordinary letter to parents cataloguing instances of drink and drug abuse, under-age sex and numerous cases of burglary in which pupils have been involved.

RAMPAGING PUPILS

TERRORISE

PRIMARY SCHOOL

A primary school in Toxteth, Liverpool, has been closed temporarily in the wake of a fortnight of violence by pupils.

Extra staff were drafted into St Saviour's Church of England School after attacks on teachers, who have been taking classes in pairs.

A gang of pupils, aged nine and ten, have slashed furniture, covered cars with swill

---

The Times 3 August 1983

One school child is beaten every 19 seconds, survey says

By Lucy Hodges, Education Correspondent

A child is beaten in an English or Welsh school once every 19 seconds, according to Stopp, the teachers' anti-caning pressure group, which claims to have carried out the most comprehensive study of caning in schools.

In a survey published today

■ **Exercise 2**

What should go into an English language course? In the following list you can see some of the aspects of language that are presented in this book, as well as some of the activities used to present and practise them. Discuss in small groups:
■ how important each of these aspects and activities is, if possible by grading them from 1 to 5, where grade 1 = essential, and grade 5 = unnecessary.
■ if there are any other activities or aspects of language that should be included in an ideal course.
■ how important it is for the students to participate in the planning of a language course.
(Note that the page numbers refer to examples in this book.)

aspects of language	activities
idioms (p. 88)	reading texts of general interest (p. 76)
vocabulary extension (p. 89)	conversation (p. 92)
structures (p. 90)	role play (p. 25)
functions (pp. 93–6)	debate (p. 71)
intonation and stress (p. 97)	giving talks (p. 46)
pronunciation (p. 109)	listening to conversations, interviews, etc. (p. 93)
spelling (p. 73)	writing articles, letters, etc. (p. 39)
	written homework

Listening comprehension

You will hear three people discussing a day excursion for a group of students. The first time you listen to the conversation, list the places suggested for visits: put ticks (√) by those which they agree to go to, and crosses (X) by those they decide not to go to. Then listen to the conversation again and answer questions 1 to 4.

suggestions	agreed?	reasons for acceptance or rejection

1 In the space provided, write down the main reason why each place was accepted or rejected.

2 What is the relationship between the participants in the discussion? Who are they? How do you know?

3 What were the exact words used in the conversation to
  a ask for opinions?
  b express opinions?

c agree? **d** disagree?

4 Discuss the arguments used in deciding which places to visit. Do you agree with them?

Function: opinions and agreement

What do you think they are saying? Fill in the bubbles.

LEARNING

■ **Exercise 1** [PW]

Look at the expressions in Pair work 8. Student B must find the most appropriate responses to what student A says.

■ **Exercise 2**

Use the tables to help you make up short conversations for these situations.

1 Three people are talking about a music group—two of them like it, but the third one doesn't.

2 In a radio programme, an interviewer asks two politicians from different parties for their opinions on student demonstrations.

3 Two friends, one a smoker and the other a non-smoker, are discussing whether or not smoking should be banned in public places such as cinemas.

Asking for an opinion

General
What do you *think/feel* (about ...)?
What are your *views on/thoughts about* ...?
What's your opinion of ...?

Informal
How do you feel about ...?
How do you see ...?

Formal
I'd be *glad/grateful* to *have/hear* your *views/opinion* on ...
What is/Could you tell me your reaction to ...?

Giving an opinion

General
(Personally,) I *think/believe/feel* ...
It seems to me/From my point of view/As far as I'm concerned, ...
In my *view/opinion* ...

Informal
If you ask me/To my mind/The way I see it ...
I reckon/I'd say ...

Formal
It's my *opinion/view/feeling* that ...
(Personally,) I consider ...
I'm convinced ...

Not giving an opinion

General

I really can't/I'd rather not say.
I (really) don't know what to *say/think.*
It's *hard/difficult* to say.

Informal

Well, I don't know (really).
Perhaps./May be./Could be./Search me.
Your guess is as good as mine.

Formal

I don't *have/hold* any (particular) *position/views* on the subject/matter.
I'd rather not/I don't want to commit myself (on . . .).
I can't/I'd rather not/I don't want to comment on . . .

Expressing agreement

General

I (*absolutely/entirely/quite*) agree.
Oh, *quite/absolutely/exactly/definitely.*
I couldn't agree more.

Informal

Yes!/Yeah!/Right!/Dead right!/Too true!
That's it (, isn't it?).
You're (so) right.

Formal

That's *exactly/precisely* my (own) *opinion/view.*
I'm of exactly the same opinion (as . . .).

Expressing partial agreement or polite disagreement

General

I see *your point/what you mean,* but . . .
There's a lot in what you say, but . . .
That's one way of looking at it, but . . .
I agree with *much/most* of what you say, but . . .
Yes, but *on the other hand/don't you think/we shouldn't forget* . . . .

Informal

OK/Mm/Yes/Could be, but . . .
I can see that, but . . .
I'd go along with most of that, but . . .

Formal

There's *some/a lot of* truth in what you say, but . . .
I agree (with you) *in principle/on the whole,* but . . .
(Personally,) I wouldn't go so far as (to say) that.

Disagreement
General (I'm afraid) I *disagree/don't agree/can't agree* (with . . .). (Oh,) I don't know (about . . .). (I think) that's nonsense.
Informal *Rubbish!/Nonsense!No way!/Never!* You must be joking. You can't be serious.
Formal (I'm afraid) I can't accept . . . (I'm afraid) I entirely disagree (with . . .) I see things rather differently (myself).

■ **Practice**

Work in threes. One student is an observer, whose job is to listen carefully to what the others say, but not to participate. The other two should choose a role each from the list, choose one of the topics for discussion, prepare a list of opinions on the topic for their particular role, and then act out the discussion, without telling anyone which role they have chosen. At the end of the discussion, the observer should try to guess which roles were being played and should give his reasons for thinking so. Then change roles, topic and observer, and repeat the activity.

roles	
■ headmaster	■ parent
■ English teacher	■ school
■ out-of-work	caretaker
16-year-old	■ university
■ politician	professor

topics
■ The schools of today are terrible.
■ English is an easy language to learn.
■ Television has a bad influence on children.
■ The purpose of education is to produce good citizens.

Reading aloud: intonation of question tags 📼

Question tags play an important part in spoken English, inviting the listener to agree or disagree with what the speaker says; by the intonation pattern he chooses, the speaker can indicate what type of response he expects to receive.

Tune 1 (falling)—the speaker expects the listener to agree.
It's always been very popular, ↘*hasn't it, John?*
You don't have to have a special outing to go to the beach, ↘*do you?*

Tune 2 (rising)—the speaker is less certain of himself; the statement becomes, in fact, a real question.
That's something else we can do any time, ↗*isn't it?*
That can't be meant seriously, ↗*can it?*

- Remember how to form question tags:
  positive statement—negative tag
  negative statement—positive tag

■ Exercise 1

Complete each statement with a question tag, and then practise saying them aloud using tune 1 (falling).

1 He's a remarkably tiresome boy, . . .?

2 There's no point in going on, . . .?

3 We'd never seen anything like it, . . .?

4 She's got courage, . . .?

5 Jane and I would love to come, . . ., Jane?

Notice also these two special types, both used with tune 2:
- *Close the door, will you, please, John?*
  imperative—positive tag (to soften a command)
- *Oh, you do, do you?*
  positive statement—positive tag (to express disbelief or sarcasm)

This form is also commonly used to show that the speaker has come to a conclusion by inference.
- *Johnny's here, is he?*
  (= I presume Johnny's here, because of your behaviour, or the time, or because I can see his car, etc.)

■ Exercise 2

Make short sarcastic or disbelieving responses to these statements.

Mary's here.—Oh, she is, is she?

1 Peter's lost all his money.

2 You must do as I say.

3 They'll be waiting for us.

4 Janet thinks she knows everything.

5 The car broke down in the middle of the road.

■ Exercise 3

Put an appropriate question tag in each gap, mark the intonation with falling or rising arrows, and read the dialogue aloud.

Lady Smythe Stop the car here, . . ., Henry? You get such a lovely view from here, . . .?
Henry Yes, madam.
Lady Smythe I mean, it's so beautiful, . . .? You don't often come across such wonderful countryside, . . .?
Henry No, madam.
Lady Smythe That's Gloucester, . . .?
Henry I believe it's Cheltenham, madam.
Lady Smythe Oh. You've been a driver all your life, . . ., Henry?
Henry Yes, madam.
Lady Smythe A bit boring, . . .? Ah, well. Drive on, . . ., please?
Henry Yes, madam.

LEARNING

Activity: language school

Imagine that you are in the process of starting a new language school in a small town on the south coast of England. The school will teach English to foreign students at all levels, in courses lasting anything between two days and one year. Students will live as guests in English-speaking families. The town is a popular holiday resort visited by thousands of British and foreign tourists every year.

You are now planning an advertising campaign, and have drawn up the following list of features which might be included in the advertising material. Read through the list and then carry out the activities.

Ideas

limited capital

only for adults

only for school children

	1	2	3
students live with British families			
overhead projectors in all classrooms			
video equipment available			
tape recorders available			
blackboards in every classroom			
film projectors available			
language laboratory			
school is close to beach			
specially written course books and other material			
purpose-built classrooms			
highly qualified administrative staff			
highly qualified teachers			
modern furniture in classrooms			
evening activities— discothèques, parties, etc.			
students' time divided between holiday and language learning			

- Individually, without discussion, rank the items in the list in terms of their importance in persuading students to come to the school. In the first column put '1' by the item you think should be stressed most strongly, '2' by the next most important item, and so on down to '15' for the least important one.
- In groups of two to four, compare your lists and produce a compromise order of priorities, which you write down as numbers 1 to 15 in the second column. Each individual must try to persuade the others in the group that his/her order is best (and give reasons), though the group must agree to a single order within a given time-limit (20 minutes, for example).
- The whole class meets to compare the decisions taken in the groups. Again, within a given time-limit, you must compromise on a final order of priorities, which you can write in column 3.
- Compose the advertising material for the school. Small groups should be given responsibility for the various features to be stressed; these groups will have to invent any necessary details, write descriptions of photographs, and of course follow the class's decisions as to how much each feature is to be stressed.
- Follow-up. Discuss the language school and its advertising campaign: is there anything else that you would expect of a language school? Do you think that this activity was realistic? Do you think that an advertising campaign can be planned in this way?

Revision: units 7 and 8

■ Exercise 1

Fill each gap in the following passage with one word; it need not be the actual word used in the original text, but it must be appropriate to the context.

The world is known to us through many ____(1)____, not just hearing, smell, vision, and, at close ____(2)____, touch and taste.

Our skins let us know whether the air is ____(3)____ or dry, whether surfaces are wet ____(4)____ being sticky or slippery. From the uniformity of slight ____(5)____, we can be aware ____(6)____ deeply a finger is thrust into water ____(7)____ body temperature, even if the finger is ____(8)____ in a rubber glove that keeps the skin completely dry. ____(9)____ other animals, with highly ____(10)____ skins, appear able to learn still more about their ____(11)____. Often they do so ____(12)____ employing any of the five senses Aristotle knew.

■ Exercise 2

Write definitions of five of these words. Give the definitions to other members of the class, who should try to guess which words they refer to.

cross-examination	harassing
exercise book	concede
drawing pin	survey
socket	glance
impeccable	plug
invariably	ruler
metaphorical	pencil
paperclip	file

UNIT 9

WORK

Reading and thinking
Reading comprehension

Who are you?

There is nothing stereotyped about choosing a career. Each one of you who has read or will be reading this chapter is unique. Ability, personality, qualifications, sex, background, prejudices and inclinations are all individual attributes which will vary in an infinite number of combinations. Their sum total will make the unique you.

5   The way in which they relate to your choice of occupation will also be a highly personal affair. The basics referred to above will be overlaid by the way you have been brought up, your parents' expectations, your education, local attitudes and a variety of other factors which can be loosely called environmental. The net result of this is simply this: no one can tell you the career to choose or which one will guarantee endless satisfaction. Many will advise but only you can choose.

10   Let us separate out some of the qualities which make up the essential you.

ABILITIES

Personal competence

  1 Reading and understanding
  2 Listening and understanding
15 3 Solving problems
  4 Thinking up new ideas
  5 Using numbers in estimating
    or calculating
  6 Memorising

  7 Making decisions
  8 Thinking quickly
  9 Deducing solutions
  10 Speaking languages
  11 Constructing things
  12 Creating artistic things
  13 Designing things

  14 Arranging things
    in an orderly way
  15 Organising events
  16 Giving advice
  17 Composing
  18 Catering
  19 Writing
  20 Demonstrating

20 | ARE THERE
OTHER QUALITIES
YOU CAN ADD?

To get a clearer view of your own strengths and weaknesses, decide on five items which you could modestly claim as reasonable strengths.

25 Insert by numbers shown above.

Now ask your parents to 'measure' you in the same way. Do not show them your own assessment until they have completed theirs.

If there are differences, discuss them. If there is wide discrepancy, come to an agreed decision as to who is wearing rose-coloured spectacles.

30 *Social skills*

1 Working in a team	6 Being patient with prickly people
2 Organising people	7 Communicating bad news
3 Taking responsibility in a group	8 Being firm with others
4 Being friendly to total strangers	9 Being tolerant of views which clash with yours
35 5 Understanding people	10 Helping people

As before, choose five which in your estimation you are quite good at.

Insert by numbers shown above.

Now ask your best friend to give an opinion.

ENVIRONMENT

40 This somewhat overworked word is being used here in a very general way to cover a variety of factors which either have had or will continue to play a big part in shaping your destiny. When making a choice of your career it is no bad thing to be aware of these influences so that you can more easily come to terms with them. Take for example the social influences of the home and school. Here is a series of statements which invite a 'true or false' response from you. See if your 45 friends agree or disagree.

fate

soci ...

	True	False
1 The number of children in a family has no bearing whatsoever on the career choice of any one child		
2 If father went to university, the chances are that if academically qualified to enter 50 a son would follow suit		
3 If an elder brother or sister failed to complete a higher education course there is a strong risk that the next child will be put off even starting		
4 No parent has the right to stop a son or daughter going on to higher education		
5 A child coming from a home where strong cultural interests exist is more likely to take 55 up a professional career than one who comes from a home where they do not figure at all		
6 No parent is powerful enough to prevent a child going on to higher education		
7 Parental occupations have no bearing whatsoever on the career choice of their children		
8 Children who are thoroughly prepared for their future career by a school do not 60 markedly make a greater success of their work than those who are not		
9 Extra-curricular activities at school have a great deal of influence on the later effectiveness of a professional adult's career		
10 The biggest single influence on a pupil's career choice is the attitude of home		

All these issues are the subject of debate. They represent a context or setting in which you have been brought up and to some degree they will have a bearing upon your life. As you are making decisions keep them in mind but do not allow the influence of any one of of them to distort your thinking.

From *Your choice at 17+* by Michael Smith and Peter March

1 What is meant by 'stereotyped' (line 1)?

2 What is the point of the word 'loosely' (line 7)?

3 What is meant by 'prickly people' (line 31)?

4 Which word is 'overworked' (line 40), and why do you think this is so?

5 What does 'these influences' (line 42) refer to?

6 Give some examples of 'extra-curricular activities' (line 59). Why might they 'have a great deal of influence on the later effectiveness of a professional adult's career'?

7 Look carefully at the statements numbered 1 to 10 (lines 46–61). Renumber them according to how strongly they support the idea that choice of career is influenced by one's home and school background; put '1' by the statement that most strongly supports this idea, down to '10' by the statement that most strongly opposes it. Discuss your new order with your fellow students.

8 Who do you think this passage has been written for?
Summarise the advice given.

Words and structures

IDIOMS

■ **Exercise 1**

Explain the meanings of these expressions as they are used in the text.

a The net result (line 8)
b the essential you (line 10)
c wearing rose-coloured spectacles (line 29)
d play a big part in shaping your destiny (line 41)
e has no bearing whatsoever (line 47)
f the chances are (line 49)
g follow suit (line 50)
h put off (line 52)

i do not figure (line 55)
j keep them in mind (line 66)

Work

■ **Exercise 2**

Fill each gap in 1 to 5 with one of these prepositions: *in, off, on, out, up.*

1 This text you've written is a little too serious—can't you work _____ a few jokes?

2 This problem's too difficult for me. I can't work it _____.

3 I can't work _____ any enthusiasm for this project.

4 We haven't found the solution yet, but we're working _____ it.

5 I need to take a lot of exercise, in order to work _____ all my superfluous energy.

Fill each gap in 6 to 9 with one of these prepositions: *at, in, off, out of.*

6 My wife's in her study, _____ work on her latest invention.

7 What measures is the Government going to take to help the millions of people who are _____ work?

8 The good news is that there are 20,000 more people _____ work this month than there were last month.

9 Mr Jones is _____ work today because of an illness in the family.

■ Exercise 3

Match up the phrases and definitions. Then write sentences that include the expressions on the left to show what they mean.

1	all in a day's work	a	able to function properly
2	have one's work cut out	b	(describing what is) normal or to be expected
3	in working order	c	efficient, competent
4	make short work of something	d	face a difficult task
5	workable	e	finish or destroy something quickly
6	working capital	f	lazy
7	working class	g	money needed for carrying on a business
8	workmanlike	h	place where machines etc. are made or repaired
9	workmanship	i	practicable, that can be done
10	work-out	j	session of physical exercise
11	workshop	k	skill in producing something
12	workshy	l	slow down production by paying exaggerated attention to the rules
13	work to rule	m	wage-earning section of the community, especially those employed in manual labour

VOCABULARY

■ Exercise 4

Fill each gap in the following passage with one word. Below the passage is a list of words which may help you. Only basic root words are given, and in some cases you will have to find other forms of these words, e.g. *occupy—occupation.*

For a ___(1)___ of reasons, I had been ___(2)___ for six weeks; so I thought it was time to look for ___(3)___. I had no academic ___(4)___ at all, but I was confident that my personal ___(5)___— my charm and enthusiasm—would get me any ___(6)___ I applied for. I'd had a very ___(7)___ background, with a wide experience of lots of different ___(8)___, and I was prepared to carry out virtually any ___(9)___ that an ___(10)___

cared to give me. Furthermore, my previous ___(11)___ had given me an excellent ___(12)___, so I was full of hope.

At the first place I went to, they looked at my clothes and hair and said, 'I'm afraid we can't give you a ___(13)___. We expect our ___(14)___ to show a ___(15)___ attitude to their ___(16)___. Come back when you're tidier and better ___(17)___.'

employ	*quality*
job	*refer*
occupy	*task*
profession	*vary*
qualify	*work*

UNIT 9
WORK

Exercise 5

Choose the word that best completes each sentence.

1 Don't jump to _____, just because you saw me with another girl.
   a conclusions **b** judgements
   c prejudices **d** results

2 Before he started work, I asked the builder to give me an _____ for the cost of repairing the roof.
   a assessment **b** estimate
   c estimation **d** evaluation

3 Unemployment is obviously an important _____, and the Government must take it into consideration.
   a fact **b** faction
   c factor **d** fiction

4 My _____ is to give her the job.
   a attitude **b** inclination
   c tendency **c** thought

5 Rose is an extremely _____ secretary.
   a effective **b** effete
   c efficacious **d** efficient

STRUCTURES

Much, many, far, and *long*

Notice how short expressions are used in negative statements and questions, while longer expressions are used in positive statements:

Q: How much money do you earn?
A: I don't earn much money,

but the job gives me $\begin{cases} \text{a great deal of} \\ \text{plenty of} \\ \text{lots of/a lot of} \\ \text{a large amount of} \end{cases}$ satisfaction.

Q: How far is to London?
A: It isn't far, but it's a long way to Edinburgh.

Q: How long does it take to get to work?
A: It doesn't take long, but it takes a long time to get home again.

Exercise 6

meaning changed! means the opposite

Make these sentences positive.

It isn't far to Tipperary.
It's a long way to Tipperary.

1 We haven't got much time.

2 It isn't long since I was at school.

3 We aren't far behind them now.

4 They haven't got many children.

5 His answer wasn't far off.

Exercise 7

Ask the questions to which these are the replies.

A: About five miles.
Q: How far (away) is the nearest shop? or How far is it to Withington?

1 About a week.

2 It's a very long way.

3 It took quite a long time.

4 Three miles away.

5 Hundreds.

Listening and speaking
Discussion and debate

Describe the scene.
What is this place?
What do you think the people are doing?
Do you think this would be a good job? Give reasons for your answer.
How important is the environment you work in—the sounds, the dust and dirt, the light, the mental and physical stress, and so on?
Are there any jobs that should not be performed by women?

■ Exercise 1

The diagram shows 17 professions that are in some way involved when someone drives a car. In small groups, discuss:
■ exactly how people in these professions might be involved with you as a driver.
■ which of these professions you would most/least like to work in.

■ Exercise 2

Make up similar diagrams for all the professions involved with the following activities.

■ Having breakfast.
■ Watching television.
■ Sitting in the classroom.

Explain in what ways they are all involved.

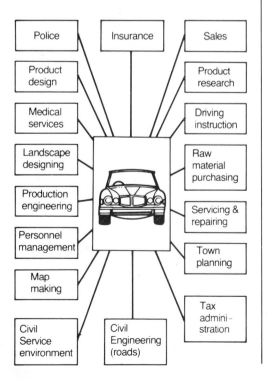

Police

Insurance

Sales

Product design

Product research

Medical services

Driving instruction

Landscape designing

Raw material purchasing

Production engineering

Servicing & repairing

Personnel management

Town planning

Map making

Tax administration

Civil Service environment

Civil Engineering (roads)

UNIT 9
WORK

■ Exercise 3

Hold a debate on one of these topics.

- Everyone should have the right to work.
- Everyone should have the right not to work.
- Automation is a blessing.
- All workers should have at least four weeks' holiday every year.
- Retirement at 60 should be compulsory for everyone.

■ Exercise 4

Write a short article for a newspaper on the subject you have just debated. Use some of the arguments that were given there.

Listening comprehension

You will hear a conversation between two people. The first time you listen, identify the situation and say who the people are. The second and subsequent times you listen to the conversation, fill in the form and answer questions 1 and 2.

1 Using the information you have written on the form, discuss the suitability of this candidate for this particular job. Write a paragraph summarising the factors for and against employing her.

2 What were the exact words used, in the last part of the interview, to
a offer advice?
b make a suggestion?
c ask for advice?

GOSLING CONFERENCE SERVICES
Job Applicant Report

Surname .... Title (Mr, Mrs, Miss, Ms) ....

First names ....

Address ....

.... Telephone ....

Job applied for .... Age ....

Educational background ....

....

Qualifications ....

....

Present job ....

....

Previous experience ....

....

Present salary .... Salary asked for ....

Positive factors   Negative factors

....

....

....

Rate the candidate on a scale of 1 to 5   1 = completely unsuitable, 5 = perfect

Function: advice and suggestions

What do you think they are saying? Fill in the bubbles.

WORK

■ **Exercise 1** PW

Look at the expressions in Pair work 9a. Student B must find the best responses to what student A says.

■ **Exercise 2**

Use the tables to help you make up short conversations for these situations.

1 Your car has stalled at a busy road junction—several people give you advice: a policeman, a taxi-driver leaning out of his car, a passenger in your car, and a pedestrian who is having difficulty crossing the road.

2 Two businessmen from different firms arrange a time and place to meet.

3 Two friends are bored; they try to help each other with advice and suggestions about what to do.

Asking for advice
General
Do you think I *should/ought to* (...)?
What *should I/ought I to/do you think I should* do?
What would you advise (me to do)?
I'd like *some/your* advice (*on/about* ...).
Informal
What would you do *in my place/if you were me*?
What do you make of ...?
Formal
I *would/should* appreciate *your/some* advice (*on/about* ...).
What would you recommend?
I was wondering what your reaction would be?

Giving advice
General
I (don't) think you *should/ought to* ...
If I were you, *I'd/I wouldn't* ...
I'd/I wouldn't ..., if I were you.
Informal
You'd better (not) ...
Take my advice and ...
The way I see it, you *should/shouldn't* ...
Formal
My advice would be to ...
If I were in your position, I *would/wouldn't* ...
I *would/wouldn't advise/recommend* ...
My reaction would be ...

Making suggestions
General Shall we ...? *You/We could/might* ...
Informal Let's ... (, shall we?) *What/How* about ... (then)? Why don't *we/you* ...? Why not ...? (Are you) coming for a ...?
Formal Perhaps you'd *care/like* to ...? *May/Might* I suggest ...? I'd like to *suggest/propose* ...

■ Practice PW

Act out the situations in Pair work 9b and 9c.

Reading aloud: advise—/s/ or /z/? 🔲

■ Exercise 1

It can be difficult to know whether endings in *-se* are pronounced /s/ or /z/. Here are some of the more common words; sort them into twelve groups—within each group every word should have the same final vowel sound and the same final consonant sound.

arise	*z*	grandiose	*s*
base	*s*	hose	*z*
blouse	*z*	loose	*s*
case	*s*	lose	*z*
cease	*s*	louse	*s*
chase	*s*	mouse	*s*
cheese	*z*	obese	*z*
choose	*z*	paradise	*s*
chose	*z*	phase	*z*
concise	*s*	phrase	*z*
devise	*z*	please	*z*
dose	*s*	precise	*s*
douse	*s*	rose	*z*
enclose	*z*	rouse	*z*
erase	*z*	spouse	*z*
fuse	*z*	these	*z*
geese	*s*	whose	*z*
goose	*s*	wise	*z*

■ Exercise 2

Practise saying the above words. One student says a word; the others call out 'one' if it ends with /s/, 'two' if it ends with /z/.

■ Exercise 3

These words are pronounced with /z/ when used used as verbs, with /s/ in other cases (nouns or adjectives): *close, excuse, house, refuse, use.* In the case of *refuse*, the stress shifts as well; thus we have *refuse* (noun, meaning 'rubbish'), but *refuse* (verb, meaning 'to say no').

In the following sentences, decide whether the words *in italics* end with /s/ or /z/. Then read them aloud.

1 *Excuse* me, can you *close* the door to my *house*, please?

2 There's no *excuse* for leaving your *refuse* so *close* to my *house*.

3 If the council wants to pull your *house* down, they can't *refuse* to *rehouse* you.

4 It's no *use* pretending.

■ Exercise 4

Improvise sentences that contain some of the words in exercises 1 and 3.

An obese goose chose a wise spouse.

cf
advise (z) advice (s)
advertise z
advertisement (s)
advertising (z)

Activity: finding a job

The class divides into groups of four to six people.

■ Each group chooses one of the advertised jobs to work with. Half of the group will be applicants for the job, while the other half will represent the company advertising the job.

■ The company representatives meet and decide what qualities they are looking for in the candidates for the job. They will have to invent details about what the company does and what the advertised job will involve. What questions should be asked? What information should be given?

■ At the same time, the job applicants meet to discuss what their strategy will be at the interview. What information will they need to know? What salary will they ask for? What qualities will they stress? They should invent backgrounds for themselves – qualifications, experience, age, etc.

■ The company representatives interview the applicants one at a time.

■ Follow-up: representatives and applicants meet to discuss which candidate was most successful, and why.

■ If you have time, reverse the roles and choose another advertisement to work with.

The Standard 12 August 1983

YOUNG & IN LOVE

Are you 17 + & in love with the idea of £120 weekly? If so we can show you the way to a smashing sales career. Details 500 1010, 32 Woodford Avenue, Gants Hill Ilford

COOK

Beautiful small hotel in Holland Park requires enthusiastic and efficient person to cook for small but exclusive restaurant. Full catering training not necessary but some cooking experience essential.
PHONE FIONA ON 01-727 2777

A FAST-growing division of a UK public company have career opportunities for graduates (min 2.2) aged 21–24. For application form write to Mrs D. Buddin. Automatic Catering Supplies Ltd. Garth Road Morden. Surrey, SM 4 4 LP.

A RESPONSIBLE person, 21–24 with driving licence for challenging job. 01-437 4429.

ATTRACTIVE young persons, aged 18–30, with good personality, required for sales promotion at the Earls Court Motorcycle Show, 19–29 August Tel: John Martin, 07017-81226 for information

CRANKS dine & wine evening restaurant W1 needs bright young people to help. Phone Margaret Chapmen/Graham Fox 437 9431.

LIGHT & SOUND ENGINEER

to assist

Stage Manager

IN LARGE WEST END DISCOTHEQUE.

Telephone 437 1447 for application form.

DOES your boss think you're worth £15,000 pa? If not call me. I'm looking for one or two self-motivated men or women to join our team. No exp necessary. Age 25–55. John Jeffries 339 4631.

DRIVERS required for prestigious high class private car hire co in the City. To work day or night shifts. If you own a 4-dr saloon not more than 3 years old please contact Mr Lewis on 01-251 3091. High earnings possible for the right persons.

Gymnasium Staff full & part time

required for luxury health club in Chiswick. Experience essential. Good rates of pay and many perks.
For further details ring John Treharne on 01-995 4600.

RESIDENTIAL HEAD PORTER

required for block of flats in

Belsize Square, NW3

Previous experience essential. Age 35 to 55. Salary negotiable.
Please contact Jennifer Wynne. 221 2929

WANTED

Aged 19–25. No experience necessary. Earn up to £200 per week and not less than £400 per mth. Smart appearance essential for good career opportunity. Call 353 7010.

★ UNEMPLOYED? ★

Are you 18–25 and single? Ring Alison on 223 9514 for an immediate interview.

Written work: connecting ideas (4)

Similarities and differences

To test a theory that four recent robberies were committed by the same gang, detectives have drawn up the following table of information.

codename	Alpha	Beta	Gamma	Delta
town?	London	London	Manchester	Birmingham
target?	bank	art gallery	jeweller's	post office
day?	Monday	Sunday	Thursday	Monday
time?	3.30 p.m.	3 a.m.	3.30 p.m.	3.30 p.m.
what was stolen?	money	paintings	diamonds	money
how valuable?	£500,000	£250,000	£120,000	£60,000
how many thieves?	4	4	3	2
how many arrested?	0	0	0	0
how did they escape?	car	van	on foot	car
explosives used?	yes	no	no	no
firearms used?	yes	no	yes	yes
face masks used?	yes	yes	yes	yes

How is Alpha similar to Beta? In what ways are Alpha and Beta similar?	There were	the same number of just as many	people in Alpha as in Beta.
What are the similarities between Alpha and Beta? What do Alpha and Beta have in common? How does Alpha resemble Beta?	Alpha and Beta are similar Alpha is similar to Beta Alpha resembles Beta	<u>in the number of</u> people involved. <u>in that</u> the same number of people were involved.	

WORK

How In what way	is Alpha different does Alpha differ	from Beta?	Less money was taken in Beta.		
			More money was taken in Alpha (than in Beta).		
			In Beta £250,000 was stolen,	whereas while	in Alpha £500,000 was stolen.
What are the differences between Alpha and Beta?			Alpha differs from Beta Alpha is different from Beta	in that more money was taken. in the amount of money taken.	
			They're different	as regards with regard to with respect to	the amount of money taken.
			They're different as far as the amount of money taken is concerned.		

■ **Exercise 1**

Imagine that you are detectives discussing the four crimes. Ask and answer questions about the similarities and differences between them.

■ **Exercise 2**

Write a report to your senior officer explaining which crimes you think may have been committed by the same gang. Give your reasons.

■ **Exercise 3**

Choose one of the following subjects and write an article for a magazine, commenting on the similarities and differences between the two things.
- Two towns that you know well.
- Two houses/flats/rooms that you have lived in.
- Two famous people (film stars, musicians, politicians, criminals, etc.).
- Two books that you have read recently.
- Two daily newspapers.
- Two television programmes or films.

THE ENVIRONMENT

Reading and thinking
Reading comprehension

Vanishing Animals

Vinzenz Ziswiler, a Swiss ecologist, in his book *Extinct and Vanishing Species,* lists about 150 species known to have vanished in the past three centuries. The list ranges from the aurochs (1627) and the dodo in the seventeenth century, to the Indian pink-headed duck in 1944. The reasons why animals vanish from the earth are various: the Tahitian parakeet
5 went because its habitat was altered by drainage. The New Zealand quail succumbed to diseases introduced by settlers. The Tasmanian 'wolf' was hunted because it was ignorantly believed to be a predator—actually it is not a carnivore, but a marsupial like the kangaroo. The nocturnal kiwi or apteryx was wiped out by weasels introduced to 'enrich' the fauna of New Zealand. Schomburgk's deer was persecuted in Siam for religious reasons.
10 It is too late to do anything about these 150 vanished species, but we could do something about the 240 further species currently threatened with extinction. These include the Bactrian camel (400 left), the oryx (200), the Sumatra rhinoceros (170), the Cape zebra (75), the cahow (70), the whooping crane (50), the Japanese crested ibis (12), the Everglades kite (15), the Bali tiger (3 or 4) and others for which the numbers are not known.
15 Not only animals but many plants are becoming extinct: about 300 species are in grave danger of being lost in Britain alone. The situation is most serious in islands where species found nowhere else in the world exist. In the Hawaiian islands, for instance, 95 per cent of the native plants are unique, and many are on the verge of extinction. It is now possible to spend a vacation in Hawaii without ever seeing a native plant. Philip Island in the western
20 Pacific is now completely eroded, with only a few plants remaining in the valleys. When Capt. Cook discovered it in 1774 it was completely covered with vegetation. There were three unique species here, of which one, the glory pea, has not been seen since 1805; a couple of years ago only one of the other two species could be found, and of this there were only a few bushes left.
25 Collectors are probably the worst menace, especially in the case of orchids and succulents: many rare African orchids are on the point of extinction. In England, the lady's slipper orchid remains only in one secret locality. Unlike Czechoslovakia and Austria, Britain has no legislation to limit picking rare plants.
Does it matter that man is wiping out whole species from the planet? Evolution is capable
30 of many quirks, and its variants are, some might say, of only museum interest. But apart from the aesthetic values of maintaining a richly varied flora and fauna there are practical reasons for doing so. Plants often turn out to have unique medical or other properties. Animals also still have much to teach. Thus the vanishing oryx can live indefinitely without drinking: hence it might become of great importance as a protein source in arid areas, as the
35 growing world population expands into them. Who knows what future peoples will want? It is sheer folly to deplete the pool of genetic variation built up so painfully over millions of years.

From *The Doomsday Book*

1 Put ticks by those factors which, according to the passage, have been responsible for species becoming extinct.

  a Draining water from the area where the species lived. ☐

  b Human illnesses. ☐

  c Human fear. ☐

  d Being hunted by men for food. ☐

  e The introduction to the area of non-native species. ☐

  f Religion. ☐

  g Collectors. ☐

2 Which of the species mentioned in the first paragraph were destroyed intentionally by man?

3 Put ticks by the statements that are true according to the text.

  a Most of the plants in the Hawaiian Islands are not found anywhere else. ☐

  b There are no native plants in Hawaii. ☐

  c Two of the species unique to Philip Island are probably extinct. ☐

  d Collectors are responsible for the erosion on Philip Island. ☐

4 Put ticks by the statements that correctly reflect the author's attitude.

  a It is sufficient to keep examples of every species in museums. ☐

  b One reason for not allowing plants and animals to become extinct is that this would make the world less beautiful. ☐

  c The oryx can teach us how to live without water. ☐

5 Using your own words, write two short paragraphs

  a describing the main causes of the disappearance of animal and plant species.

  b giving the main reasons why we should 'do something about the species currently threatened with extinction'.

Words and structures

IDIOMS

■ Exercise 1

Explain the meanings of these expressions as they are used in the text.

a wiped out (line 8)

b do something about (line 10)

c being lost (line 16)

d on the verge of (line 18)

e the worst menace (line 25)

f of only museum interest (line 30)

g turn out (line 32)

h built up (line 36)

■ Exercise 2

Two-part verbs with *out*

Match up the two-part verbs and definitions.

1 back out	**a** become unconscious
2 black out	**b** trap by a trick
3 break out	**c** draw attention to
4 catch out	**d** escape
5 die out	**e** exclude
6 fall out	**f** gradually cease to exist (family or species, usually)
7 point out	
8 rule out	**g** make useless through excessive use
9 stick out	
10 wear out	**h** protrude
	i quarrel
	j withdraw (from an agreement)

Now choose the most appropriate two-part verbs from the above list to fill the gaps in these sentences, making any necessary adjustments to verb forms.

1 The Covingham family _____ at the end of the 15th century, since the sixth earl had no children.

2 When the explosion came, I _____ for a second.

114

3 Some reporters are very sadistic—they enjoy _____ the people they are interviewing.

4 Those shoes are _____. You'll have to buy a new pair.

5 That possibility is not very likely, but we cannot _____ it _____ completely.

Now write sentences of your own to include the five two-part verbs that were not used in 1–5.

■ Exercise 3

Make sure you know the meanings of these words:

outburst	*fall-out*
outcome	*knock-out*
outcry	*layout*
outlay	*look-out*
outlet	*turn-out*

Now choose words from the list to complete these sentences.

1 It's impossible to predict the _____ of these negotiations.

2 In a nuclear attack, the greatest threat to life will come from the radioactive _____ after the actual explosion.

3 Pat wrote the text, while Sally was responsible for the _____.

4 Boxing is an excellent sport, because it provides an _____ for young people's energies.

5 We can be very pleased with the _____ at last week's meeting—we've never had as many as 200 before.

VOCABULARY

■ Exercise 4

Find words in the text *Vanishing Animals* that match these definitions.

1 Active in the night. *nocturnal*

2 All the animals of a region. *fauna*

3 Belonging to or originating in the place in question. *native*

4 Gradual process of development or change in life forms. *evolution*

5 Group of animals with many characteristics in common. *species*

6 Having died out, no longer in existence. *extinct*

7 Reduce, empty out until little remains. *deplete*

8 Treated cruelly. *persecuted*

9 Usual natural surroundings of animals and plants. *habitat*

10 Worn away. *eroded*

THE ENVIRON- MENT

■ **Exercise 5**

Write the correct numbers in the boxes.

bay	16 ☐	lake	6 ☐
coast	2 ☐	lighthouse	21 ☐
dam	15 ☐	mainland	1 ☐
estuary	4 ☐	marsh	5 ☐
forest	10 ☐	mountain	13 ☐
headland	20 ☐	peninsula	19 ☐
hill	8 ☐	reef	17 ☐
inlet	12 ☐	river	9 ☐
island	18 ☐	reservoir	14 ☐
		tributary	11 ☐
		valley	7 ☐
		wood	3 ☐

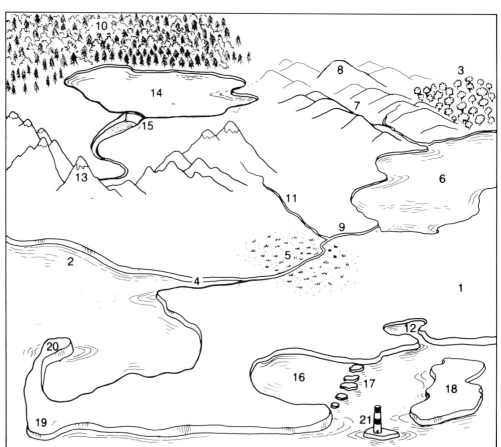

STRUCTURES

The extra *it*

Does it matter that man is wiping out whole species from the planet? (line 29)

It is used here as an extra or preparatory subject. The real subject of the verb *matter* is '(the fact) that man is wiping out whole species from the planet'; stylistically it is preferable to put long subjects that are infinitives, gerunds or clauses at the end of their sentences, with an extra *it* close to the verb.

But contrast the *it* in the clause 'actually it is not a carnivore' (line 7), where *it* makes direct concrete reference to something previously mentioned—the Tasmanian wolf.

■ Exercise 6

Look carefully at these examples from *Vanishing Animals* and the contexts in which they appear. In which cases is *it* an extra subject of the type described above, and in which cases does it refer to something concrete?

1 It was completely covered with vegetation. (line 21)

2 It is too late to do anything about these 150 vanished species. (line 10)

3 It is sheer folly to deplete the pool of genetic variation ... (line 36)

4 It might become of great importance as a protein source ... (line 34)

5 It is now possible to spend a vacation in Hawaii without ever seeing a native plant. (line 18)

6 It was ignorantly believed to be a predator. (line 6)

■ Exercise 7

Make sentences of your own with the subjects given here as well as the extra *it*.

People are so shy.
It's a shame that people are so shy.

Go for a run every morning.
It's out of the question for me to go for a run every morning.

1 Go for walks in the countryside.

2 Big industries are responsible for a great deal of pollution.

3 See you again after such a long time.

4 Demand that our society reverts to a more primitive state.

5 We, as individuals, are responsible for our own destiny.

■ Exercise 8

It can also be used as an extra object, when the real object is a clause or infinitive.

I dislike it when people disagree with me.
I leave it to you to decide what needs to be done.

Make sentences that have the phrases in exercise 7 as the objects of the following expressions. You will have to add words like *to*, *when*, *if*, etc.

1 I find it impossible to believe.

2 I put it to you.

3 The bad weather has made it difficult.

4 I consider it to be intellectually immature.

5 I found it very stimulating.

Listening and speaking
Discussion and debate

Describe the scene.
What do you think has led up to this situation?
What do you think has happened to the people who lived here?
Describe their feelings and thoughts now.
How would you react if you knew that your home might soon be destroyed by some sort of natural catastrophe?
What preparations would you make?

■ Exercise 1

Here are some natural and man-made catastrophes that threaten the world. If you can think of any more, add them to the list. Which are the most serious? Which are you most/least afraid of?
- air pollution
- sea pollution
- war
- killing animals to extinction
- flooding
- drought
- earthquakes
- volcanic eruptions

forest fire
avalanche

■ Exercise 2

Choose one of the above problems and give a short talk on the dangers involved and methods that can be used to prevent and combat these dangers.

Rumania is situated in the south-east of Europe, between 43° 37' 07" and 48° 15' 06" N and 20° 15' 44" and 29° 41' 24" E, extending for some 300 miles from north to south and for some 400 miles from west to east.

Physical Features

Rumania has a total area of 91,400 square miles. Its frontiers extend over 1,970 miles—669 miles of land frontiers, 1,148 on rivers and 153 on the sea. It has common boundaries with the U.S.S.R., Bulgaria, Hungary and Yugoslavia.

The area of the country is almost equally divided between plains (roughly 33% of the total), hills and plateaux (36%) and mountains (31%).

The *Danube Delta*, covering an area of over 1,500 square miles, is the lowest-lying plain in Rumania—a plain still in process of formation. It is a type of scenery which stands quite by itself, a corner of nature which is unrivalled for the abundance and variety of its vegetation and of its land and water fauna. There is nothing like it anywhere else in Europe.

Climate

In general the climate of Rumania is a continental one: relatively uniform, without any great differences between one part of the country and another in spite of its geographical diversity.

The coldest month is January, the warmest July (except in the alpine areas of the Carpathians, where February is the coldest month and August the warmest). In January the mean temperature ranges between − 5° and − 10° C. in the mountains and between − 2° and − 5° in the plains; in July it reaches 23° along the Danube and in Dobruja, 20° in Moldavia and Transylvania, 10° to 12° in the high mountains (only 8° in the Retezat, Făgăras and Bucegi Mountains). The extreme temperatures so far recorded are 44.4° C. (in 1951, near Brăila, in the Bărăgan) and − 38.5° C. (in 1942, in the Brașov depression).

The rainfall varies from area to area, the lowest rates (14–16 in. annually) being recorded on the Black Sea coast, the highest (40–60 in.) in the mountainous areas. There is much rain in spring; less in summer and autumn.

Hydrography

The main rivers are the Someș, the Mureș, the Jiu, the Olt, the Arges, the Dimbovița, the Ialomița, the Siret and the Prut. All of them flow, directly or indirectly, into the Danube, which has a total length within Rumania of over 670 miles, finally dividing into three arms and flowing into the Black Sea.

Fauna and Flora

Rumania has a very varied fauna and flora.

The Rumanian forests—found mainly in the mountains and hills, and covering an area of 25,000 square miles—contain a variety of game. Deer, roe-deer, bears, wolves, boars, lynxes, martens, squirrels, capercailzies, etc.—all these are found in abundance. The steppe is the haunt of hares and bustards.

The Danube basin possesses more than 70 species of fish. In the mountain streams there are trout, and rarer species like the grayling and the salmon trout; in the rivers of the plains and the lower hills there are perch, carp, and barbel. And finally there is the sturgeon, which makes its way up the Danube from the Black Sea in the spawning season.

From *Nagel's Rumania Travel Guide*

■ Exercise 3

Look at the information about the geography of Rumania. Use this as a model for talking about your own country. What do you know about its climate, physical features, hydrography, fauna and flora, industries, population, etc?

■ Exercise 4

Write a brief description of your country along the lines of the discussion.

THE ENVIRON-MENT

Listening comprehension

You will hear a conversation between three people. The first time you listen to it, identify the situation and say who the people are; describe the scene. The second and subsequent times you listen to the conversation answer questions 1 to 4.

1 Mark the following on the map.
   a The names of the three marked towns.
   b The A626, the B6105, and the B6110 roads.
   c Arrows that show the routes to be taken by motorists from Pennington to Garth, and from Baldeswell to Garth.
   d Shaded areas on the roads to show where roads are impassable.

2 Why is Garth important?

3 Imagine you are a policeman in
   a Baldeswell.
   b Pennington.
   Give instructions to motorists about how to reach Garth, and give reasons why they must take these routes and not any others.

4 What are the exact words used
   a by the policeman to say that the motorists must stop and get out of their car?
   b by the radio announcer, to advise people to drive carefully?
   c by the policeman to say that they can decide themselves?

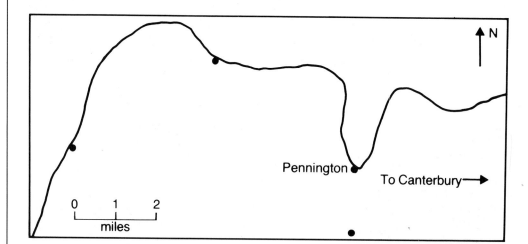

Function: orders and obligation

What do you think they are saying? Fill in the bubbles.

THE ENVIRON-MENT

UNIT 10
THE ENVIRONMENT

■ **Exercise 1** PW

Look at the sentences in Pair work 10. Student B must find the most appropriate responses to what student A says.

■ **Exercise 2**

Use the tables to help you find suitable remarks in these situations.

1 You are going through customs. The customs official wants to look at your luggage; you're not keen because you have quite a lot of cigarettes and perfume. You also have some chocolate, but you are not sure if you have to declare it.

2 You have toothache. A friend suggests going to the dentist, but you don't want to.

3 A film director gives some actors instructions about what they must and must not do. The actors think that some things might be difficult or dangerous.

Telling someone (not) to do something

General
(*Do/Don't do* that) ... (, please). (*or any suitable imperative*)
Will/Would you (not) ... (, please).
..., *will/would* you (, please).
I'd like you (not) to ... (, please).

Informal
Go/Come and do *that/this*. (*or any other imperative*)
Just do it! (*or any other imperative*)

Formal
Would you be so kind as to ... (, please)?
(I'm afraid) it is my *duty/obligation* to *insist/ask you to/tell you to* ...

Asking about obligation

General
Do I (really) *have/need* to (...)?
Am I *supposed/meant/expected* to ...?
Is it (absolutely) *necessary/essential/vital/compulsory* (*to/that* ...).
What *do I have to/must I* do?
What am I *meant/supposed/expected* to do?

Informal
Have I got/Do I have to (...)?
(Surely) I haven't got to (..., have I)?

Formal
Is/isn't ... *compulsory/obligatory*?
Are/Aren't we under an obligation (to ...)?

THE ENVIRON-MENT

Saying someone must do something

General

(*I think/I'm afraid*) you're *meant/supposed/expected* to ...
(*I think/I'm afraid*) you *should/ought to/have to/must/can't avoid* ...
(*I think/I'm afraid*) you'll have to (...).

Informal

(I'm afraid) you've got to (...).
(I'm afraid) you can't get *out of/away with* ...

Formal

(*I'm afraid/I think*) you're under an obligation to ...
You are obliged to (...)
(*I'm afraid/I think*) ... is *compulsory/obligatory*.

Saying someone must not do something

General

I don't really think you *should/ought to* ...
You're not (really) *allowed/meant/supposed* to ...
... isn't (really) allowed.

Informal

You'd (really) better not (...).
You *can't/mustn't* (...).

Formal

(*I think/I'm afraid*) you're under an obligation not to ...
On no account must you ...
... is (*absolutely/completely*) forbidden.

Saying someone need not do something

General

You *needn't/don't need to/don't have to* ...
It *isn't/won't be* necessary (to ...).
There's no need (to ...).
There's no reason why you should (...).

Informal

(It's) up to you.
You haven't got to ...
I *don't/can't* see why you *should/shouldn't* (...).

Formal

You are under no obligation (to ...).
You're not *obliged/required* to (...).
The decision is yours.

■ Practice

Work in pairs. Talk about the etiquette of formal meetings in your own country. What must you do? What must you not do? What do you not need to do?

Reading aloud: *Russian, Christian, Norwegian, Indonesian* 📼

/ʃ/ ca<u>sh</u>
/tʃ/ ca<u>tch</u>
/dʒ/ ca<u>dge</u>
/ʒ/ ca<u>s</u>ual

- The endings -*tion*, -*tian*, and -*tial* are pronounced with /ʃ/ except
  a when preceded by *s: question, Christian* /tʃ/
  b in the word *equation* /ʒ/
- The endings -*sion*, -*sian*, -*sure*, -*sual* are pronounced with /ʒ/ except when preceded by *r, s* or *n: tension, pressure, diversion* /ʃ/
- -*sian* in adjectives of nationality can be pronounced in a variety of ways. *Indonesian*, for example, is pronounced /ʃən/ or /ʒən/ or /ziən/.
- *ch* is pronounced /tʃ/ at the end of words except when followed by *e* in certain words of French origin: *moustache, pastiche, attaché*, etc. are pronounced /ʃ/. Another exception is the word *ache* /k/.
- *ge* is pronounced /dʒ/ except in certain words of French origin: *rouge, beige, sabotage, espionage, camouflage, prestige, mirage*, etc. are all pronounced with /ʒ/. But note that there are a large number of words with similar endings pronounced with /dʒ/, e.g. *courage, advantage, privilege*, etc.

■ Exercise 1

Sort these words into four groups: with /ʃ/, /tʃ/, /dʒ/ and /ʒ/.

allege	cohesion
besiege	combustion
courageous	nation
creature	nouveau riche
detach	partial
division	passion
exhaustion	patient
expansion	pleasure
fission	region
fuselage	richer
infectious	seizure
just	strategy
lecture	touch
magic	usual
manage	

■ Exercise 2

Practise saying the words in the list above. One student says a word; the others call out 'one' if it has the sound /ʃ/, 'two' if it has /tʃ/, 'three' if it has /dʒ/, and 'four' if it has /ʒ/.

■ Exercise 3

Look through the text on p. 113 and see how many words you can find that have the sounds /ʃ/, /tʃ/, /dʒ/, and /ʒ/.

■ Exercise 4

Improvise sentences that contain some of the words in exercise 1.

Richer nations manage to be patient.

Activity: the island RC

In Role card 10, each student has an incomplete map. Complete your map by describing what you can see and by asking the other students what features are shown on their maps. You must not show your map to anyone else.
When you are ready, answer these questions:
- Describe the different routes you can travel from Camble to Stenning. What would you see on the way?
- Describe the shortest route from Bridgenorth to Worth. How far is it?
- How many forests and woodland areas are there on the island?

Revision: units 9 and 10

■ Exercise 1

Fill each gap in the following passage with one word; it need not be the actual word used in the original text, but it must be appropriate to the context.

1 The number of children in a family has no ____(1)____ whatsoever on the career choice of ____(2)____ one child.

2 If father went to university, the ____(3)____ are that if academically qualified to enter a son would ____(4)____ suit.

3 If an elder brother or sister failed to complete a higher education ____(5)____ there is a strong risk that the next child will be put ____(6)____ even starting.

4 No parent has the right to stop a son or daughter going on to ____(7)____ education.

5 A child coming from a home where strong cultural interests exist is more ____(8)____ to take up a professional ____(9)____ than one who comes from a home where they do not figure at all.

6 ____(10)____ parent is powerful ____(11)____ to prevent a child going on to higher education.

7 Parental occupations have no bearing ____(12)____ on the career ____(13)____ of their children.

8 Children who are ____(14)____ prepared for their future career by a school do not markedly ____(15)____ a greater success of their work than those who are not.

9 Extra- ____(16)____ activities at school have a great ____(17)____ of influence on the later effectiveness of a professional adult's career.

10 The biggest ____(18)____ influence on a pupil's career choice is the attitude of home.

____(19)____ these issues are the ____(20)____ of debate.

■ Exercise 2

Write a brief story or description that contains all the expressions in one of the boxes. Then delete these expressions and pass what you have written to someone else, to see if he/she can fill in the gaps.

catch out
on the verge of
evolution
estuary
I put it to you

die out
menace
nocturnal
reef
it is too late

point out
outlet
persecute
reservoir
it is sheer folly

rule out
outcome
erode
peninsula
it's a shame

stick out
turn-out
species
headland
I leave it to you

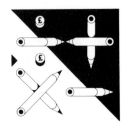

UNIT 11

MONEY

Reading and thinking
Reading comprehension

Spending money to save money

1 Wise buying is a positive way in which you can make your money go further. The way you go about purchasing an article or a service can actually save you money or can add to the cost.

Take the simple example of a hairdryer. If you are buying a hairdryer, you might think that
5 you are making the best buy if you choose one which you like the look of, and it is the cheapest in price. But when you get it home you may find that it takes twice as long as a more expensive model to dry your hair. The cost of the electricity plus the extra cost of your time could well make your hairdryer the most expensive one of all!

So what principles should you
10 **adopt when you go out shopping?**

● If you keep your home, your car or any valuable possession in tiptop condition you'll be saving money in
15 the long term.

Wise buying means getting the best value for money. You can make your money go further by buying the 'own brand' in your favourite supermarket instead of an expensively advertised 'famous name' brand. Or you can buy in bulk. But do guard
40 *against the temptation to use more as a result!*

● Before you buy a new appliance, talk to someone who owns one. If you can, use it or borrow it to check it suits your particular purpose.

20 ● Almost half the things we buy in supermarkets we didn't intend to buy before we entered, according to a recent survey. Combat this by compiling a detailed shopping list—
25 and sticking to it.

When you are choosing an expensive new appliance like a washing machine, don't be bewitched by all those knobs for the programmes you will never make real use of. You are paying heavily for the privilege. Choose the appliance to give you what
45 *you know you need now, and in the near future.*

● Before you buy an expensive item, or a service, do check the price and what is on offer. If possible, choose from three items or three
30 estimates.

● Don't throw away those money-off coupons. Use before they 'expire', but don't buy the item unless you really need it. Swop coupons
35 with friends.

Radio, television, video and other electric appliances may need service from time to time. It may well pay to shop where you will get this, even though it means paying a little extra, and not be tempted by that 'special discount' offer with no after-sales
50 *services.*

from 'TSB Money Guide' by Marie Jennings

1 Which of the alternatives in each of the three groups of products illustrated here does the author recommend? What are her reasons?

2 Explain how a cheap hairdryer might in fact cost more than an expensive one.

3 Why should you 'swap coupons with friends'?

4 Which of the following does the author advise you to do in order to make your money go further? Put ticks in the appropriate boxes, and explain your answers by referring to the text.
   a Buy the cheapest model. ☐
   b Buy the most expensive model. ☐
   c Make sure the appliance really suits your purpose. ☐
   d Write a shopping list and stick to it. ☐
   e Buy articles that you like the look of. ☐
   f Buy in bulk. ☐
   g Buy the most technically advanced product. ☐
   h Use all your money-off coupons to buy goods. ☐
   i Buy your favourite supermarket's own brand. ☐

5 Which of the pieces of advice in the text do you agree with? Can you think of any more advice that you might give to a friend on the subject of shopping?

Words and structures

IDIOMS

■ **Exercise 1**

Explain the meanings of these expressions as they are used in the text.

a make your money go further (line 1)
b making the best buy (line 5)
c getting value for money (line 36)
d buy in bulk (line 39)
e in the long term (line 14)
f it may well pay to . . . (line 47)
g after-sales service (line 49)

■ **Exercise 2**

Money talk

Explain the meanings of the words in bold.

1 Stop **talking shop**, you two! You're on holiday now.

2 It pays to **shop around**, if you've got time.

3 I've never seen a team play so badly—they were **all over the shop**.

4 His illness **put paid to** his chances of getting promotion.

5 They have high quality products, but you have to **pay through the nose** for them.

6 You have to **pay on the nail** in this establishment. We don't allow credit.

7 It's **a buyers' market** at the moment as far as houses are concerned.

8 We're thinking of putting our house **on the market**.

9 That restaurant is a bit too **up-market** for my liking.

10 I think this new project will be **a real money-spinner**.

■ **Exercise 3**

Improvise a brief story or description that includes three of the expressions from exercise 2.

VOCABULARY

■ **Exercise 4** RC

In Role card 11, each student has two words and two definitions, all of them to do with financial matters. Try to match them up without showing your page to anyone else. Then choose the most appropriate words from amongst the ones you have been discussing to fill the gaps in these sentences.

UNIT 11
MONEY

1 The _____ to *Gardening Magazine* costs about £14 a year.

2 This dress was a fantastic _____! It only cost £25.

3 The main advantage with a _____ is that you don't have to carry cash around with you.

4 My landlord has decided to increase my _____ next year.

5 I couldn't buy the house because the bank refused to let me have a _____.

6 If you buy expensive things, like cameras and watches, when you're abroad, you have to pay _____ when you return home.

7 We offer a _____ of 10% on purchases over £100.

8 My salary is not very good, but I like the job because of all the _____, like the use of a company car and occasional trips abroad.

9 Our pay rise has been eaten up by _____, so our standard of living is no higher than it was last year.

10 Gold would be a good _____; it's bound to increase in value.

STRUCTURES

Conditional sentences

Remember the main types of conditionals:

I Real
If he comes, I'll leave/I shall leave/I will leave.
Ia *If you heat chocolate, it melts.*
Ib *If he thought that I'd agree/I should agree/I would agree, he was mistaken.*
Ic *If you're in town, drop in for a cup of tea.*
II Unreal
If he came, she'd leave/she would leave.
III Impossible
If he had come, she'd have left/she would've left/she would have left.

■ Exercise 5

Put the verbs into the correct forms.

1 You'd get annoyed if I (not tell) the truth.

2 I won't give it back unless you (promise) to behave yourself.

3 If it wasn't so crowded, Brighton (be) an interesting place.

4 We would never have asked you if we (not think) you'd agree.

5 Put the kettle on now if you (want) some tea.

6 If you follow my advice, you (manage) all right.

7 You were a fool if you (believe) her.

8 If I'd thought more about it, I (find) the answer.

9 People notice you if you (dress) expensively.

10 If you dressed more expensively, people (notice) you.

Willingness

The idea of co-operation or willingness can be introduced into conditional sentences:

Real *If you'll help me with this, we can go out later.*
Unreal *If you would agree to leave, I'd feel much happier.*

Note that *will* and *would* are equivalent to 'are/were willing to', and may not be used when there is no suggestion of co-operation:

If he won a lot of money, he wouldn't stay in England.

Insistence

Will is also used in conditional sentences with the meaning of 'insist on', in these examples of the sort of thing a mother might say to a tearful child:
If you will pull the cat's tail, what do you expect?

(= *If you insist on pulling . . .*)
If you <u>will</u> misbehave, you must accept the consequences.

■ Exercise 6

Make complete sentences from the following cues. Use *will* or *would* in the conditional clauses whenever this is possible.

1 /If/Doug/play/, /we/have/chance/win.

2 /I/go/cinema/, /if/you/pay.

3 /If/they/make/too much/noise/, /you/have to/kick/them/out.

4 /If/they/give/us/discount/, /we/all/be able/go.

5 /If/you/have/car/, /you/be able/visit/us.

Doubtfulness

'Real' and 'unreal' conditionals can be made more doubtful, or less likely, with the introduction of *should* and *was/were to*.

Real

If you $\begin{Bmatrix} should\ see \\ see \end{Bmatrix}$ *Mary Jane,*

[handwritten: sollte]

tell her I love her.

Unreal

If she $\begin{Bmatrix} was/were\ to\ smile \\ smiled \end{Bmatrix}$ *at you,*

you'd fall in love too.

- *Should* and *were to* are not essential; they add the meaning 'by any chance'.
  If, by any chance, you see Mary Jane . . .

- Conditionals of this type can be expressed without *if* and with subject-verb inversion.
  Should you see Mary Jane, tell her I love her.
  Were she to smile at you, you'd fall in love too.

The form *were she to . . .* is used in the written language only. *Were* is used for all persons.
Were I/you/she/they to . . .

■ Exercise 7

Rewrite the following conditional clauses to start with *should* or *were*, and add suitable main clauses.

1 If you remember where you saw him, . . .

2 If the government agreed to freeze prices, . . .

3 If I became President, . . .

4 If the weather's bad, . . .

5 If you talked to me like that, . . .

6 If they are not able to come, . . .

Inversion with impossible conditionals

Subject-verb inversion can also take place with 'impossible' conditionals.

$\begin{rcases} If\ I\ had\ known, \\ Had\ I\ known, \end{rcases}$ *I would have met you*

at the station.

■ Exercise 8

Write sentences beginning with *had*.

He answered the phone.
Had he not answered the phone, he'd have missed the good news.

1 The car ran out of petrol.

2 She said 'Thank you'.

3 They didn't understand English.

4 I wasn't ill.

5 We were very tired.

6 You didn't agree with me.

Listening and speaking
Discussion and debate

Describe the scene.

Where do you think this is?

What are all the people doing?

Would you find it interesting to be here?

Describe the differences between this and any other market that you have been to.

How would you set about selling these objects: a car, an antique brooch, a house, some English text books, an oil painting that you yourself have painted?

Where would you go if you wanted to buy these objects?

Can you think of any other ways of buying and selling?

■ Exercise 1

How helpful do you think it is to plan your spending in advance with the help of tables like the one here? Is there anything else that you think should be included in a budget planner? Are there any items here which are not relevant to your way of life?

Budget Planner

OUTGOINGS	Monthly	Quarterly	Annual
Mortgage/rent			
House and contents insurance			
Maintaining the property			
Water rates			
Electricity			
Gas/other fuel			
Telephone			
Life insurance			
TV rental/Licence			
Food/cleaning materials			
Clothing, shoes etc			
Fares			
Personal loan repayments			
Credit card repayments			
Membership subscriptions			
Papers, magazines			
Regular savings			
Holidays			
Car Insurance			
Car expenses and Petrol			
Entertainment/Drinks/Cigarettes			
Other expenses			
ESTIMATED EXPENDITURE	£	£	£

■ **Exercise 2**

Give a short talk on one of these topics.

■ Collecting antiques.
■ Taxes.
■ Investments.
■ Gambling.
■ Saving for a rainy day.
■ Prices, wages and inflation.

Listening comprehension

You will hear a conversation in a shop between a customer and an assistant. The customer mentions four faults with the article he has bought. The first time you listen, write down in note form what the faults were and the replies given by the assistant. The first one has been done for you. Then listen again and answer questions 1 to 5.

faults	assistant's replies
1 *colour ran*	*should have looked at the label*
2	
3	
4	

1 What threats did the customer make? Put numbers (1, 2, 3 . . .) by the threats he made, to show the order in which he made them. Put crosses by the threats that he didn't make.
  a To insult the assistant. ☐
  b To phone the police. ☐
  c To get annoyed. ☐
  d To stop buying things in this ☐
    shop.
  e To speak to the manager. ☐
  f To provoke the assistant. ☐
  g To use force. ☐

2 How do you think the assistant intended to complete these remarks?
  a If you'd looked at the label, sir, . . .
  b If you use excessive force, . . .

3 What do you think had actually happened before this conversation took place? Was the customer's story true?

4 Describe the assistant's attitude. Did she behave correctly?

5 What were the exact words used
  a by the customer, to say that he was going to complain about something?
  b by the customer, when he threatened to speak to the manager?
  c by the assistant, when she tried to persuade him not to continue making his complaints?

Function: complaining, threatening and persuading

What do you think they are saying? Fill in the bubbles.

■ Exercise 1 [PW]

Look at the sentences in Pair work 11a. Student B must find the most appropriate response to what student A says.

■ Exercise 2

Use the tables to help you find suitable remarks in these situations.

1 A shop assistant tells you it's time to close the shop. You want to try on one more piece of clothing.

2 You think you've been badly treated by a policeman. You go to the police station to complain.

3 A friend arrives late for a date, as usual. You're annoyed.

4 A colleague threatens to resign from his/her job. You try to persuade him/her to stay.

5 At a dance, someone keeps bumping into you.

Complaining

General

I'd like/I want to *complain/make a complaint* about ...
(*I'm sorry to say this but/I'm afraid*) ... *is most unsatisfactory/just isn't good enough.*
What's the meaning of this?
I object (to ...).

Informal

(*Really!/Look!*) I'm fed up with ...
I've (just about) had enough (of ...).
I wish you *would/wouldn't* (...).
You can't go around ...

Formal

I wish to *complain/make a complaint/lodge a complaint* (about ...).
I'm not at all satisfied (with ...).

Threatening

General

If you do that again, I'll (have to) ...
I wouldn't (do that), if I were you, (or ...).
Unless/If ..., I'll (have to) ...

Informal

(Do that again) and I'll ...
Don't ... or I'll ...
Don't you dare!/Just you try!

Formal

If you *don't/cannot* ..., I shall be *forced/obliged* to ...
(I'm afraid) *if/unless* you ..., I (shall) have *no/little* alternative but to ...
You'd be *very/most* unwise (not) to ...

Persuading

General

Please let me (...).
I (really) think *you should/you'd* do well to ...
Are you (really) sure you *won't/can't/wouldn't* ...?

Informal

Go on!/Come on!/Please!
Just this once!/Just for me!

Formal

How can I persuade you (to ...)?
Are you (quite) sure you won't reconsider?
Can/Can't/Couldn't/Could I persuade you (...)?

133

■ **Practice** PW

Act out the situations in Pair work 11b and 11c.

Reading aloud: *who, how or hoe*?

The sounds /u:/, /au/ and /ou/ can be spelt in many different ways. Here are some examples; the first two in each list are the most common ways of spelling the sounds.

/u:/		/au/		/ou/	
oo	*soon*	ou *round*		o-(e)	*home*
u-(e)	*rule*	ow *clown*			*homing*
	ruling			oa	*boat*
ew	*grew*			ow	*show*
ou	*route*			o	*no*
o-(e)	*move*			oe	*doe*
	moving			ew	*sew*
				ou	*though*
ui	*bruise*				
ue	*blue*				
oe	*shoe*				

■ **Exercise 1**

Sort these words into three groups: with /u:/, /au/ and /ou/.

aloud
brew
brow
chose
cold
cow
cue
dough
flow
flower
folk
house
howl
juice
knows

mould
now
plough
prove
rude
shoot
shout
soap
soup
sour
suit
through
throw
tomb
whole

■ **Exercise 2**

Practise saying the words in the list above. One student says a word; the others call out 'one' if it has the sound

/u:/, 'two' if it has the sound /au/, and 'three' if it has the sound /ou/.

■ **Exercise 3**

Look through the passage on p. 126 and see how many words you can find with the sounds /u:/, /au/ and /ou/.

■ **Exercise 4**

Improvise sentences that contain some of the words in the list in exercise 1 above.

The cow chose cold soup and juice.

Activity: the Stock Exchange

A game for any number of players.

The Start

Each player has
■ an Accounts Sheet
■ a pencil
■ 600 shares with a face value of £1 each, divided as follows: 100 in gold, 100 in silver, 100 in platinum, 100 in copper, 100 in nickel, and 100 in tin

STOCK EXCHANGE – ACCOUNTS

CREDIT	DEBIT	SHARE HOLDINGS
		GOLD 100
		SILVER 100
		PLATINUM 100
		COPPER 100
		NICKEL 100
		TIN 100

GOLD
SILVER
PLATINUM
COPPER
NICKEL
TIN

TOTALS

BALANCE

The object

The object of the game is to earn as much money as possible by buying and selling shares at the right time. This usually means buying when the price is low, and selling when the price is high.

The game

Every few minutes you will hear a report on changes in the values and prices of your shares. Each report also includes a prediction about future market movements. Between each report you may buy, sell or exchange any or all of your shares, as long as you can find someone to trade with on terms that are acceptable to both parties. The price of shares is whatever the buyer and seller agree on: it need not be determined by the price quoted in the reports, which should be seen merely as a guide.

Keeping accounts

Each time you trade shares, you must make a note of the transaction on your Accounts Sheet. Suppose, for example, that after the first report you trade shares with various other players:

- you buy 20 copper shares at £1.10 each (= £22)
- you buy 10 copper shares at £1.20 each (= £12)
- you sell 10 gold shares at 90p each (= £9)
- you receive 15 silver shares in exchange for 12 platinum shares.

You should then mark your Accounts Sheet as shown in the illustration.

The end

There are ten Market Reports altogether, and the game ends when you have listened to the last one, or earlier if all the players agree. Calculate the final value of your share holdings by multiplying the number of shares in a particular metal by the price for that metal given in the last report you listened to. Suppose, for example, that you have 200 shares in gold, and that the price quoted is £1.15. The value of your holding is therefore 200 × £1.15 (= £230); this figure should be written in the *Credit* column in the appropriate place. Then add up all your credits, take away the sum of your debits, and write the result next to *Balance*. The player with the largest balance is the winner.

During the game, remember:
- Do not follow the predictions you hear blindly; they will usually be right, but not always.
- Use the language you have learnt for persuading (and perhaps even threatening!)

STOCK EXCHANGE – ACCOUNTS

CREDIT	DEBIT	SHARE HOLDINGS
£9	£22 £12	GOLD 1̶0̶0̶ 90
		SILVER 1̶0̶0̶ 115
		PLATINUM 1̶0̶0̶ 88
		COPPER 1̶0̶0̶ 1̶2̶0̶ 130
		NICKEL
		TIN

GOLD
SILVER
PLATINUM
COPPER
NICKEL
TIN

TOTALS

BALANCE

Written work: connecting ideas (5)

Attitudes

■ Exercise 1

The following is a letter to the editor of a newspaper. Read it carefully, and then fill each gap with the most appropriate of the alternatives given below.

17, Crouch House Road,

Edenbridge,

Kent TN 8 5 SP

29th August 1983

Dear Sir,

    I was shocked to read in your newspaper that the Palace Theatre is to be knocked down and replaced by an amusement complex, whatever that may be. (1)_____ the new building will contain one-armed bandits, bingo halls, ten-pin bowling and so on, all of which will,(2)_____, provide a boost to the community's economy. This is,(3)_____, an admirable goal.(4)_____, however, the aims of culture should bear far more weight than crass financial considerations; a living theatre is, after all, essential if our civilisation is to survive.

    If people want to fritter away their time and money on what are,(5)_____, mindless pursuits, then (6)_____ they must be allowed to do so. But (7)_____ it need not be done at the expense of those who appreciate the value of true culture. (8)_____ the Council will reconsider their decision if enough of us can make our voices heard.

    Yours faithfully,

Cyril P. Barlow

1 a Frankly **b** Presumably
  c Quite properly

2 a generally **b** honestly
  c of course

3 a admittedly **b** fortunately
  c seriously

4 a As a matter of fact
  b In my opinion **c** Naturally

5 a broadly speaking **b** eventually
  c to be frank

6 a actually **b** obviously
  c quite likely

7 a indeed **b** surely **c** undoubtedly

8 a Perhaps **b** To my surprise
  c Unfortunately

■ Exercise 2

Write a letter to a newspaper on one of the following topics. Use expressions from exercise 1 to show your attitude.

- The preservation of a well-known monument or building.
- The building of a new motorway, a new sports centre, or a multi-storey car park.
- Any issue of national topical interest, e.g. unemployment, inflation, crime, hooliganism, schools, etc.

UNIT 12

THE NEWS

Reading and thinking
Reading comprehension

These headlines appeared in British newspapers recently. Read them carefully and discuss which of them would arouse your interest enough for you to want to read the accompanying articles. Then choose one or two of the headlines, and make up short stories to go with them.

ALCOHOL TAX?

Arms Go-ahead

Atlantic Crossing Warm-up

Blow Restores Sight

BAN ON FOOTBALL FANS

CANCER LINK

Head Hides

Fish Deadlock

Hospital Move for Stuntman

Married Clergy Eligible for Priesthood

LABOUR PAPER MOVE BLOCKED

Murder Case Doctor Back

POCKET TV

Nuclear Dumps at Sea Ended

Reforms Agreed

Self-Shearing Sheep

SWEET RIVALRY

Turk Leaps to Death

40,000 US TARGETS IN RUSSIA

THE NEWS

Now read the openings of the stories that actually accompanied the headlines, and answer the questions below.

a South Africa's parliament has approved the Government's constitutional reform Bill, which gives limited political power to Indians and Coloureds but excludes the country's 20 million blacks.

b TUC* moves to set up a popular newspaper sympathetic to the Labour movement seem doomed to fail at next week's congress.

c The US has identified 40,000 possible targets for nuclear attack in the Soviet Union, compared with 2,600 in 1960, says the International Institute for Strategic Studies.

d The Government's imminent approval of two new artificial substitutes for sugar is expected to produce unprecedented commercial competition and allegations of health risks.

e EEC fisheries ministers were heading for deadlock last night after two almost fruitless days' negotiation and bartering here in Luxembourg over who should have the right to fish herring from the North Sea.

f The incorrect use of suntan lamps and the development of skin cancer have been linked in two independent medical reports, from London and Sydney, Australia.

g Mr *** ********* has gone into hiding after giving up the headship of Dartington Hall independent school. He resigned after he and his wife were pictured naked in *The Sun* newspaper.

h All dumping of nuclear waste in the world's oceans has been halted because of pressure from British environmentalists and trade unions.

i A West Country** sheep farmer who is planning a round-the-world solo voyage in a £12,000 rowing boat will prepare for his epic journey by rowing across the Atlantic this winter.

j A woman has restored her blind husband's sight by hitting him on the head with a plastic bucket.

k Mr ******* ********, the gynaecologist cleared of the attempted murder of a baby, has had his suspension lifted by the North-West Thames Regional Health Authority.

l Sir Clive Sinclair launched the first British flat screen pocket television set, costing £79.95, less than a third of the price of its nearest rival.

m Congress has passed President Reagan's $187,500m arms bill. It authorizes production of nerve gas, banned since 1969, and 21 huge MX nuclear missiles.

n A new pressure group, Action on Alcohol Abuse, has suggested that higher taxes and advertising restrictions on alcohol could curtail alcoholism.

o Married clergy who convert to the Roman Catholic Church are to be eligible for ordination to the priesthood, Cardinal Basil Hume, the Archbishop of Westminster is expected to confirm today.

p A left-wing Turkish activist whom the government was trying to deport yesterday committed suicide by jumping from a sixth floor window of the Berlin court house where his case was being heard. He was Mr Kemal Altun aged 23 and his death quickly unleashed a furore in Germany.

q Australian scientists believe that within five years, using genetic engineering techniques, it might be possible to insert new genes into sheep that could result in an animal which would 'shear itself' when fed a chemical.

r Attendance at football matches should be temporarily restricted to home team supporters as one measure to curb hooliganism, Mr Leslie Curtis, president of the Police Federation said yesterday.

s Mr Richard Smith, the stunt driver whose crash was seen live on BBC television on the Noel Edmonds Late Late Breakfast Show last Saturday, was moved to another hospital yesterday, but because of his injuries, he had to reject an offer from Mr Edmonds to fly him in his private helicopter.

*The TUC (Trades Union Congress) is a federation of the major British trade unions.

**The south-west part of Great Britain.

1 Match up the headlines with the articles.

2 True or false? Put ticks by the statements that accurately reflect what the article writers mean.

a In South Africa, the political power of Indians is to be curtailed.

b It is probable that none of the existing popular newspapers is sympathetic to the Labour movement.

c The USA knows which places the Russians will attack in a nuclear war.

d The production of artificial substitutes for sugar will probably be dangerous to health.

e The EEC ministers are probably going to be imprisoned.

f Suntan lamps cause skin cancer if used in the wrong way.

g A school headmaster appeared naked in a newspaper photograph.

h Nuclear waste is no longer thrown into the sea.

i The journey across the Atlantic is part of a round-the-world trip.

j The husband lost his sight when he was hit with a bucket.

k The gynaecologist was not allowed to work for a time.

l The pocket TV set produced by Sir Clive Sinclair is the only one of its kind.

m The production of nerve gas is forbidden in the USA.

n There are no restrictions on advertising alcohol in the UK.

o It will soon be possible for all Roman Catholic priests to be married.

p The Turkish left-wing activist jumped from a window while being deported.

q The new animal created by genetic engineering techniques will live on chemicals.

r There will be less hooliganism if home team supporters are kept away from football matches.

s Mr Smith was hurt while moving to another hospital.

Words and structures

IDIOMS

■ **Exercise 1**

Explain the meanings of these words and phrases as they are used in the articles.

a moves (b)
b set up (b)
c gone into hiding (g)
d giving up (g)
e epic journey (i)
f live (s)
g lifted (k)
h launched (l)
i pressure group (n)

■ **Exercise 2**
Go *go-ahead* (headline)

Replace the underlined words in each of the following sentences with the correct form of one of these expressions:

go all the way
go off the deep-end
go the whole hog
go to pieces
go to the dogs

1 When I told him the bad news, he <u>broke down</u>.

2 There's no need to <u>lose your temper</u>.

3 Instead of just replacing one tile, why don't we <u>do the job completely</u> and repair the whole roof? *go the whole hog*

4 The country <u>has become a complete mess</u> since the present goverment came to power. *has gone to the dogs*

5 I'm afraid I can't <u>agree completely</u> with everything you say. *go all the way*

■ Exercise 3

Choose the word or phrase that best completes each sentence.

1 We'd better go _____ this chapter again.
a about **b** by **c** over **d** round

2 The bomb went _____ with a loud bang.
a away **b** off **c** out **d** up.

3 I think I have a good chance, to go _____ the judge's remarks.
a after **b** by **c** from **d** with

4 Paul has decided to go _____ the local tennis championships.
a in for **b** into **c** on to **d** up for

5 The firm's likely to go _____ , unless business improves.
a back **b** down **c** out **d** under
- water, sea.

VOCABULARY

■ Exercise 4
Synonyms

Find words in the newspaper articles that mean the same as the following.

1 Accusations. *allegations d*

2 Competitor. *rival c*

3 Control. *curb s*

4 Diminish. *curtail n*

5 Joined together. *linked f*

6 Let loose. *unleashed p*

7 Put in. *insert g*

8 Replacements. *substitutes t*

9 That has never happened before. *unprecedented d*

10 Weapons. *arms m*

■ Exercise 5

Choose the word that best completes each sentence.

1 You must tell me the result now. I can't bear the _____.
a suspenders **b** suspending
c suspense **d** suspension

2 The white cliffs are the most _____ feature of the landscape.
a eminent **b** imminent
c permanent **d** prominent

3 This year's _____ for non-European immigrants has already been filled.
a amount **b** number
c quantity **d** quota

4 In Britain, members of the _____ usually wear a special white collar that fastens at the back of the neck.
a church **b** clergy
c priests **d** vicarage

5 You can tell how many dollars your pounds are worth by looking at this _____ table.
a conversing **b** conversion
c convertible **d** converting

6 Restriction of personal freedom is acceptable as a _____ to an end: the well-being of the majority.
a means **b** measure
c method **d** way

STRUCTURES

Infinitive constructions
expected to produce (d)

a Verbs followed by the infinitive only:

He <u>appeared</u> to be drunk.

b Verbs followed by an object and the infinitive:

I <u>expect</u> you to be home by ten o'clock.

homework

c Verbs followed by *what, where, who, how,* etc. and the infinitive:

I can't underline{decide} what time to leave.

d Verbs followed by an object and *what, where,* etc. and the infinitive:

Peter underline{showed} us which way to go.

■ **Exercise 6**

Read through the following sentences and sort the underlined verbs into four groups, a, b, c and d as in the examples above, depending on which construction they are followed by. You will see that some verbs have to be put into more than one group.

1 At school, they underline{taught} us to be polite in all situations.

2 Don't underline{ask} me how to get to London.

3 Haven't you underline{learnt} how to deal with questions like that?

4 Her performance only underline{encouraged} the audience to leave.

5 He underline{taught} us what kind of expressions to use in formal situations.

6 I underline{asked} him to accompany me.

7 I'll underline{consider} what to do with you later.

8 I think I can underline{guess} how to operate it.

9 I've underline{told} you what to look for.

10 I underline{want} to leave.

11 I underline{want} you to leave.

12 They'll underline{try} to underline{force} us to give in.

13 They've underline{arranged} to start at four o'clock.

14 You underline{deserve} to be shot.

15 You haven't underline{forgotten} who to invite, have you?

■ **Exercise 7**

Choose the word that best completes each sentence.

1 I _____ to resign.
a chose **b** forbade
c informed **d** told

2 I couldn't _____ who to ask for.
a attempt **b** command
c desire **d** remember

3 She _____ us to accept the proposal.
a resolved **b** scorned
c threatened **d** urged

4 They _____ us how to work the machine.
a begged **b** demonstrated
c explained **d** showed

5 We __(a)__ to __(b)__ her to join us.
a) **a** considered **b** managed
   c recalled **d** wondered
b) **a** inquire **b** offer
   c persuade **d** refuse

■ **Exercise 8**

Make up sentences based on the following cues, using the four infinitive constructions already practised.

ask/get to Norwich
I asked him how to get to Norwich.

1 learn/speak Swahili

2 decide/car/choose

3 undertake/solve/problem

4 implore/stay

5 find out/get to China

6 forbid/go out after dark

7 explain/do in an emergency

8 understand/work the machine

9 tempt/earn some easy money

10 teach/address the Queen

Listening and speaking
Discussion and debate

Describe the scene.

What are all these people doing? What do their jobs involve?

Would it be fun to work here? Do you think the people here can influence the news in any way?

■ **Exercise 1**

Read through the list of contents of *The Times* newspaper. What would you expect to find under each of the headings? In what order would you read articles under the various headings? Put '1' by the one you would look at first, '2' by the one you would look at second, and so on. Put crosses by those that you would not look at at all. Then discuss your order with the other students. Try to get hold of an English language newspaper and compare its contents with the list here. What are the differences, if any?

■ **Exercise 2**

Hold a debate on one of these topics.

■ Newspapers don't just report the news: they make it.
■ News censorship is a necessary evil.
■ The news is under the control of those who advertise in the news media.
■ A newspaper's main function is to entertain.

Leader page, 13
Letters: On courts martial, from Mr D S Mindel, and Professor Colonel G I A D Draper; Liberals, from Mr G M L Smith
Leading articles: Liberals; Mrs Thatcher in Germany, Russians at Edinburgh conference
Features, pages 8, 9, 12
Hongkong: how a harder British line could help Peking; curtain up on the Argentine elections; barrelling across the Atlantic. The bubbly battle: Spectrum on American "champagne"; Penny Perrick talks to Clare Francis on the Wednesday Page
Obituary, page 12
Trinidad and Tobago: Four-page Special Report on the richest nation in the Caribbean after the end of the oil boom

Home News	2–4	Law Report	14
Overseas	4–6	Night Sky	14
Appts	14, 21	Property	29
Arts	18	Sale Room	2
Bridge	14	Science	14
Business	19–22	Sport	23–26
Court	14	TV & Radio	31
Crossword	32	Theatres etc	31
Diary	12	Weather	32
Events	32	Wills	14

■ Exercise 3

Half of the class works for TV channel 1, while the other half works for channel 2. In your two groups, plan an evening's television programmes for your channel, with details of times and types of programmes (films, news, documentaries, etc.). Then meet as a whole class to adjust your plans to fit together with the other channel's programmes. Remember, though, that

- you want as many viewers as possible for *your* channel.
- you don't want viewers to complain that all the good programmes are shown simultaneously.

■ Exercise 4

Write a brief description of each of the programmes you have agreed on, as if for the TV page in a daily newspaper.

---

8 30 NATURE. Tony Soper with the living-world magazine, last of the series, looking at the sixth sense which enables salmon to find their way across thousands of miles of ocean to spawn in the same river in which they were hatched. Now scientists think they have the answer — magnetism.

9 0 SWEET BIRD OF YOUTH. The Paul Newman season continues with Richard Brooks' cleaned-up but still-powerful version of Tennessee Williams's play. Made in 1961, it's set in the small town from which the no-good Newman character was once sent packing by local politician Ed Begley; where he now returns, still hoping to impress the folks, as a gigolo with faded, drunken actress Geraldine Page in tow.

10 55 NEWSNIGHT. With news, interviews, analysis, special reports, weather, sport.

Listening comprehension

You will hear a conversation between three people. The first time you listen to it, identify the situation, say who the people are, and write in the table headings for the four topics they discuss. The first one has been done for you. The second and subsequent times you listen, answer questions 1 to 4.

topic		surprise	excitement	pleasure	relief	disappointment	anger	lack of interest
1 *Royal baby*	man							
	woman							
2	man							
	woman							
3	man							
	woman							
4	man							
	woman							

UNIT 12
THE NEWS

1 Put ticks in the appropriate boxes to show how the man and woman reacted to the various news items.

2 Using the information you have written in the table, describe the two people's reactions and give the reasons behind these reactions.

The man's reactions to the news about the Royal baby was one of ...; he explained that ...

3 What were the exact words used to express the following?
   a Surprise.
   b Excitement.
   c Pleasure.

d Relief.
e Disappointment.
f Anger.
g Lack of interest.

4 What do you think the interviewer and the newspaper he was working for learnt from this interview? Were the two people's answers what you would expect? How would you yourself react to these news items?

Function: reacting to news and information

What do you think they are saying? Fill in the bubbles.

■ **Exercise 1** PW

1 Look at the sentences in Pair work 12a. Student B must find the most appropriate responses to what

student A says.

2 Do Pair work 12b. Here student B speaks first, and student A must find suitable replies.

■ **Exercise 2**

Use the tables to help you find suitable remarks in these situations.

1 A colleague tells you that you haven't been promoted.

2 You're with a friend waiting for a train—there's an announcement that the train will be 30 minutes late.

3 You're driving to work with a friend—there's a traffic jam because someone has parked in the middle of the road.

4 A stranger you're talking to at a hotel suddenly tells you he's a famous pop star.

5 You've parked by a 'No Parking' sign, but manage to drive away just before a traffic warden gets to you.

6 Your bank manager tells you he can't give you the loan you have asked for.

7 Your boss tells you that your company has made a large profit.

8 You're going through customs with too much alcohol and tobacco—but the customs official doesn't stop you.

9 A friend has managed to get two tickets for the football Cup Final.

Expressing surprise
General   *Really!?/What!?*   That's *amazing/extraordinary/very surprising*!   *That is/What* a surprise!
Informal   I don't believe *it/you*.   You must be joking!   (Well, I) never!   Fancy (that)!
Formal   I find *it/that extraordinary/incredible/very surprising*.   I must say, that *surprises me/comes as a (total/complete) surprise*.

Expressing satisfaction
General   *That's/How marvellous/wonderful*.   I'm (*very*) *pleased/(really) delighted* (about . . .).
Informal   (That's) *great/fantastic/smashing/terrific*!
Formal   It gives me great *pleasure/satisfaction* (to . . .).   I can't say how *pleased/delighted* I am (about . . .)

THE NEWS

Expressing dissatisfaction or anger

General
Oh *no/dear*!
What a nuisance!
How *annoying/irritating*!
... *annoys me/irritates me/makes me cross.*

Informal
I can't stand ...
I'm fed up with ...
... (really) makes me mad.

Formal
I'm *extremely/most displeased/unhappy* (about) ...
I *resent/object* to ...

Expressing relief

General
That's/What a relief!
Thank goodness (for that)!

Informal
Phew!
Thank goodness for that (...).

Formal
That's/It's a great relief.
I'm very *relieved/glad* to hear (about) ...

Expressing disappointment

General
(Oh,) I am disappointed.
That's/What a (great) *pity/shame/disappointment.*

Informal
Oh, no.
Just *my/our* luck.

Formal
(I must say) I had hoped ...
... comes as a great disappointment.

Expressing excitement

General
How|That's exciting|thrilling|sensational!

Informal
Wow!
Great!|Fantastic!|Hooray!

Formal
I'm very *enthusiastic (about . . .)|excited (by . . .)*.
. . . is most exciting.

Expressing boredom

General
That isn't|I don't think that's very *interesting|exciting.*
How *dull|boring|unexciting!*

Informal
. . . leaves me cold|turns me off|is a waste of time|bores me stiff.
So what?

Formal
(To be *honest|frank*) I find . . . *rather|very tedious|uninteresting.*

■ **Practice** PW

Act out the situation in Pair work 12c.

Reading aloud: repeat questions 📼

Questions that ask for information to be repeated are spoken with a special intonation pattern: the question word is low in pitch and stressed, and the voice then rises continuously to the end of the question.

I'm flying to xxxxx.
↗ *Where?* or
↗ *Where are you flying to?* or
↗ *Where did you say you were flying to?*
I'm leaving at xxxx o'clock.
↗ *When?* or
↗ *When are you leaving?* or
↗ *When did you say you were leaving?*

Questions that express surprise use the same pattern in an exaggerated form.

I won a million pounds!
↗ *How much?* or
↗ *How much did you win?* or
↗ *How much did you say you'd won?*

■ **Exercise 1**

Ask short or long questions to elicit the information that is unclear.

1 I live in xxx.

2 I've decided to buy the xxx one.

3 I've never been introduced to xxx.

4 Ann's having a party on xxx.

5 I'll xxx when we're ready.

6 I went there because of the xxx.

7 She used to go there xxx times a year.

8 It only took us xxx days to get there.

9 We can walk to the station. It's only xxx xxx away.

10 xxx's such an odd fellow.

■ **Exercise 2**

Work in pairs. Both students write down five short statements similar to those in exercise 1, and then replace one word in each statement with a made-up word (such as *plerm*, *trumble*, etc.—use your imagination!). Each student then reads out one statement in turn, including the made-up word, and the other student must ask a question to find the missing information.

Activity: local news

■ In pairs or small groups, think up an event that could make an interesting story in a local newspaper. You can use the headlines here to help you. When you have chosen a subject, work out the details of the story: imagine that you are participants in or witnesses to whatever has happened.

THEATRE TO CLOSE

The Repentant Thief

Two Injured in High Street Pile-up

Motorway Plans Approved

A SCANDAL SAYS FIRE CHIEF

Local Man Gets Medal

POP STAR OPENS FETE

Church Repair Appeal £100,000 Needed

UNITED LUCKY TO GET A DRAW

■ Now carry out interviews and write articles for the local newspaper. Each pair should act as reporters, interviewing another pair and then writing up their story for the newspaper.

■ Use the articles you have written as the basis for a news programme on a local radio station. Give yourselves a fixed time at which the programme will go on the air (for example fifteen minutes after all the articles have been completed), and a fixed time at which it must finish (say, five minutes later).

■ Make all the necessary preparations: decide in which order you will present the news items, whether or not you will have any live or taped interviews in the programme, who is going to read the news, who is going to carry out interviews, etc. Then, at the time you have decided on, act out the programme; make sure you don't exceed the time limit you have set yourselves.

Revision: units 11 and 12

■ Exercise 1

Fill each gap with one word; it need not be the actual word used in the original text, but it must be appropriate to the context.

If you are buying a hairdryer, you might think that you are making the best ___(1)___ if you choose one which you like the look ___(2)___, and it is the cheapest in price. But when you get it home you may find that it takes twice as long as a more expensive model to dry your hair. The ___(3)___ of the electricity plus the extra cost of your time could well make your hairdryer the most expensive ___(4)___ of all!

So what principles should you ___(5)___ when you go out shopping?

If you keep your home, your car or any valuable ___(6)___ in tiptop ___(7)___ you'll be saving money in the long ___(8)___.

Before you buy a new appliance, talk to someone who ___(9)___ one. If you can, use it or borrow it to ___(10)___ it suits your ___(11)___.

Almost half the things we buy in supermarkets we didn't intend to buy before we entered, ___(12)___ to a recent survey. ___(13)___ this by compiling a detailed shopping list—and ___(14)___ to it.

Before you buy an expensive item, or a service, ___(15)___ check the price and what is ___(16)___ offer. If possible, ___(17)___ from three items or three estimates.

Don't throw away those money-off ___(18)___. Use before they 'expire', but don't buy the item ___(19)___ you really need it. Swap coupons ___(20)___ friends.

■ Exercise 2

Choose five of the expressions below and write them down. Give them to another student, who should then improvise a brief story or description that includes all of them.

allegation
armour plating
ban
curb
curtail
dump
environmentalist
fracture
go-ahead (adjective)
go in for
go into hiding
go off
go to pieces
go to the dogs
imminent
to insert
launch
linked
pressure group
quota
restore
restriction
rival
set up
stunt
substitute
suspension
sympathetic
unleash
unprecedented

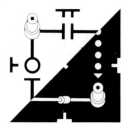

UNIT 13

MACHINES

Reading and thinking
Reading comprehension

The Pyramid

Constructing a Pyramid

1 Make your pyramid model as close to scale to the Great Pyramid as possible. One need not become fanatic, but the more correct the proportions, the better the results.

5   Place your pyramid at least four feet from walls, radiators, TVs, radios, fluorescent lights, or any electrical appliance. It should not sit on anything metal.

   Pyramids seem to work better with a base or
10 bottom. This may be taped along one side making a convenient hinge arrangement.

   Make an orientation mat by tracing the square base of your pyramid on a larger sheet of paper or cardboard. Draw a north-south and an east-west
15 line crossing exactly in the center of the square, and extending out beyond the square so you can see the lines once you position your pyramid on the square. The area where the lines cross is directly under the apex. If working with a bottom, also
20 draw a cross on that to let you know where to put material.

   The most 'active' section of the pyramid is supposed to be the bottom third. When possible, place experimental material in the king's chamber,

Pattern for Pyramid and Base

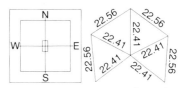

measurement in centimeters
(not drawn to scale)

Cut or score the sides and assemble the pyramid with the flap on the inside using glue or tape.

25 or so-called focal-point position, in the middle of the pyramid, one-third of the way up to the apex.

   Cardboard is the easiest material out of which to make a pyramid. Plastic, wood, and even metal or layers of foil and cardboard are commonly used.
30 Color of material seems to make little difference, nor does opacity; tests with transparent plastic succeed.

   The basic testing model is the six-inch pyramid. Each side is an isosceles triangle with equal sides of
35 eight and seven-eighths inches and the base of nine and three-eighths inches. For more exact models of the Cheops pyramid, it is best to work in centimeters.

Razor-Blade Sharpening

The old-fashioned blue blades are the ones that
40 deliver results. Place a blunt blade on a two-inch matchbox or other holder directly under the apex of a six-inch pyramid. Sharp sides face east-west, the ends north-south. Leave it there at least a week, longer if it doesn't prove ready. On removal,
45 it should again give you smooth shaving. Replace blades under pyramid regularly after each use. Drbal claims up to 200 shaves with a single blade. Many clean-shaven pyramid builders speak of using a single blade for a month or two and claim marked
50 difference between treated and control blade shows most clearly after four weeks' use. Drbal observes that the crystallinelike structure of the blade edge tends in time toward its original form. The pyramid, he feels, <u>enhances</u> this tendency. Put
55 a blunt control blade aside for the same length of time as the one in the pyramid. Keep on shaving one side of the face or one leg with the control and one with the treated blade. It is claimed that dull kitchen knives or dull scissors can also be shar-
60 pened with appropriate-sized pyramids.

Mummifying

Just about anything that goes bad is a candidate for the king's chamber. The most commonly preserved items are eggs (in and out of shells), sprouts, flowers, vegetables, hamburger, and whole meat.
65 Put an equal portion aside as a control; you might also cover it with a square cardboard box. Samples are usually left under the pyramid for one to eight weeks.

   In 1953 Verne Cameron put two ounces of raw
70 pork, which was about half fat, under a four-inch pyramid. He set the structure 'in a bathroom where it was hot, steamy, or draughty by spells—not conducive to preservation of foods, certainly. In about three days the pork had a faint odor, but it
75 lost this, and in about nine days was completely mummified.' He reported that the pork remained 'perfectly <u>edible</u> after several months. A large chunk of <u>watermelon</u> [placed in a pyramid] dried down to the texture of a dried apricot but is still
80 sweet and good.'

From *Handbook of Psychic Discoveries* by Sheila Ostrander and Lynn Schroeder.

1 Tick the statements that are true.

  a The model should be nearly ☐
  the same size as the Great
  Pyramid.

  b It must not be close to any ☐
  electrical equipment.

  c It must have a base hinged ☐
  to one of its walls.

  d It should be made out of ☐
  cardboard.

  e It doesn't matter what ☐
  colour it is.

  f It need not be transparent. ☐

2 In the basic testing model, what
should be the lengths in inches of
the lines A . . . . . .
            B . . . . . .
            C . . . . . .
            D . . . . . . ?

Mark the position of the following.

  a The apex.

  b The focal-point position.

3 What happens if you put razor blades
inside a model pyramid?

4 What is the 'control blade' for?

5 Some of the sentences in the paragraph headed 'Razor-Blade Sharpen-
ing' are written in a sort of note
form, with some articles (*a, the*)
omitted. Write these sentences out
with the articles reinserted.

6 What happens if you put food inside
the king's chamber?

7 What was the point of putting the
pyramid in a bathroom?

8 Summarise in two sentences what
the model pyramid can be used for.

9 What clues can you find in the text
to show that it is the work of an
American author?

Words and structures

IDIOMS

■ Exercise 1

Explain the meanings of these expressions as they are used in the text.

  a as close to scale . . . as possible
  (line 1)

  b deliver results (line 40) 44

  c doesn't prove ready (line 51) 44

  d marked difference (line 56) 49

  e tends in time (line 60) 53

  f a candidate for . . . (line 68)

  g by spells (line 79)

■ Exercise 2
Geometrical figures

Fill each gap with one of these words:
circle (2)
round (2)
rounds
square (3)
triangle
Then explain what the sentences mean.

1 Dr Stephen always made his
_____ in the afternoon.

2 I'm exhausted. But a hot bath and a
_____ meal will put me right.

3 We're caught in the vicious _____
of inflation: prices go up, so wages
go up, so prices go up, and so on.

4 Our profit was about £1 million, in
_____ figures.

5 Steve's a bit of a _____ peg in a
_____ hole.

6 The eternal _____ of Jim's and
Lee's love for Marilyn could only be
resolved by murder.

7 Their refusal to negotiate puts us
back to _____ one.

8 Well, we seem to be back where we
started; we've come full _____.

UNIT 13
MACHINES

VOCABULARY

■ Exercise 3

Write the correct numbers in the boxes.

angle	17	semicircle	4
circle	11	sphere	6
cone	19	spiral	16
crescent	21	square	15
cube	5	triangle	7
cylinder	1	wedge	18
ellipse	9	circumference	14
pentagon	2	diameter	10
polygon	20	radius	8
pyramid	12	tangent	13
rectangle	3		

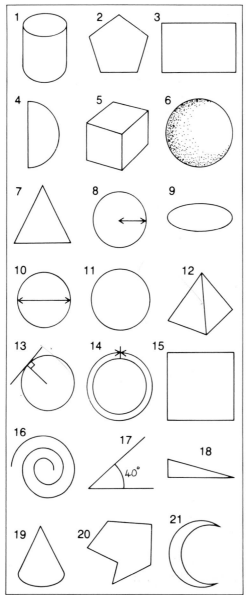

■ Exercise 4

Fill each gap with the adjective formed from the root word given.

1 The magician wore a _____ hat. *cone*

2 A ball is a _____ object used in many games and sports. *sphere*

3 Some comets have _____ orbits round the sun. *ellipse*

4 The capacity of motorbike engines is usually measured in _____ centimetres. *cube*

5 The flute is a _____ instrument with holes in it. *cylinder*

6 He was a tall, thin man with _____ features. *angle*

■ Exercise 5

Complete the table.

adjective	noun	verb
broad		
deep		deepen
	height	
long		
wide		

■ Exercise 6

What is being described here?

It is twenty-five metres long and about fifteen metres wide. At one end its depth is four metres, but the bottom slopes up towards the other end, which is only one metre deep.

■ Exercise 7

Describe the dimensions of one of these things, as in exercise 6, and see if the rest of the class can guess what it is.

a cupboard	a table
a box	a railway carriage
a dictionary	an aeroplane
a cigarette packet	a classroom

■ **Exercise 8**

Fill each gap with the correct form of one of the verbs in exercise 5.

1 The traffic is so heavy here that the road will have to be _____.

2 It's no longer fashionable to have the hem above the knee, so I'll have to _____ all my dresses.

3 Travel helps to _____ the mind.

4 The mystery _____ when they couldn't find the body.

5 The emotional effect of the scene was _____ by the sudden appearance of the villain.

■ **Exercise 9**

Find words in the text on p. 150 that match these definitions.

1 Allowing light to pass through.

2 Direction in relation to the points of the compass.

3 Emphasises, adds something to.

4 Fit to be eaten.

5 Helping to produce or promote.

6 Mark with grooves or scratches.

7 Put together (the parts of something).

8 Quality of a material that does not allow light to pass through.

STRUCTURES

Relative clauses

The old-fashioned blue blades are the ones that deliver results.
He put two ounces of raw pork, which was about half fat, under a four-inch pyramid.

The first example here shows a 'defining' relative clause: it defines *ones*, and is essential to the meaning and grammatical structure of the sentence. The second example includes a 'non-defining' relative clause: it describes *pork*, but here the meaning is perfectly clear even if the relative clause is omitted.
Note:
Commas are used around non-defining clauses, but are not used around defining clauses.
Whom is nowadays restricted to formal usage, but must be used after prepositions.

Choice of pronoun in relative clauses

■ **Defining clauses—people**

subject	Anyone $\frac{who}{that}$ wants may come.
object	The person $\begin{array}{l}whom\\who\\that\\I\ met\end{array}$ I met knew nothing.
with preposition	The person $\begin{array}{l}to\ whom\ I\ talked\\who\ I\ talked\ to\\that\ I\ talked\ to\\I\ talked\ to\end{array}$ was nice.
possessive	The man whose dog bit me lives next door.

MACHINES

■ Defining clauses—things

subject	This is the chair $\frac{\text{which}}{\text{that}}$ is most popular.
object	This is the chair $\begin{array}{l}\underline{\text{which I mentioned.}}\\ \underline{\text{that I mentioned.}}\\ \underline{\text{I mentioned.}}\end{array}$
after indefinite pronouns (all, nowhere, some-thing, etc.)	Everything $\frac{\text{that I own}}{\text{I own}}$ is in this room. Everything <u>that is in this room</u> is mine.
with preposition	This is the chair $\begin{array}{l}\underline{\text{about which I spoke.}}\\ \underline{\text{which I spoke about.}}\\ \underline{\text{that I spoke about.}}\\ \underline{\text{I spoke about.}}\end{array}$
possessive	This is the chair $\begin{array}{l}\underline{\text{whose properties I described.}}\\ \underline{\text{the properties of which I described.}}\end{array}$

■ Non-defining clauses—people

subject	This man, <u>who is Chinese</u>, is very rich.
object	This man, $\frac{\text{whom}}{\text{who}}$ I like very much, is rich.
with preposition	This man, $\begin{array}{l}\underline{\text{about whom I know little,}}\\ \underline{\text{whom I know little about,}}\\ \underline{\text{who I know little about,}}\end{array}$ is rich.
possessive	This man, <u>whose mother you met</u>, is rich.

■ Non-defining clauses—things

subject	This ring, <u>which was given to me</u>, is valuable.
object	This ring, <u>which I inherited</u>, is valuable.
with preposition	This ring, $\frac{\text{about which I spoke,}}{\text{which I spoke about,}}$ is valuable.
possessive	This ring, $\begin{array}{l}\underline{\text{whose beauty is undeniable,}}\\ \underline{\text{the beauty of which is undeniable,}}\end{array}$ is a fake.

MACHINES

■ Exercise 10

Fill each gap with a suitable relative pronoun, where necessary.

1 Did you understand everything _____ he told you?

2 The device _____ you use to make straight lines is called a ruler.

3 Anyone _____ dress is unsuitable will be left behind.

4 The train on platform 4, _____ leaves at 9.15, is the Cornwall Flyer.

5 I want you to meet the man _____ designed the X-15z.

6 The vehicle _____ capabilities most interest me is the SXAP.

7 The vicar, _____ I spoke to yesterday, is coming to tea.

8 There's the old woman _____ we were watching yesterday.

9 I am the last person in _____ you should confide.

10 The thing _____ you fasten two bits of paper with is called a paperclip.

11 My sister, _____ is much richer than I am, wants to borrow some money.

12 The X-15z, _____ we designed and built, can do anything _____ you tell it to.

13 This is the machine _____ can provide the answer.

14 Here's the stone from _____ we extract the radioactive metal.

15 The man _____ we spoke to this morning is an inventor.

16 The president, _____ generosity is well known, will speak on behalf of the poor and needy.

■ Exercise 11

Which sentences in exercise 10 contain 'non-defining' relative clauses?

■ Exercise 12

Underline all the relative clauses in exercise 10. Then write new clauses of your own to replace them.

1 *Did you understand everything that happened in the film?*

Listening and speaking
Discussion and debate

Describe the scene.
What is this object?
What is it doing?
What is it made of?
What is its purpose?
Do you think that objects like this exist in reality?
What differences do you think there would be in our lives if robots were commonplace?

UNIT 13
MACHINES

■ **Exercise 1**

Read the articles here. What is your reaction to them? What dangers might arise as a result of improved technology? Divide into groups of three or four. Each group should make a list of *either* the five most serious dangers *or* the five greatest benefits of technology. Then hold a debate: each person should present and explain one of the dangers/benefits, as well as countering the arguments of the previous speaker.

COMPUTER TAKES OVER

Panic broke out at the offices of Ibis Financial Services in Windsor yesterday, when the firm's computer made a bid to take over operations. In an apparent effort to rationalize the structure of the company, it printed and mailed notice of dismissal to all but three

Two Plus Two Makes Five?

A report published today shows that 50% of all school-leavers are unable to perform the simplest mathematical operations. The increasing reliance on pocket calculators is largely to blame, says Mr A. Peterson of

■ **Exercise 2**

Write a speech advocating one of the following.

■ A return to pre-technological society, with suggestions as to how this might be achieved.
■ Further technological development along lines that you think most valuable.

Listening comprehension

Listen to the conversation and try to identify the situation. Who are the people and why are they here?
Listen to the conversation again and answer questions 1 to 6.

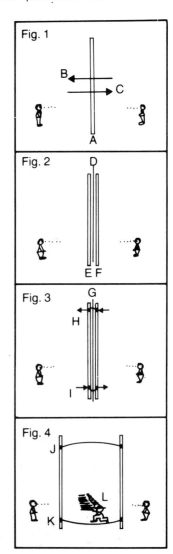

1 Look at the illustrations:

figure 1
What do A, B and C represent? What can the two observers see?

figure 2
What do D, E and F represent? What can the observers see?

figure 3
What do G and the curved lines H and I represent? What can the observers see?

figure 4
What do J, K and L represent? What can the observers see?

2 What is the name of the material used in the process described here? What makes it suitable?

3 Put ticks by the statements that are true.

a The process can make anything invisible. ☐

b At present the process cannot be detected when it is in operation. ☐

c It is possible to turn off the process so that objects become visible again. ☐

4 Use your own words to describe how the process works.

5 'I'm sure you can all see the possibilities.' What possibilities do you think the speaker is referring to?

6 What were the exact words used to

a ask someone to repeat something?

b check that everyone has understood?

c say that something is going to be explained with other words?

d ask about the spelling of a word?

Function: checking understanding and asking about language

What do you think they are saying? Fill in the bubbles.

UNIT 13
MACHINES

■ **Exercise 1** PW

Look at the expressions in Pair work 13a. Student B must find the most appropriate respones to what student A says.

■ **Exercise 2**

Use the tables to help you find suitable remarks in these situations.

1 You are making a formal presentation of a project you've been working on. The audience is a group of eminent scientists.
   ■ You want to make sure that they have understood you.

■ One of them asks a question, but his accent is unfamiliar and you don't understand him.
   ~~don't understand him.~~
■ You're afraid they haven't understood a point you have tried to make, so you're going to repeat it but with different words.

2 Someone is introduced to you: you want to make a note of his/her name, but are not sure how to spell it or pronounce it.

3 You ask a friend about the usage of some of the idioms on p. 151.

Asking someone to repeat something

General
Pardon?/Sorry?/What did you say?
(I'm sorry,) I didn't (quite) *catch/hear* ...?
(I'm sorry,) what was the last/first word/sentence?
Would/Could you repeat *that/the first word*, please?

Informal
What was that (again)?
Who?/Where?/When?/What?
(Sorry,) I didn't get (any of) that.

Formal
I beg your pardon?
I'm sorry, would you mind repeating that, please?

Checking that someone has understood you

General
Do you *see/know* what I mean?
I hope *that's clear/that makes sense.*
..., if you *see/know* what I mean.

Informal
Do you see?/Right?/OK?
Get it?/Got it?
Are you with me?

Formal
Do I make/Am I making/have I made myself clear?
..., if you *follow/understand me/my meaning.*

Saying something in another way

General
In other words, ...
Let me/To put it another way, ...
What I *mean is/meant was* ...
That's to say/i.e. ...

Informal
All/What I'm *trying to say/getting at/driving at* is ...
All I mean is ...

Formal
If I can/Let me just rephrase that: ...
Perhaps I *could/should* make that clearer by saying ...

Asking about language

Pronunciation
How do you/What's the correct way to say/pronounce this *word/name/expression?*
Do you say ... or ...?
Is that the *correct/right pronunciation/stress/intonation?*

Spelling
How do you spell ...?
Do you spell ... with one 't' or two?
Is this the *right/correct* way to spell ...?

Usage
Is it correct to say ...?
How/When do *you/we* use ...?
Can you give me an example of *when/how* you *use/say* ...?
Is/Was that the *correct/right word/expression?*
What should I say *if/when* ...?

Meaning
What does ... mean?
What's another *word for/way of saying* ...?
Does ... mean the same as ...?

■ **Practice** PW

Act out the situations in Pair work
13b and 13c.

Reading aloud: *weight* or *height*?

There are many different ways of spelling the sounds /ei/ and /ai/. Here are some examples:

	/ei/		/ai/
a-(e)	name	i-(e)	line
	naming		lining
ai	rain	y	fly
ay	say	ie	die
ei	vein	igh	light
	weight	uy	buy
ey	obey	eye	eye
		y-(e)	rhyme
			rhyming
		*ai	aisle
		*eight	height

*More commonly used for the sound /ei/.

■ Exercise 1

Sort these words into two groups: with /ei/ and with /ai/.

ache	fiver	pry
ail	freight	raise
ale	fright	rise
arrange	guy	tray
deign	idle	try
deny	I'll	waste
dine	isle	weighed
fail	mate	whale
favour	might	while
file	prey	wide

■ Exercise 2

Practise saying the words in the list above. One student says a word; the others call out 'one' if it has the sound /ei/, and 'two' if it has the sound /ai/.

■ Exercise 3

Look through the text on p. 150 and see how many words you can find that contain the sounds /ei/ and /ai/.

■ Exercise 4

Improvise sentences that contain some of the words in the list in exercise 1.

Activity: how good an inventor are you?

Imagine that you work for a multinational concern that manufactures all sorts of gadgets, from cigarette lighters and hinges to computers and spaceships. You are an inventor, whose job is to come up with ideas for new products.

- Working in groups of three or four, invent a machine or device, of any kind whatsoever. Decide:
  —what its purpose is.
  —how it works.
  —what it looks like: dimensions, shape, colour, etc.
  —how it is to be manufactured, e.g. materials and equipment needed, is it to be handmade or mass-produced? etc.
  —how big the potential market is, and how much the device will cost.

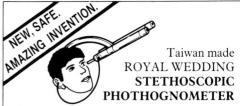

- Now imagine that you are going to present your invention to the company's board of directors. Plan the presentation very carefully, so as to emphasize the facts that will interest the directors most. Make drawings, graphs, information sheets, etc., where you think these will be useful. Make use of any equipment there may be in the classroom, such as the blackboard, flip-charts, overhead projectors, etc.

- Make the presentation to the rest of the class. Here are some phrases that you might be able to use:
  —I'm going to talk about …
  —I'd like to start by *describing/talking about* …
  —There are *two/three* important *things/points* to notice …
  —Well, I think that's all I have to say *about/on* that particular *point/subject*.
  —If we now *turn to/look at* the question of …
  —*To sum up/In conclusion*, I'd like to say …

The 'directors' may ask questions during or after the presentation.

Written work: numbers

a

26	*twenty-six*	
132	*a hundred and thirty-two*	
7,641	*seven thousand, six hundred and forty-one*	
3,936,278	*three million, nine hundred and thirty-six thousand, two hundred and seventy-eight*	

Notice particularly the use of commas, hyphens, and *and*. Only numbers up to one hundred need be written out in full.

b *hundreds of prizes, thousands of people, dozens of excuses, five hundred prizes, six thousand men, two dozen eggs*

Notice the use of *of* and the plural *-s*.

c $\frac{1}{2}$ *a half* $\frac{2}{3}$ *two-thirds*
$\frac{3}{4}$ *three-quarters* $\frac{5}{8}$ *five-eighths*

Only the simplest fractions should be written out in full.

d 23·41   *twenty-three point four one* (not *forty-one*)

Decimals need never be written out in full.

Note that in decimals a 'point' (·) is used *not* a comma, which is used only after millions and thousands (see **a** above).

e the number 0

- Say *zero* in temperatures.
  three degrees below zero (− 3°)
- Say /ou/ (the letter 0) in telephone numbers.
  three six 0 double-seven 0 five (360 7705)
- Use *nought, zero* or *0* in decimals.
  0.05 is spoken as:
  nought point nought five or
  zero point zero five or *0 point 0 five*
- Use *nil* in most games and sports.
  three nil (3–0)
  However some sports have their own conventions, e.g. 40–0 in tennis is spoken as *forty love*.
- In British English, use *nought* for
  —the figure 0:
  he wrote down two noughts and a seven
  —scores in examinations, etc.:
  I got nought out of ten

f dates

1939 *nineteen thirty-nine* or
     nineteen hundred and thirty-nine
1908 *nineteen 0 eight* or
     nineteen hundred and eight

These need never be written out in full.

■ **Exercise 1**

Write these numbers out in full.
1 25,492   **2** 48   **3** 98,765,432
4 100,036   **5** 7,000,000   **6** $\frac{1}{3}$
7 $\frac{3}{7}$ **8** $\frac{7}{8}$ **9** $\frac{1}{2}$
10 $\frac{2}{5}$

■ **Exercise 2**

Say these numbers aloud.

- decimals
  1 132·91   **2** 6·08   **3** 1111·403
  4   2·22   **5** 0·001

- telephone numbers
  1 377 0026   **2** 01-222 3488   **3** 002740
  4 936 4002   **5** 770025

- dates
  1 1801   **2** 1740   **3** 1066   **4** 1492
  5 1909

UNIT 14

POLITICS

Reading and thinking
Reading comprehension

1 Politics is perhaps the only profession for which no preparation is thought necessary.
R.L. STEVENSON, *Familiar Studies of Men and Books*.

2 It was but the other day that a man sent me a letter asking what matter one should put into a political speech. To which I answered, having an expert knowledge in this, that the whole art of a political speech is to put *nothing* into it. It is much more difficult than it sounds.
HILAIRE BELLOC,
A Conversation with an Angel

3 The professional politician woos the fickle public more as a man engaged than married, for his is a contract that must be renewed every few years, and the memory of the public is short.
J. T. SALTER,
Boss Rule

4 An honest politician is one who, when he is bought, will stay bought.
SIMON CAMERON,
remark

5 If we meet an honest and intelligent politician, a dozen, a hundred, we say they aren't like politicians at all, and our category of politicians stays unchanged; we know what politicians are like.
RANDALL JARRELL,
Mademoiselle

6 Democracy always makes for materialism, because the only kind of equality that you can guarantee to a whole people is, broadly speaking, physical.
KATHERINE FULLERTON GEROULD,
Modes and Morals

7 Political language—and with variations this is true of all political parties, from Conservatives to Anarchists—is designed to make lies sound truthful, and to give an appearance of solidity to pure wind.
GEORGE ORWELL,
A Collection of Essays

8 If the conscience of an honest man lays down stern rules, so also does the art of politics.
F. S. OLIVER,
Politics and Politicians

9 To the politician we are something of a dark horse. He does not know what we want; he wishes he did. Do we know ourselves? Vaguely we know that we don't want the politician.
ROSE MACAULAY,
A Casual Commentary

10 Those of you who regard my profession of political life with some disdain should remember that it made it possible for me to move from being an obscure lieutenant in the United States Navy to Commander-in-Chief in fourteen years with very little technical competence.
JOHN F. KENNEDY,
The Kennedy Wit, edited by Bill Adler

11 A democracy can be distinguished, if its citizens are distinguishable; if each has an area of choice in which he really chooses. To keep that area of choice as large as possible is the real function of freedom.
G. K. CHESTERTON,
All Is Grist

12 An empty stomach is not a good political adviser.
ALBERT EINSTEIN,
Cosmic Religion

13 Government, even in its best state, is but a necessary evil; in its worst state, an intolerable one.
THOMAS PAINE,
Common Sense, 1

1 Put ticks next to the statements that agree with ideas expressed in the quotations; put crosses by those that do not correspond to quotations. Discuss your answers with the rest of the class.

a People who eat a lot should not become politicians. ☒

b All politicians can be bribed. ☑

c You need no special training to become a politician. ☑

d Being a politician costs a lot of money. ☒

e It's unpleasant to have a government, but you must have one anyway. ☑

f It's a common belief that politicians are stupid and dishonest. ☑

g Politicians have to concern themselves more with the long-term future than with the near future. ☒

h It is impossible to achieve complete equality. ☑

i In a democracy, people should have only limited areas within which they can make choices. ☒

j Politicians find it difficult to know what people want. ☑

k When politicians talk, their purpose is either to avoid saying anything at all or to make lies sound like the truth. ☑

l Politicians must be honest, and must obey their consciences. ☑

m Politicians can achieve important positions without knowing anything. ☑

2 What threads can you find running through these quotations? Think about people's attitudes to politicians, and politicians' attitudes to their jobs and to the people they represent.

3 Which quotations don't fit in with the general pattern?

Words and structures

IDIOMS

■ **Exercise 1**

Explain the meanings of these expressions as they are used in the quotations.

a necessary evil (13)
woos the fickle public (3)
memory . . . is short (3)
makes for (6)
broadly speaking (6)
something of a dark horse (9)
but the other day (2)

■ **Exercise 2**
Make
makes for (6)

Match up the phrases and definitions. Then write seven sentences of your own, each containing one of the phrases with *make*.

1 make a clean breast of something	**a** accept, manage
2 make believe	**b** confess
3 make do (with something)	**c** fantasise, pretend
4 make good	**d** restore, compensate
5 make hay while the sun shines	**e** treat jokingly
6 make light of something	**f** use advantageously
7 make the best/most of	**g** use an opportunity to the full

■ Exercise 3

Choose a suitable preposition to fill each gap, and write a word or phrase of explanation.

Could you make *out* the cheque to Hall and Sons, please? (Explanation: *write*)

1 Last night thieves broke in and made _____ with the silver.

2 Their task complete, they turned south and made _____ home.

3 The house was made _____ to me just before my father died.

4 I don't know what to think. What do *you* make _____ his behaviour?

5 Please accept this gift, I hope it'll make _____ for some of the trouble I've caused.

■ Exercise 4
Animal idioms
a dark horse (9)

Match up the expressions and definitions in the table below.
Then choose the most suitable expressions to fill the gaps in the sentences.

1 Your remarks about political blackmail really stirred up _____.

2 We had _____ at the seaside last summer. It was wonderful!

3 I think the whole expedition is _____. There's no such place as Atlantis.

4 I'm not invited to family reunions any more. I'm considered _____ because of my political convictions.

5 James opted out of _____ and went to live on a South Sea island.

VOCABULARY

■ Exercise 5

Complete the table; in some cases there are several possibilities.

personal nouns	adjectives	abstract nouns
	political	
	socialist	
conservative		
anarchist		
communist		
dictator		
		republic
		democracy

1 a black sheep		a	a disreputable member of a family
2 a dogsbody		b	a foolish and useless enterprise
3 a hornet's nest		c	an enemy who pretends to be a friend
4 a lame duck		d	an extremely enjoyable time
5 the rat race		e	a person or company in trouble, helpless
6 a red herring		f	competition for improved status and wealth
7 a whale of a time		g	someone who has to do all the boring jobs
8 a white elephant		h	something that distracts attention from the problem being dealt with
9 a wild-goose chase		i	something that is expensive but useless
10 a wolf in sheep's clothing		j	trouble, a threatening situation

Exercise 6

Write five sentences, each including one of the words in the table in exercise 5 to illustrate its meaning.

STRUCTURES

Inversion of subject and verb
so also does the art of politics (8)

So, neither, nor
John likes coffee.
So do I. (I like coffee, too.)
Peter can never forget.
Neither/Nor can I. (I can never forget either.)

■ Exercise 7 | PW |

In Pair work 14a, both students have five remarks. Student A reads one of his remarks, and student B should respond with a short answer of agreement, beginning with *so*, *neither*, or *nor*. Then student B reads one of his remarks, and so on.

Here, there
Here comes the bus.
Here is the man I was telling you about.
There goes the woman of my dreams.

- *do*, *does*, and *did* are not used in this type of inversion.

- There is no inversion when the subject is a pronoun. *Here it comes. Here he is. There she goes.*

- With verbs other than *be*, *come* and *go*, inversion of this type is old-fashioned or literary. Instead, put *here* or *there* at the end of the sentence, and keep the normal subject-verb order.
Aunt Elizabeth lives here.

■ Exercise 8

Rearrange the words into the best order to make statements (not questions).

1 schoolteacher/there/old/is/my

2 comes/he/now/here

3 are/build/going/here/motorway/the/they/to

4 a/can/have/here/picnic/we

5 is/Mrs/your/Jones/cake/of/here/piece

Negative adverbs
Not only did John smoke, but he also drank.
Never again will I trust an old friend.
Rarely are we given the opportunity to make our voices heard.
Little did he know it, but his time was up.

- Inversion takes place after initial negative adverbs and conjunctions.
- These adverbs, when placed at the beginning of a sentence, are also followed by inverted subject and verb: *barely, hardly, scarcely; seldom; few, little* (but not *a few, a little*); *only.*

■ Exercise 9

Make complete sentences from the following cues, adding articles and changing the verb forms where necessary.

1 Never/I/see/such/brilliant/acting.

2 Pete/not/play/piano; /nor/he/play/clarinet.

3 Hardly/we/leave/building/, /when/it/explode.

4 Not only/President/smile/yesterday,/but/he/laugh/too.

5 Not until ten years later/they/find/out/truth.

6 No sooner/I/get/into/bath,/than/telephone/ring.

7 Only under exceptional circumstances/civilians/be allowed/into/camp.

8 Nowhere else in England/there/be/such/inspiring/scenery.

9 Not even after/I/explain/it/three/times/he/understand/what/I/mean.

Listening and speaking
Discussion and debate

Describe the scene.
What are the two women saying to each other?
What are the men doing?
What is the purpose of activities like this?
What can they achieve?

■ **Exercise 2**

Imagine that a national election is to take place soon, and that you are one of these people.

an unemployed 18-year-old.	a housewife.
	a stockbroker.
an unemployed 45-year-old.	an old age pensioner.
an army officer.	a coal-miner.
a bank manager.	a shopkeeper.
a trades union official.	a clerk.
	a student.

Invent some details for your new character, and then talk about the political issues that are of greatest importance to you.

What do you want the politicians to talk about? Which issues do you think will decide the election?

■ **Exercise 3**

Write a balanced essay with one of the quotations on p. 162 as its title.

■ **Exercise 1**

The following are some of the methods used in attempts to create political change. If you can think of any more, add them to the list. Under what circumstances are they useful and/or justifiable tools?
- Writing and performing songs and plays.
- Writing letters to members of parliament.
- Voting at elections.
- Canvassing support in the form of signatures to petitions.
- Publishing articles in newspapers and magazines.
- Mass demonstrations.
- Boycotting certain products or groups of people.
- Going on strike.
- Hijacking aeroplanes.
- Armed revolution.

Listening comprehension

You will hear some questions and answers. The first time you listen, identify the situation and write down headings for the topics discussed. The second and subsequent times you listen, answer questions 1 to 5.

topics

1
2
3
4

1 Put ticks by the statements which are true, according to what the speaker says.

The candidate's party intends to
a get rid of unemployment altogether. ☐
b put a stop to traffic congestion in the town centre. ☐
c fight against pollution. ☐
d work to help old-age pensioners. ☐
e convict the majority of teenagers. ☐
f do something about violent teenagers. ☐

The candidate's party
g is not in the present government. ☐

2 Write down the key words in what the speaker says. The first topic has already been done for you.

1 *top priorities—halt unemployment—meaningful jobs—confident—bring about— foreseeable future*
2
3
4

3 Use the key words you have written in question 2 as the basis for reconstructing, in your own words, what the speaker said.

4 Which questions did the speaker actually give concrete answers to? Would you be satisfied with these answers?

5 What were the exact words used by the speaker to express
a an intention to do something, or not do something?
b optimism about a future event?
c pessimism about a future event?

POLITICS

Function: plans, optimism and pessimism

What do you think they are saying? Fill in the bubbles.

HOLIDAY NEXT SUMMER?

SPAIN.

WONDERFUL!

AWFUL!

■ **Exercise 1** PW

Look at Pair work 14b. Student B must find appropriate responses to what student A says.

■ **Exercise 2**

Use the tables to help you find suitable remarks in these situations.

1 Say what you hope to do, plan to do, plan not to do, are optimistic and pessimistic about:
   ■ next summer
   ■ at the weekend
   ■ when you retire
   ■ this evening

2 The chairman of a large company talks about some of his company's plans for the following year.

3 Talk about plans that you have changed, and give reasons.

   play tennis
   I was going to play tennis, but I can't now that it's raining.

   ■ weekend in Paris
   ■ go to party
   ■ not talk about politics
   ■ get married

Expressing plans and intentions
General   I'm (not) *going/planning* to ...   I've decided *that/(not) to* ...   I (don't) think I'll ...   I'*ll/won't* be ... -ing.
Informal   I (don't) reckon I'll ...   I'm (not) thinking of ...
Formal   It's my (firm) intention (not) to ...   I have *every/no* intention of ...   I (don't) intend to ...

POLITICS

Changing plans

General

I *was/wasn't* (actually) *going/planning* to ..., but ...
(*Actually/As a matter of fact*) I'd decided *that/(not) to* ...
I *had/hadn't planned/meant* to ..., but ...

Informal

I *was/wasn't* thinking of ..., but ...
I *hadn't/had* thought of ...

Formal

It *was/had been* my intention (not) to ...
I had (fully) intended (not) to ...

Expressing hopes

General

I hope/I'd like/I'm hoping ...
..., I hope.

Informal

Let's hope (for)...
..., with a bit of luck.

Formal

We must hope (for ...)
I *do hope/trust* ...

Expressing optimism

General

... will be *wonderful/good/nice* (, I'm sure).
... is bound to be *wonderful/a success/enjoyable*.

Informal

Everything'll *be/turn out fine/great/OK*.
I don't see how ... can *fail/go wrong*.

Formal

I feel quite *confident/sure about/that* ...
I have every confidence (in ...).

POLITICS

Expressing pessimism
General I'm not (at all) *sure/happy (about/that ...).* I'm rather doubtful (about ...) ... is *bound/going* to *fail/be a failure/lose/be awful.*
Informal There's no way (...). I don't see how ... can possibly work.
Formal (To *tell you the truth/be honest*,) I have my doubts (about ...). I'm not *particularly/very confident/optimistic/sure* (about ...).

■ **Practice** PW

Act out the situations in Pair work 14c
and 14d.

Reading aloud: /ð/ or /θ/?

■ **Exercise 1**

Sort the following words into two
groups: those that contain the sound
/ð/, as in *this*, and those that contain
the sound /θ/, as in *thing*.

author	rhythms
bath	sixth
births	smooth
breathe	soothe
cloth	than
clothes	theatre
either	then
enthusiasm	theory
growths	there
heathen	though
leather	through
months	thump
mouths	weather
Mr Smith's	with
mythical	worth
panther	youths

■ **Exercise 2**

Practise saying the words in the list
in exercise 1. One student says a word;
the others call out 'one' if it contains
/ð/, 'two' if it contains /θ/.

■ **Exercise 3**

Make up sentences that contain some
of the words in exercise 1.

There's the sixth heathen.

■ **Exercise 4**

Look at the listening comprehension
script on pp. 216–17. Make a note of all
the words that contain /ð/ and /θ/, and
practise saying them aloud. Then read
the dialogue aloud.

Activity: election platform

1 Party political pamphlet

The following is an extract from a party political pamphlet published before the UK Parliamentary elections of 1982. Read it carefully, and discuss what you agree with and disagree with. Are the ideas well presented? Would you vote for this party?

PROGRAMME OF EMERGENCY ACTION

Within days of taking office, we will launch a programme of emergency action to save Britain. These are some of the things we will do:

● **GET BRITAIN GROWING by starting huge programmes of reconstruction. We'll build ourselves out of the slump, as well as boost services.**
Increase investment in industry. **We'll also steer jobs to the regions and inner cities.**
Act to control imports. **We'll make sure that extra spending creates jobs in Britian.**
Introduce a crash programme of employment and training. **We'll create new jobs, especially for young people.**

● **START TO REBUILD INDUSTRY by means of an agreed five-year plan. We'll use new public enterprise to lead the way in new technology.**
Agree a national assessment with unions and employers. **We'll decide together how to share out our national wealth.**

Set up a new National Investment Bank. **We'll make British investment work for Britain.**
Repeal Tory laws which damage industral relations. **We'll give new rights to people at work.**

● **CREATE A FAIRER BRITAIN by spending more on public services and by reforming taxation. We want everyone to have an equal opportunity.**
Raise child benefit to £8. **We'll give real help to families.**
Spend much more on health and personal social services. **We'll make sure help goes to those in need, not those who can afford to pay.**
Invest in education. **We'll improve standards all round, from nurseries to adult education.**
Freeze rents for a year. **We'll aim to build 50 per cent more houses.**

● **PROMOTE EQUALITY by extending women's rights at work. We'll improve child care, and appoint an Equality Minister.**
Introduce a programme to aid ethnic minorities. **We'll make sure the law does not discriminate.**

● **IMPROVE THE QUALITY OF LIFE by protecting the environment. We'll ban lead in petrol and begin to clean up our inner cities.**
Help public transport. **We'll keep fares down and invest to expand.**
Clamp down on waste. **We'll begin a crash programme to conserve energy.**

● **TAKE POSITIVE ACTION IN INTERNATIONAL AFFAIRS by promoting peace and development. We'll introduce an effective non nuclear defence policy**
Work to remove the nuclear threat here and abroad. **We'll cancel plans for Trident and Cruise and phase out nuclear weapons and bases in Britain.**
Increase aid to developing countries. **We'll work to eliminate world poverty.**
Open talks with the Common Market. **We'll negotiate our withdrawal.**

---

2 Election campaign

- Decide first what type of election you are going to hold: national, local, school, society or club, etc.
- Divide into groups, each representing a different party or faction. Each group decides on three or four issues to be stressed in the election campaign, as well as its policy on these issues.
- Within each group, prepare and write an election manifesto with headlines and brief outlines of your policies. Each member of the group could perhaps be responsible for one issue.

- Hold an election debate. In turn, spokesmen from each group present their manifestos. Students who are not spokesmen form the audience and may ask questions between each presentation. The teacher should act as a chairman, to ensure that order is kept and that spokesmen do not speak for too long.
- Follow-up: Discuss the differences and similarities between the various manifestos and policies. Which would you vote for in reality?

Revision: units 13 and 14

■ Exercise 1

Fill each gap with one word; it need not be the actual word used in the original text, but it must be appropriate to the context.

The old-fashioned blue blades are the ones that ____(1)____ results. ____(2)____ a blunt blade on a two-inch matchbox or other holder directly under the ____(3)____ of a six-inch pyramid. Sharp sides ____(4)____ east–west, the ends north–south. Leave it there at ____(5)____ a week, ____(6)____ if it doesn't ____(7)____ ready. On removal, it should again give you smooth ____(8)____. Replace blades under pyramid regularly after each use. Drbal claims ____(9)____ to 200 shaves with a single blade. Many clean-____(10)____ pyramid builders speak of using a single blade ____(11)____ a month or ____(12)____ and claim marked difference between treated and control blade shows most clearly after four ____(13)____ use. Drbal observes that the crystallinelike ____(14)____ of the blade edge tends in ____(15)____ toward its original form. The pyramid, he feels, ____(16)____ this tendency. Put a blunt control blade ____(17)____ for the same length of time as the one in the pyramid. ____(18)____ on shaving one side of the face or one leg with the control and one with the treated blade. ____(19)____ is claimed that dull kitchen knives or dull scissors can also be ____(20)____ with appropriate-sized pyramids.

■ Exercise 2

Write a brief story or description that contains all the expressions in one of the boxes. Then delete these expressions and pass what you have written to someone else, who should try to fill in the gaps.

disdain make believe make off a dark horse dictatorial
the other day make light of make over a red herring republicanism
woo make do make out a lame duck anarchy
a necessary evil make the most of make up for a wild-goose chase materialistic
fickle make good make for the rat race conservatism

THE FUTURE

Reading and thinking
Reading comprehension

We haven't conquered space. Not yet. We have sent some 20 men on camping trips to the Moon, and the US and the Soviet Union have sent people up to spend restricted lives orbiting the Earth. During the next few weeks, for instance, the US Space Shuttle will take Spacelab into orbit, showing that ordinary (non-astronaut) scientists can live and work in space – for a few days only.

All these are marvellous technical and human achievements, but none of them involves living independently in space. The Russians have been sustained by food parcels – even oxygen parcels – sent up from Earth. And they haven't gone far into space. The residents of Sheffield are farther from London than those of the Shuttle or the Soviet's Salyut. It is only in fiction, and in space movies, that people spend long periods living more or less normally deep in space.

But in a couple of decades – by the year 2000, say – this could have changed. There could be settlements in space that would house adventurers leading more or less normal lives. They would have to be near normal for the settlements to endure, because only eccentrics would want to spend years in space on a diet of survival foods.

The pictures on these pages show where the settlers would live. They seem like science fiction – but they are not. They are based on plans produced by hard-headed people: engineers and scientists, headed by Gerard O'Neill of Princeton University, summoned to a conference by NASA. They are space enthusiasts, of course, but they are not dreamers.

The settlement is a gigantic wheel, a tube more than 400ft in diameter bent into a ring just over a mile across. The wheel spins gently once a minute. It is this leisurely rotation that makes this settlement different from the Shuttle and Salyut, and infinitely different from the Lunar modules that took man for the first time to any non-terrestrial soil, because the spin produces a force that feels like gravity. Every space trip has shown that the human body needs gravity if it isn't to deteriorate, and gravity also makes normal activities practicable. Nobody would want to live for long in a space settlement where everything – people and equipment and the eggs they were trying to fry – drifted weightlessly around.

With gravity, life in space can be based on our experience on Earth. We can have farming and factories and houses and meeting-places that are not designed by guesswork.

The main settlement, as the picture on this page shows, is inside the tube, and the artificial gravity makes the "hubwards direction" equivalent to "up". The "ground" is inside the tube, farthest from the hub.

The need for gravity is one of the reasons for building a space colony, rather than sending settlers to an existing location such as the Moon or the planets. The Moon is irretrievably inhospitable. Its gravity is tiny – and any one place on the Moon has 14 days of sunlight followed by 14 of night, which makes agriculture impossible and puts paid to any hope of using solar energy.

In the settlement, which floats in permanent sunlight, the day-length is controlled. A gigantic mirror about a mile in diameter floats weightlessly above the ring of the settlement. It reflects sunlight on to smaller mirrors that direct it into the ring, through shutters that fix the day length.

The sunlight is constant during the "daytime," so farming is productive to an extent which can be reached on Earth only occasionally. The aim is to provide a diet similar to that on Earth, but the balance will be shifted.

The farms will be arranged in terraces with fish ponds and rice paddies in transparent tanks on the top layer; wheat below; vegetables, soya and maize below that.

The population of the settlement is fixed at about 10,000 people: farm output can be accurately planned. Research reports suggest that about 44 square metres of vegetables will be needed for each person, and just over five square metres of pastures.

The picture here shows where the people will live. It doesn't look very different from modern small towns on Earth, and this is deliberate. Science-fiction films feature vast glass tower blocks and subterranean warrens, But real-life space settlers won't want these. Throughout history, settlers have tried to put up buildings like the ones they left behind, because these are familiar: space settlers will do the same.

By Tony Osman from *The Sunday Times Colour Magazine*, 31 July 1983 (See illustration on page 177.)

THE FUTURE

1 What is the main difference between trips into space actually undertaken so far and the settlement described here?

2 In what respects would life in the space settlement be 'normal'?

3 In what way would farming in the settlement be better than farming on Earth? Why?

4 What reason is given for making life in the settlement as much like life on Earth as possible?

5 What associations do these words conjure up, and why does the author use them?
   a camping trips (para. 1)
   b adventurers (para. 3)
   c hard-headed (para. 4)
   d warrens (para. 13)

6 Why are there quotation marks round 'hubwards direction', 'up', 'ground', and 'daytime'(paras. 7 & 10)?

Words and structures

IDIOMS

■ **Exercise 1**

Explain the meanings of these expressions as they are used in the text.

a more or less normally (para. 2)
b survival foods (para. 3)
c headed by (para. 4)
d puts paid to (para. 8)
e real-life space settlers (para. 13)

VOCABULARY

■ **Exercise 2**

Choose the word that best completes each sentence.

1 Let's hold a symposium on genetic surgery. It's a very _____ subject.
   a actual b current
   c modern d topical

2 Your idea won't work; it's just not _____.
   a practicable b practical
   c practised d practising

3 It's important that the temperature should remain _____.
   a consistent b constant
   c continual d continuous

4 There's little chance that mankind would _____ a nuclear war.
   a endure b revive
   c survive d sustain

5 In the central plains of North America the corn _____ stretch as far as the eye can see.
   a fields b meadows
   c paddies d pastures

6 The assistant _____ nervously while I made up my mind.
   a drifted b floated
   c hovered d orbited

7 The drawing shows three _____ circles.
   a concentric b eccentric
   c egocentric d geocentric

8 Claudius remained in _____ until the year 54 AD.
   a energy b force
   c power d strength

9 The law has been in _____ since January.
   a energy b force
   c power d strength

10 Owing to the _____ of circumstances, I shall be unable to attend.
   a energy b force
   c power d strength

■ **Exercise 3**

Find words in the text that match these definitions.

1 Become worse.
2 Force that draws matter towards the centre of the Earth.
3 Kept alive.
4 Made by humans, not natural.
5 Making judgements or estimates without sufficient evidence.

6 Periods of ten years.
7 People who are very keen on something.

8 Successful actions.
9 Underground.
10 Very large.

STRUCTURES

The subjunctive

1 Expressing indirect commands, advice, etc.

I *propose/demand/suggest* It's *vital/essential* I was *adamant/insistent/keen* My *advice/proposal* is	that	John *be given* the job. everyone *try* his hardest. she *open* it at once. Jackson *head* the delegation.

■ *Should* can always be used in this type of sentence.
... that John *should be given* the job.

■ The same verb form (the same as the infinitive) is used for all persons and all tenses.

■ It is also possible to use the normal indicative form in sentences of this type.
I suggest that John is given the job.

■ **Exercise 4**

Turn the commands into suggestions, demands, proposals, etc., using the expressions in table 1.

Go and get them, John.
I suggest/It's vital/My proposal is that John (should) go and get them.

1 Take notes, Pat.
2 This must be kept secret.
3 Write them a letter, Smith.
4 Hawkins must be sacked.
5 Forget what I said, Leslie.
6 The submarine must be intercepted.

2 Expressing attitudes or emotions

I	am was	disappointed annoyed angry	that	he *should ignore* our invitation. she *should want* to leave. children *should be allowed* to smoke.
		don't like the idea		
It doesn't surprise me				
It's		ridiculous shocking extraordinary		

■ The subjunctive form without *should* cannot be used in sentences of this type.

■ Straightforward indicative forms may be used to make concrete references to actual events.

It's ridiculous that children <u>are allowed</u> to smoke.
This refers to particular situation in which smoking is allowed. The inclusion of *should* shows that the speaker is referring to ideas rather than facts.

THE FUTURE

■ Exercise 5

Talk about your attitudes to the following, using some of the expressions in table 2.

children/smoke
It's quite ridiculous that children should be allowed to smoke.

1 more money/weapons
2 you/treated so badly
3 rich people/high taxes
4 police/more powers
5 bank robbers/long prison sentences
6 scientists/energy/space travel

3 In conditionals

> If I were you, I'd leave at once.

■ *Was* is commonly used instead of *were*. Verbs other than *be* always have the normal past simple form in this type of conditional.

4 After *wish* and *if only*

I wish	they had come (but they didn't). they were here (but they aren't).
If only	they would come (but I'm not sure that they will).

■ Exercise 6

Make wishes that are the opposites of these statements.

They didn't come.
I wish they had come.
They are here.
If only they weren't here.

1 I saw him.
2 I don't know him.
3 He's so careless.
4 They were frightened.
5 They can't make it.
6 We have to do it immediately.
7 She didn't get there on time.
8 They're not going to come.

5 After *I'd rather* ... and *it's (about/high) time* ...

I'd rather	he weren't so rude. you left me alone. you didn't hit me.
It's (*about/high*) time	they got a new car.

■ Exercise 7

Change the sentences as in the examples.

His hair's too long.
It's time he had a haircut.
Please don't come.
I'd rather you didn't come.

1 It's very late.
2 This typewriter's very old.
3 He doesn't know how to behave.
4 I'm very tired.
5 Our flat's too small for us.
6 Please wait a minute.
7 Please don't be so negative.
8 Please don't stand there.
9 Please come a bit closer.
10 Please let me do it on my own.

■ Exercise 8

Prepositions and gerunds

Fill the gaps with suitable prepositions, when necessary, and put the verbs in brackets into the correct form.

1 It is no use _____ (cry) over spilt milk.

2 Don't try to dissuade me _____ (go).

3 There's no point _____ (go) over that again.

4 Please forgive me _____ (arrive) so late.

5 You are quite mistaken _____ (think) that I am your enemy.

6 He prides himself _____ (be) an excellent cook.

7 He takes pleasure _____ (hurt) people's feelings.

8 She's quite capable _____ (look) after herself.

9 He was publicly criticised _____ (encourage) the men to strike.

10 They suggested _____ (start) at eight.

11 Let's concentrate _____ (find) a solution.

12 You tricked me _____ (give) you all my money.

13 He has that annoying habit _____ (crack) his knuckles.

14 She's busy _____ (finish) her new novel.

15 I may be tolerant; but I draw the line _____ (be) called a fool.

16 I insist _____ (help) you.

17 I am accustomed _____ (be) treated with respect.

18 Please refrain _____ (interfere).

19 I'm thinking _____ (travel) by boat.

20 They made a pretence _____ (congratulate) one another.

21 You're very good _____ (imitate) others.

22 We anticipate _____ (complete) the project next month.

23 If you persist _____ (make) ridiculous comments, you'll have to leave.

24 She confessed _____ (murder) her husband.

25 We must reconcile ourselves _____ (become) poor.

Listening and speaking
Discussion and debate

Describe the scene in your own words. What would it be like to live here? What problems might arise? How do you think people will live in the future? What differences, for instance, do you think rising population, decreasing energy resources and improved technology will make to the way we live?

■ Exercise 1

What methods do we use to look into the future (e.g. horoscopes, weather forecasts, etc.)? Which are the best methods? Why are people so interested in the future?

■ Exercise 2

Choose one of these areas as the subject of a debate entitled: 'The future of . . .'.

television	education	travel
newspapers	medicine	finance
politics	sport	entertainment
the police	food	crime
the army	transport	literature

■ Exercise 3

Write an essay on the subject of the debate, based on some of the ideas discussed.

UNIT 15
THE FUTURE

Listening comprehension

You will hear a conversation between two people. The first time you hear it, identify the situation—who are these people, where are they, and why have they met? The second and subsequent times you listen answer questions 1 to 6.

1 Which of these statements do you know to be true? Tick the boxes.

   a The man and woman are old friends. ☐
   b The man knows that his girlfriend has found another boyfriend. ☐
   c The woman has a crystal ball that speaks to her. ☐
   d In the story the woman tells, the weather is bad. ☐
   e The man doesn't know any girls with dark hair. ☐
   f The man is already married. ☐
   g The man has to pay more money in order to find out who is going to be his wife. ☐

2 During their conversation, they talk about two other adults. Write down what you know to be true about them.

3 What did the woman mean with the expression 'trick of the light'?

4 Describe in your own words the story that the woman 'sees' in her crystal ball.

5 Can you find any instances of the woman's getting information from the man and then using what he tells her, rather than getting it from the crystal ball?

6 What were the exact words used in the conversation to express the following?
   a Worry or fear.
   b Reassurance or comfort.
   c Regrets for things done or not done in the past.

Function: worry, past regrets and reassurance

What do you think they are saying? Fill in the bubbles.

Look at the sentences in Pair work 15a. Student B must find the most appropriate responses to what student A says.

■ **Exercise 2**

Use the tables to help you find suitable remarks in these situations.

1 A woman is nervous because she is about to go on trial for shoplifting. A friend tries to cheer her up.

2 The headmaster of a school is talking to the parents of a very difficult pupil, who he thinks is badly behaved and stupid. He is worried about the future, and regrets having accepted the child as a pupil.

3 A friend of yours is nervous about an important interview. You reassure him/her.

4 You lent one of your favourite books to a friend, who then lost it. You blame yourself.

5 You bought a cheap second-hand car, but it broke down almost immediately. You tell a friend that you regret the purchase.

Expressing worry and fear

General
I'm (very) *worried/uneasy* (about . . .).
I'm (really) *terrified/frightened/afraid* (of . . .).
I find . . . (very) *worrying/upsetting*.

Informal
I'm scared (stiff) *that/of* . . .
I'm worried sick (*by/about* . . .).

Formal
I'm (*very/extremely*) *concerned/anxious/apprehensive* (about . . .).
. . . gives some cause for *concern/anxiety*.

Giving reassurance

General
There's no need to *worry/get upset* (about . . .).
You really needn't worry (about . . .).
There's nothing to worry about.
Everything'll *be/turn out fine/all right* (in the end).

Informal
There, there./Cheer up!/Steady on!/Don't worry.
Come on! It's not as bad as all that.
No need to get so worked up (about . . .)

Formal
There's (really) no *reason/cause* to be *worried/nervous/apprehensive/alarmed* (about . . .).
(I assure you) you need have no *fears/worries* (about . . .).

THE FUTURE

Expressing past regrets
General I wish *I'd (never)/I hadn't* . . . *I can't think/I don't know* why I (didn't) . . . I *should/shouldn't* have . . .
Informal What *an idiot/a fool* I *was/have been* (to . . .). How *silly/stupid* of me (to . . .). If only *I'd/I hadn't* . . .
Formal I (really) regret (not) having . . . It was *foolish/thoughtless/careless* of me (not) to . . .

■ Practice PW

1 Act out the situations in Pair work 15b and 15c.

2 Act out in pairs a visit to the fortune-teller. Think up new fears, worries, hopes and predictions.

Reading aloud: revision

Look at the listening comprehension dialogue on p. 217.

■ Exercise 1

Make lists of all the words in the dialogue that contain the same vowel sounds as these words and then say them aloud.

bear	night
beer	late
earn	who
bean	how
bin	hoe

■ Exercise 2

Make lists of all the words in the dialogue that contain the underlined consonant sounds in these words and then say them aloud.

Norwe<u>g</u>ian	Chri<u>st</u>ian
mea<u>s</u>ure	preci<u>se</u>
Ru<u>ss</u>ian	ri<u>se</u>

■ Exercise 3

Mark with rising or falling arrows the final stressed syllables in every word group or sentence.

■ Exercise 4

Find examples of the following and then practise saying all the examples aloud.

1 Question tags.

2 Questions with falling intonation.

3 Questions with rising intonation.

4 A question that starts with a question word but has rising intonation.

5 A group of words with 'list' intonation.

■ Exercise 5

Read the dialogue aloud, paying close attention to pronunciation, intonation and stress.

Activity: looking back from the future

Read the passage carefully. It is taken from a book called *The 80s—a look back*, published in 1979 and containing satirical articles supposed to have been written in 1990 about what happened in various countries in the 1980s.

Work in groups.

■ Choose a country or area of the world and discuss what might happen there during the 1990s. You may choose either a satirical or a realistic approach.

■ Plan an article on the lines of your discussion that looks back from the year 2000.

■ Each member of the group takes responsibility for one aspect of the topic and writes one or two paragraphs about it. These are then put together to make a complete article.

■ Read the article aloud to the rest of the class.

For Sale: One country. Quaint. Needs work. Best offer.

This extraordinary advertisement appeared in the classified sections of most of the prominent First World newspapers one morning in early 1982. It presaged the greatest single land sale of the decade.

The buyer was an American leisure and entertainment conglomerate, and the seller was the United Kingdom itself. By a simple Act of Parliament that stipulated a payment of three million dollars to each Member in return for the Lords' and Commons' relinquishing all governmental power, the United Kingdom overnight became Walt Disney's United Magic Kingdom — a carefree, fun-for-the-whole-family amusement park; admission 50p, no passport required.

It was an instant park: the ready-made, fully operating insanity of 1982 Britain provided a wealth of amusements that needed no improving. Clean and tasty food was replaced by typical British cuisine; and lucky visitors could snack on roast beef sandwiches with a 65-to-1 bread-to-beef ratio or cold sausages that tasted like tubes of pork toothpaste. Sullen, soggy skies needed no special-effects wizardry. Everything from the phone system to the plumbing to BBC Radio exactly duplicated the hilarious eccentricities of yesteryear. And without the expense to Disney of a single penny.

From *The 80s—a look back*
Edited by Tony Hendra, Christopher Cert and Peter Elbling.

THE FUTURE

Written work: capital letters

■ Exercise 1

Read the text and notice how capital letters are used. Make a list of all the words with capital letters, and formulate a set of rules about their use, beginning with the rules given.

Capital letters are used for:
1 the first word in every sentence (e.g. *On*).
2 the personal pronoun I.

On April 1st I said to Mrs Smith, 'You know, I've just read a review in *The Times* of an interesting book called *Have a Good Trip*. It's all about going on holiday. Let's go to London at Easter. We can take the early morning train, the Inter-City Flyer, to Victoria Station, and go and stay with a friend of mine who lives in Park Lane. He's a Dane and married to a Spanish girl, but he speaks very good English. If he's not there, we can stay at a hotel— the Hilton's very good. We can take a sightseeing trip up the River Thames to Hampton Court Palace, and have a look at the paintings in the National Gallery, and perhaps spend a day at the Tower of London. Then we could come back home on Sunday evening.'

'Well, I'm not sure,' said Mrs Smith. 'If you'd suggested flying Concorde to the South Pacific, or Tibet, or the Rockies, or something exciting like that, I'd have agreed. Perhaps next year.'

■ Exercise 2

Rewrite the following story, putting in capital letters where necessary.

when i got to london, i decided to take a taxi to the grand hotel. it was the middle of december, and snow was falling heavily. the traffic was chaotic, and we finally came to a halt half-way up regent street. after a while, the driver turned round and said, 'do you like going to the cinema? the palace cinema is just over there—they're showing *groans and shouts* by the italian director verdini. i think sir lawrence olivier is in it.'

'well, yes, but i don't think . . .'

'look,' said the taxi-driver, 'it's rush hour on a friday afternoon in the middle of winter, and it's snowing. we'll be stuck here until christmas if we don't get out now.'

so we did. when we came out of the cinema two hours later the taxi was still where we had left it, and the traffic was just starting to get moving. 'now i'll take you to the hotel, sir,' said the taxi-driver. 'sorry it's taken longer than expected.'

APPENDIX

Pair work A

1a You are waiting alone at a bus stop when a friend comes up. You can see your bus coming in the distance.

1b You see an acquaintance in a café. Go and sit at the same table.

1c You're talking to a close friend when you realise you're almost late for an appointment.

1d You are standing alone at a party. You intend to leave very soon. A stranger approaches.

1e You are a married couple who have invited an old school friend of the husband to lunch. The wife has not met him/her before.

1f You are two people who arrive at a party at the same time. You have never met before. Your host, whom you both know, is standing at the door.

2a You are a passenger on a charter flight between London and Rome. Signal to one of the cabin staff to come over to you, and ask about two of the following, one from each list:

- You want to smoke.
- You want to change places.
- You want to have a look at the cockpit and talk to the pilot.
- You want to stand in the gangway and entertain the passengers.

- You are thirsty.
- You think a person nearby is making too much noise.
- You want the pilot to turn back, since you've left something important behind.
- There's someone nearby smoking evil-smelling cigars.

2b You are a security guard on duty at Heathrow Airport. Someone comes up to you.

3a 1 Here are the books I promised you.
2 Do you fancy going to the pictures?
3 Thank you very much.
4 Is there anything I can do?

3b You have just arrived at a rather formal party. Your host comes up to you.

3c You have just received a formal invitation to an acquaintance's wedding. You ring up to accept or decline.

3d A close friend is having his/her birthday. Give him/her a present.

3e You are a salesman entertaining a potential client at a restaurant. Offer him/her various dishes from the menu, drinks, bread, butter, etc.

3f A relative to whom you lent a lot of money a few months ago comes up to you.

3g You have just arrived at a new school and are feeling a bit lost, since you don't know anybody else, and you don't know where you are supposed to go. Someone comes up to talk to you.

3h You telephone to invite a friend to go out with you. Choose activities from this list: opera, cinema, the theatre, a boxing match, a discotheque, an Indian restaurant, a Chinese restaurant, a party, a fashion show, a day on the beach, a jazz concert.

Don't be satisfied until you have agreed to do two things together!

4a 1 Do you enjoy listening to music?
2 I'm for going to the cinema this evening.
3 Aren't the Beatles great?
4 Would you rather go to a play or a film?
5 Do you think it's a good idea to book the tickets in advance?

4b You find yourself sitting next to a stranger at a party. Introduce yourself and then get on to the subject of hobbies. Your interests are riding horses, collecting coins, the blues, and watching horror movies; you find everything else uninteresting. You could start by talking about the music at the party.

4c Someone with rather bizarre clothes and a strange hair-style comes up to you. You don't recognise him/her at first, but eventually you realise that it is your boss's wife/husband, so you must be polite.

4d You're at an art gallery with a friend, in a room with four paintings: you hate the first one, love the second one, find the third one dull, and think the fourth one is fairly attractive. Talk about your likes and preferences.

5a A colleague from work comes up to talk to you. Find out what has happened and respond accordingly.

5b Choose one of these situations. You are 17 years old, and go home looking miserable to tell your father/mother what has happened.
- Your boyfriend/girlfriend has left you.
- You failed your driving test.
- You've lost some money.
- You failed to get a job/pass an exam/win a 100 metres race/find a nice birthday present for your aunt.

5c You are a radio reporter interviewing some of the thousands of runners who have just completed a marathon race. Ask one of them how well he/she did and if he/she is satisfied with his/her performance; respond accordingly.

6a The following crimes were committed yesterday:
- 1 p.m.—Paris airport blown up
- 2 p.m.—nuclear-powered submarine stolen in Glasgow
- 3 p.m.—West German embassy occupied in Stockholm
- 4 p.m.—Prime Minister assassinated in London
- 5 p.m.—National Bank robbed in Geneva
- 6 p.m.—newspaper magnate kidnapped in Dublin

6b 1 Right. Who spilt the paint?
2 Sorry about making a fool of myself last night.
3 It was your fault.
4 I really must apologise for my child's behaviour.

6c You're driving fairly slowly when a child runs out into the road and you have to brake quickly. The car behind bumps into your car, causing slight damage, though you yourself are not hurt. You think the driver behind was either driving too fast or not concentrating. Go and talk to him/her.

6d Yesterday you telephoned a friend and arranged to meet at the Tower Restaurant at 8 p.m. He/She didn't arrive, and after waiting half an hour you went home. You see him/her in the street.

6e You are driving through a part of the country that you haven't been to before, on the way to an important meeting. A colleague is sitting next to you reading the map and giving you directions. Suddenly you realise that your colleague has no idea of where you are or how you are going to get to your destination. You are very annoyed, though if he/she apologises you will calm down and offer to help.

6f You are one of ten people chosen at random to take part in an identification parade—a witness to a crime is going to try to pick out the person seen committing it. Of course, you had nothing to do with the crime—you don't even know what is supposed to have happened.

7 Try to find out where the following places are: the theatre, the bank, the tobacconist's, the concert hall, the cinema, the swimming-pool, the grocer's, the newsagent's, the greengrocer's, the hairdresser's, the bus station, the Chinese restaurant, the supermarket, the Italian restaurant. Mark the ones that student B knows about with the same symbol that he/she has.

8 1 What do you feel about school uniforms?
2 Which party do you think will win the next election?
3 I think it would be best if everybody spoke the same language.
4 I'd be glad to hear your views on the tax system.

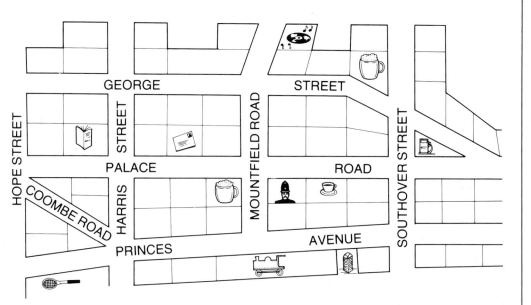

9a 1 What would you do in my place?
2 Let's go to the cinema.
3 Do you think I should tell him what I think?
4 If I were you, I wouldn't tell anyone about it.
5 I'd like to propose a meeting sometime next week.

9b Student B is an Employment Counsellor, whose job is to visit different places of work and offer help and advice to anyone who has any kind of personal problems. Imagine that you have *one* of these problems:
- You dislike one of your colleagues.
- You find the work boring.
- You find the work too difficult for you.
- You feel insecure and shy; you can't communicate with your colleagues.

Think for a few minutes about what your work involves and about the details of the problem you have chosen. Then ask the Employment Counsellor for advice.

9c You are a Family Guidance Counsellor. Anyone who has problems to do with the family (marriage, difficult children, finding somewhere to live, etc.) can come to you for free advice. See if you can help student B with his/her problem.

10 1 Is it all right if I leave my car here?
2 Pass the salt, will you, please.
3 I'm afraid you'll have to open it.
4 Taking photographs is not allowed.
5 Actually, you don't have to wait.

11a 1 Do that again, and I'll have to teach you some manners!
2 I'm fed up with your leaving things lying around.
3 It'd be most unwise to come any closer.
4 Please! Just this once!

11b You are staying at a hotel which you saw advertised as follows: 'Luxury hotel, quiet location, view of sea, shower and colour TV in every room, world famous cuisine and room service, indoor swimming-pool, bar, casino, ballroom.'

However, hardly anything in the advertisement is true. You paid in advance. Complain to the manager and try to get your money back.

11c You work at the Complaints Desk of a large department store. A customer comes up to you to make a complaint. He/she doesn't look very honest, so you try to avoid having to replace the article in question or refund the money paid for it.

12a 1 I've lost my pen.
2 I've never been to the cinema.
3 Joe's not well.
4 Pat wasn't seriously hurt.
5 There's a political debate on this evening.
6 We're going to get married.

12b 1 Yes, it's a shame, isn't it?
2 Yes, it was very exciting.
3 Yes, I was surprised, too.
4 Yes, that was close.

12c You and student B are old friends who are meeting for the first time in a couple of years. Talk about some of the things that have happened to you since you last met, and react with surprise, relief, disappointment, etc. to what student B tells you. Here are some suggestions for things you can talk about:
- You've got a new job/no job.
- A friend of yours was/wasn't injured seriously in an accident.
- You've had a book/filmscript/composition/article accepted for publication (or rejected).
- You or a friend of yours has just won/failed to win a prize.
- You've travelled quite a lot to some interesting places.
- You've met some old friends that you have in common—invent a few things that have happened to them.

13a 1 Are you with me?
2 I'm going to *brabble*. (*non-existent word*)
3 Sorry, I didn't quite catch that.
4 What does *crotian* mean? (*non-existent word*)

13b Imagine that you are the inventor of the device illustrated here. Describe its construction and function to student B. Let your imagination run wild, but help your listener by checking that he/she understands all the time, and by using the phrases you have practised to repeat things and say things in a different way.

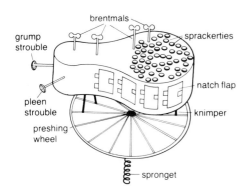

13c Student B will describe a device to you. Imagine that you are going to have to describe it to someone else later, so you must make sure that you understand everything, and can spell and pronounce all the technical terms used.

14a 1 Jane can't swim.
2 They travelled by bus.
3 You should help them.
4 I hardly ever go to the cinema.
5 Mary didn't bring a present.
14b 1 I don't see how it can fail.
2 I have no intention of making a fool of myself.
3 I'm thinking of going into politics.
4 I wasn't actually planning to visit them.
5 There's no way your plan'll work.

14c You are a candidate in the forthcoming parliamentary election. You are going to be interviewed by a journalist. Think of three or four things that you intend to do if elected. The journalist may ask you about other issues, but you should try to steer the discussion back to the topics you have prepared. If he accuses you of having changed your attitude to one of the issues, agree with him and give reasons for having done so.

14d You are interviewing a 16-year-old school-leaver about his/her plans and hopes for the future. Prepare some questions and then act out the interview.

15a 1 If only I'd listened to him.
2 I'm worried sick by the thought of the exam.
3 The lack of security gives some cause for concern.
4 There's no need to get upset.

15b Imagine that you are worried about your present situation at work. There are some things that you regret having done, for example:
- You were rude to your boss.
- You were away on holiday when something very important happened at work.
- You made a mistake which cost the firm a lot of money.

You also have certain fears for the future, for example:
- You might lose your job.
- You might not be promoted.
- You might have to pay for the mistake you made.

Talk to student B, who is one of your colleagues, about your troubles.

15c Your are on holiday abroad, and have just met student B, who is also on holiday. Respond with sympathy and reassurance when he/she talks about his/her problems.

Pair work B

1a You go up to a friend who is waiting at a bus stop.

1b You're sitting at a café. An acquaintance that you don't like very much sits down at the same table.

1c You are talking to a close friend.

1d At a party you see someone you don't know standing alone. Go and talk to him/her.

1e You have been invited to lunch by an old school friend, whose wife you haven't met before. Unfortunately, you must leave almost immediately since you have a plane to catch.

1f You are giving a party. Two guests arrive, and you are not sure if they know each other.

2a You are working as one of the cabin staff on a charter flight between London and Rome. One of the passengers signals to you.

2b You have just arrived at Heathrow Airport from abroad. You see a security guard and ask him about one of these items:

- You want to leave your luggage for a short while.
- You've lost your four-year-old daughter.
- A drunk has been annoying you and other travellers.
- You want to know the time.
- You want a light for your cigarette.
- You want to spend the night in the arrival hall, since you have no means of getting to your final destination today.

3a 1 Don't mention it.
2 I won't, if it's all the same to you.
3 It's very good of you to offer, but I think I can manage.
4 Many thanks.

3b You are the host at a rather formal party. You go up to a guest who has just arrived, greet him/her, and offer something to eat or drink.

3c You are getting married. An acquaintance to whom you have sent an invitation rings you up.

3d It is your birthday. A close friend comes up with a present.

3e You are a business man being entertained at a restaurant by a sales representative from another firm. Respond to what he/she says, but do not volunteer any conversation.

3f You have borrowed some money from a relative. Give it back to him/her.

3g You see a new student obviously feeling rather lost at your school, which you have been attending for some time. Offer to help.

3h A friend telephones to invite you out. You enjoy the following: watching films, going to the theatre, eating Indian food, parties and jazz, but you are not keen on opera, boxing, discotheques, Chinese food, sunbathing or fashion shows.

4a 1 No, I don't think it's necessary.
    2 Well, actually, I can't stand them.
    3 Yes, I love it.
    4 Me too.
    5 Why don't you choose?

4b At a party, you find yourself sitting next to a stranger who starts talking to you. Let him/her direct the conversation, and express your own real opinions and preferences on the subjects brought up.

4c You're just had your hair done at the most fashionable hairdresser's in town, and you're wearing some new exciting clothes that you've just bought. You see someone who you think is an employee of your husband/wife. Go and find out his/her opinion of your appearance.

4d You're at an art gallery with a friend, in a room with four paintings: you find the first one quite interesting, the second one dull and lifeless, you hate the third one, and you like the fourth one very much. Talk about your likes and preferences.

5a Choose one of these situations. Then tell one of your colleagues at work what has happened.

- You are going to be promoted/lose your job/get married/get divorced.
- You have won the football pools/lost a lot of money playing roulette.
- Your house was burgled last night.
- You scored three goals in an important football match yesterday.

5b Your 17-year-old son/daughter comes home looking miserable. Find out what the matter is and respond accordingly.

5c Together with thousands of other runners, you have just completed a marathon race when a radio reporter comes up to you. Invent a result for yourself and decide whether or not you are satisfied with it. Then act out the interview.

6a The four suspects were seen at the following times and places:
The Rat—Stockholm at 2.50 p.m. and Dublin at 6.15 p.m.
The Mole—Glasgow at 1 p.m. and Stockholm at 3.40 p.m.
The Viper—Paris at 2 p.m. and Geneva at 4.15 p.m.
The Spider—Glasgow at 1.45 p.m. and London at 4.30 p.m.

6b 1 You're joking! I had nothing to do with it.
    2 There's no need.
    3 Forget it.
    4 I did, but I didn't mean to.

6c You're driving along the road when the car in front brakes very sharply and you have no time to avoid a collision. There is some slight damage to both cars, but you are not hurt. You realise that you are responsible for the accident in legal terms, but you think that the accident wouldn't have occurred if the other driver had been concentrating more.

6d Yesterday a friend telephoned and arranged to meet you at the Town Restaurant at 8 p.m. You waited for twenty minutes, but when he/she didn't turn up, you went home. You see him/her in the street.

6e A colleague of yours is driving you to a very important meeting. You are travelling through a part of the country that neither of you knows, and so you have promised to read the map and give directions. Unfortunately you realize that you are lost, and have no idea how to get to your destination. You think the map which the driver has given you must be out of date, and things have been made more difficult by the fact that he/she has been driving so fast.

6f You were a witness to a recent bank robbery, and have been asked by the police to pick out the person you saw from a group of ten people who have been chosen at random. Student A is one of them, and you are fairly certain that he/she is the robber.

7 Try to find out where the following places are: The Rose and Crown pub, a café, the library, a record shop, the chemist's, the Town Hall, the police station, a public telephone, a garage, a discothèque, the railway station, public tennis courts, the post office, the castle. Mark the ones that student A knows about with the same symbol that he/she has.

8 1 Your guess is as good as mine.
2 Well, to be quite frank, I consider it to be quite unjust.
3 It seems to me that they're completely unnecessary.
4 I see your point, but wouldn't we lose a lot too?

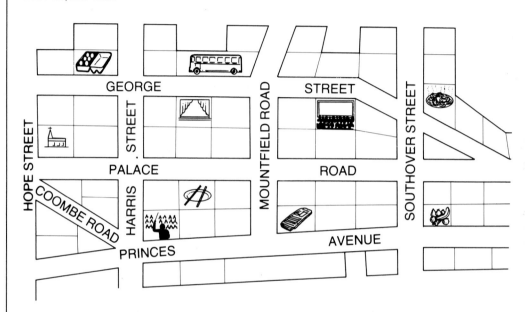

9a 1 I'd love to.
    2 When I want your advice, I'll ask
       for it.
    3 Would Tuesday morning be
       convenient?
    4 Look for a new job, I think.
    5 No, you'd better not annoy him.

9b You are an Employment
Counsellor. It is your job to visit
different places of work and offer help
and advice to anyone who has any
kind of personal problems. See if you
can help student A with his/her
problem.

9c Student A is a Family Guidance
Counsellor, whose job is to provide free
advice to anyone with problems to do
with the family. Imagine that you have
one of these problems:

- you are 18 years old, and think your
  parents are too restrictive.
- you are a parent with a very difficult
  18-year-old child.
- you think your spouse spends too
  much spare time outside the home,
  at clubs and social activities that
  don't involve the rest of the family.
- your boyfriend/girlfriend is married
  to someone else, and refuses to get a
  divorce.

Think for a few minutes about the
details of the problem you have
chosen. Then ask the Counsellor for
advice.

---

10 1 Oh, I'm sorry. I didn't know.
    2 Oh, good. That'll save a bit of
       time.
    3 I don't think you should,
       actually.
    4 Do I really have to?
    5 Certainly. There you are.

11a 1 For the last time, no!
    2 I'm sorry. I'll try to be tidier in
       the future.
    3 Just you try!
    4 Oh yes? What are you going to
       do about it?

11b You have just become the manager
of a hotel. One of the guests comes up
to complain. You don't know very
much about the hotel yet, but try to
find answers to the guest's complaints
and apologise if you think it necessary.

11c You recently bought something
very expensive (e.g. a computer, or a
washing machine) from a department
store. Think of four or five things that
have gone wrong with it, and then try
to persuade the assistant at the
Complaints Desk to refund your
money.

12a 1 That's marvellous.
    2 That sort of thing leaves me
       cold.
    3 What a nuisance!
    4 What a relief!
    5 What a shame!
    6 You must be joking!

12b 1 Wow!   2 Oh dear!
    3 Phew!   4 Fancy that!

12c You and student A are old friends
who are meeting for the first time in a
couple of years. Talk about some of the
things that have happened to you since
you last met, and react with surprise,
relief, disappointment, etc. to what
student A tells you. Here are some
suggestions for things you can talk
about:

- You, or a friend of yours, are going
  to write a play/book/filmscript/
  composition.
- You, or someone you know, were
  found guilty, or not guilty, of a
  driving offence.
- You lost your job, but managed to
  find another one.
- You, or a friend of yours, got
  married/engaged/divorced.
- You have taken up an unusual
  hobby.
- You were very ill for a time, but are
  better now.

13a 1 I don't know. You'll have to look it up.
2 Sorry, what was the last word?
3 Yes, it's a terrible line, isn't it?
4 Yes, that's quite clear.

13b Student A has invented a device, and is going to describe it to you. Imagine that you are going to give a talk about the device later; you must make sure that you understand everything about it, and can pronounce and spell all the technical terms.

13c Imagine that you are the inventor of the device illustrated here. Describe its construction and function to student A, giving help by checking all the time that he/she has understood and by using the phrases you have practised to repeat things and say things in a different way. Use your imagination!

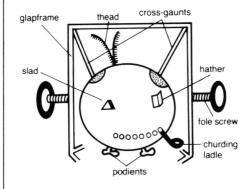

14a 1 I don't like doing this.
2 The Smiths won't approve.
3 We're going to New York.
4 I'd love to go to the party.
5 Paul never wears a tie.

14b 1 But you will reconsider, won't you?
2 How can you be so confident?
3 I'm afraid you already have.
4 Of course it will. It can't go wrong.
5 What on earth for?

14c You are a journalist, and are going to interview a candidate for the forthcoming parliamentary election. Prepare some questions:
- about his intentions if elected; for one of his answers you could accuse him of having changed his attitude since the last time you interviewed him.
- about his hopes for the future.
- to find out what he is optimistic and pessimistic about.

Then act out the interview.

14d You are a 16-year-old school-leaver, and are going to be interviewed about your plans and hopes for the future. Prepare what you are going to talk about, and then act out the interview.

15a 1 I assure you, you need have no fears about that.
2 It's not your fault—you couldn't have known what would happen.
3 That's easy for *you* to say.
4 There, there! You'll be all right.

15b Student A is one of your colleagues at work. Respond with sympathy and reassurance when he/she comes to tell you about his/her worries.

15c You are on holiday abroad, and have just met student A, who is also on holiday. Tell him/her about your fears:
- You forgot to lock the door to your flat or house, and none of your possessions at home is insured—you have one or two antiques.
- You forgot to ask your neighbour to water your plants and feed your cat.
- You didn't tell your boss that you were going on holiday.
- You have bought something that you don't think the customs will let you take back home.

Role card—student 1

1 Your name is A. Renton. Your interests are painting, the theatre and running. You know B. Winfield and M. Spencer very well. You have met J. Waller and A. Gardener briefly on a previous occasion.

6a The man on the top floor was Polish.
6c You are spying for the Germans.
Passwords: batch price tank
Code letters: C G I I L N T

7a A pair of deer dared to peer.

ROLE CARD 1

10

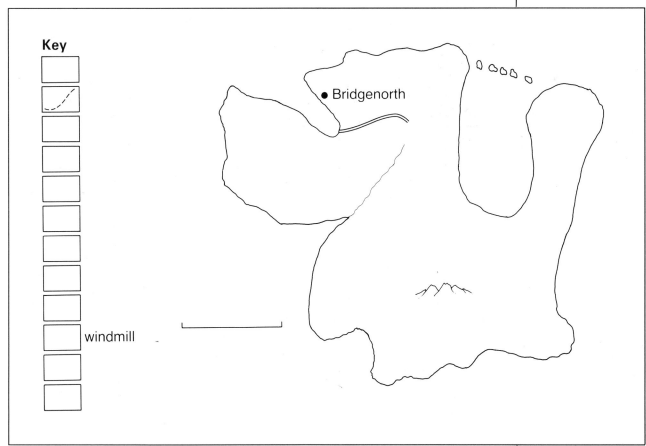

Key

windmill

● Bridgenorth

11 Your words: ■ assets
  ■ insurance
Your definitions:

Costs that arise while you are doing a job.
Money that a person gets, e.g. salary.

Role card—student 2

7b

1 Your name is R. Gibson. Your interests are football, running and sailing. You know D. Odling and J. Waller very well. You have met A. Watson and M. Spencer briefly on a previous occasion.

6b The American was 41 years old.
6c You are spying for the Italians.
Passwords: blues   thank   year
Code letters: C D E N R

7a June chose cold soup.

10

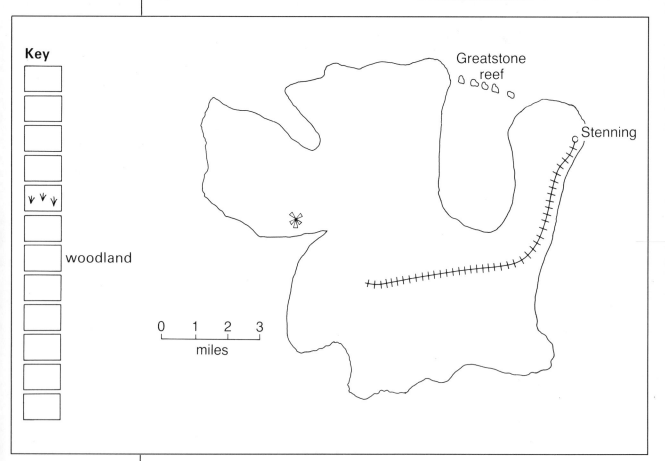

Key

woodland

0   1   2   3
miles

Greatstone
reef

Stenning

11 Your words: ■ interest
■ bargain
Your definitions:
One of the equal portions into which the capital of a company is divided, giving its owner the right to a part of the profits.
Tax that must be paid on certain imports, exports and exchanges of property.

Role card—student 3

1 Your name is M. Powell. Your interests are theatre, football and photography. You know A. Gardener and A. Watson very well. You have met B. Winfield and D. Odling briefly on a previous occasion.

6a Max, 53, was being blackmailed by Mrs Cooper.
6c You are spying for the French.
Passwords: bash bird prize
Code letters: A I N S P

7a Please, policeman, seize his niece.

ROLE CARD 3

10

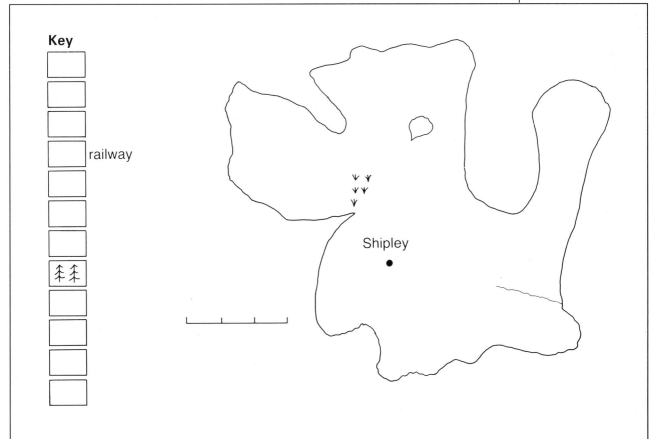

Key

railway

Shipley

11 Your words: ■ budget
■ investment
Your definitions:
Money paid e.g. for membership of a club, or for receiving a magazine or newspaper.
A sum deducted from the normal price.

Role card—student 4

7b

1 Your name is M. Spencer. Your interests are bird-watching, photography and sailing. You know C. Lavender and A. Renton very well. You have met R. Gibson and S. Franks briefly on a previous occasion.

6b The Russian was holding a piece of rope.
6c You are spying for the Americans.
Passwords: cheer praise sank
Code letters: E E T T

7a I fear their beards and hair are very fair.

10

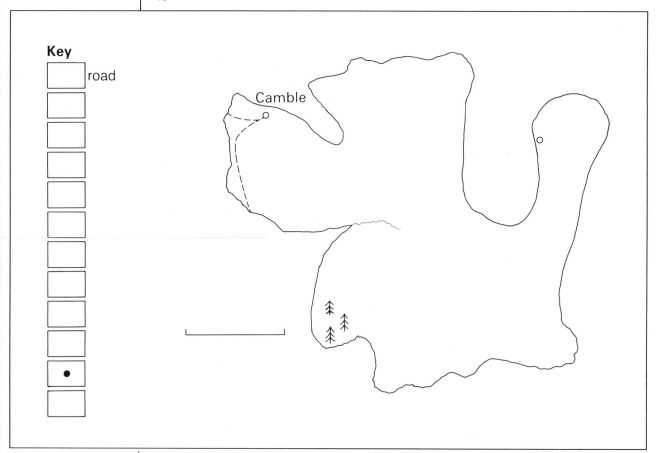

Key

☐ road
☐
☐
☐
☐
☐
☐
☐
☐
⊡
☐

Camble

11 Your words: ▪ profit
▪ credit card
Your definitions:
Money paid regularly for the use of e.g. a house or a flat.
What you own, including house, car, furniture, money, etc.

Role card—student 5

1 Your name is J. Taylor. Your interests are gardening, the cinema and bird-watching. You know A. Watson and D. Odling very well. You have met A. Gardener and J. Waller briefly on a previous occasion.

6a Tom was on the second floor.
6c You are working for the British.
Passwords: badge   beard   blouse
Code letters: E E G L T U

7a The rude fool stole a stool.

10

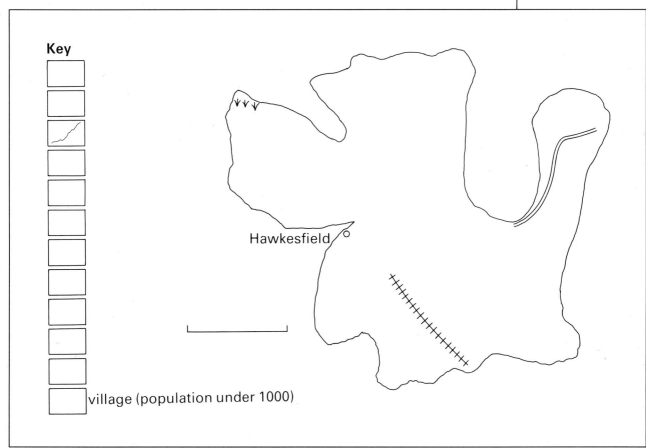

Key

village (population under 1000)

Hawkesfield

11 Your words: ■ debt
■ fee
Your definitions:
The provision of financial protection against certain events, such as illness, theft.
Additional payment beyond what is due or expected.

Role card—student 6

7b

1 Your name is B. Winfield. Your interests are the cinema, cooking and football. You know A. Renton and S. Franks very well. You have met C. Lavender and M. Powell briefly on a previous occasion.

6b The 22-year-old, who was jealous of Mrs Cooper, and the man holding a bottle of poison were on adjoining floors.

6c You are working for the French.
Passwords: bash   bird   prize
Code letters: E E G O

7a While the vine is fine, the wine is vile.

10

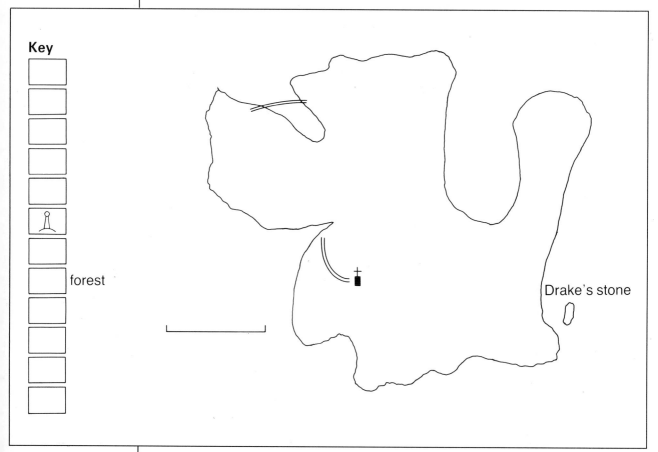

Key

forest

Drake's stone

11 Your words: ■ discount
■ overdraft
Your definitions:
A method used frequently to finance the buying of a house: the owner borrows money in exchange for temporarily transferring ownership to the lender.
An article or service bought for less than the normal price.

Role card—student 7

1 Your name is A. Watson. Your interests are running, gymnastics and cooking. You know M. Powell and J. Taylor very well. You have met S. Franks and R. Gibson briefly on a previous occasion.

6a The 28-year-old and the Pole were on adjoining floors.
6c You are working for the Russians.
Passwords: Bert   blows   jeer
Code letters: B E J N S

7a Fred thought he fought three thin Finns.

10

7b

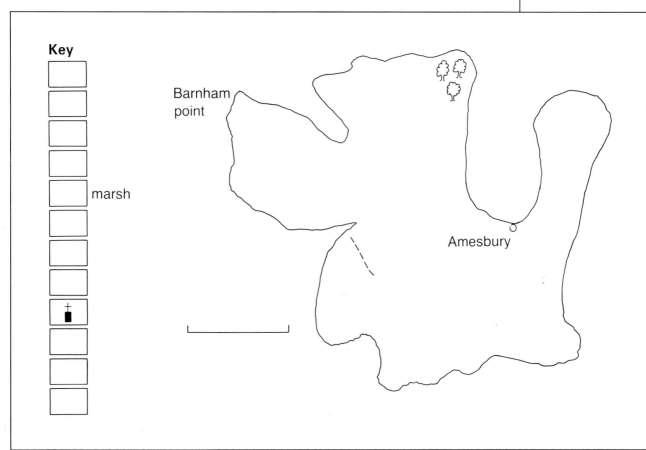

Key

marsh

Barnham point

Amesbury

11 Your words: ■ rebate
■ duty
Your definitions:
A sum of money placed so as to increase its value.
Advantages other than money gained from the job you do.

Role card—student 8

1 Your name is J. Waller. Your interests are gymnastics, the cinema and the theatre. You know R. Gibson and C. Lavender very well. You have met J. Taylor and A. Renton briefly on a previous occasion.

6b The Indian had political reasons for wanting to kill Mrs Cooper.
6c You are working for the Germans.
Passwords: batch   price   tank
Code letters: E E E L N

7a I wish the witch would share her chair.

10

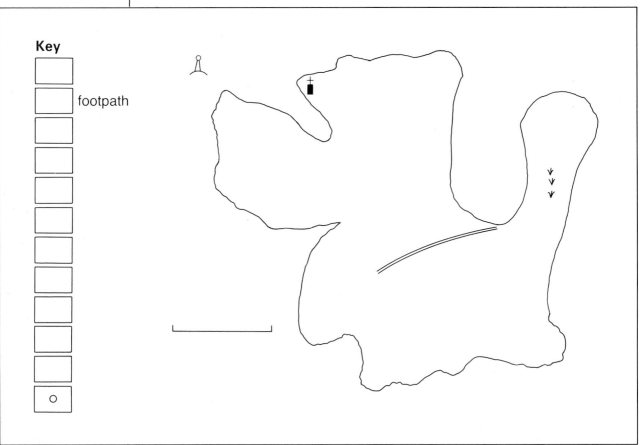

Key

footpath

11 Your words: ■ rent
■ expenses
Your definitions:
Money paid for professional services, e.g. doctor, lawyer, private school.
An estimate of spending and income over a period of time, e.g. a year.

Role card—student 9

1 Your name is D. Odling. Your interests are local history, painting and photography. You know J. Taylor and R. Gibson very well. You have met M. Powell and C. Lavender briefly on a previous occasion.

6a Jo, who was 76, could hear the 53-year-old in the flat above.
6c You are working for the Italians.
Passwords: blues   thank   year
Code letters: E O R U V

7a He hates heights, but he won't fight fate.

10

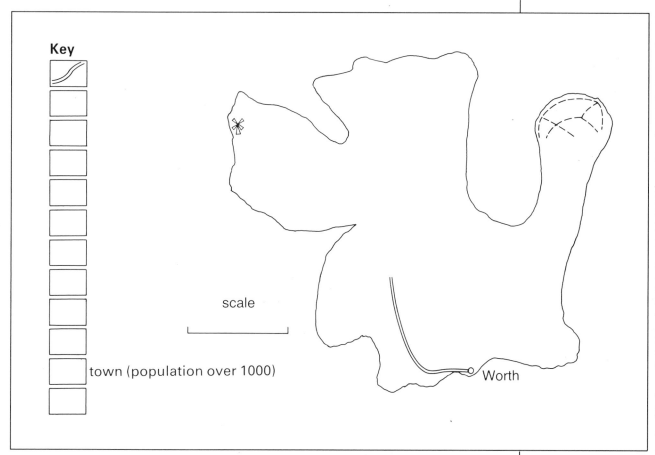

Key

town (population over 1000)

scale

Worth

11 Your words: ■ bonus
■ share
Your definitions:
The amount of money you owe to the bank if you take out more than you have put in.
Rise in the level of prices or fall in the real value of money.

Role card—student 10

7b

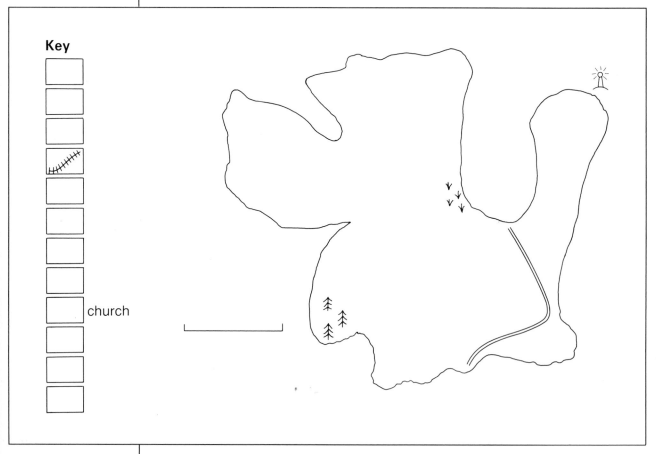

1 Your name is A. Gardener. Your interests are gardening, painting and sailing. You know S. Franks and M. Powell very well. You have met A. Renton and J. Taylor briefly on a previous occasion.

6b The man with a hammer in his pocket was going to inherit Mrs Cooper's fortune.

6c You are working for the Russians.
Passwords: Bert   blows   jeer
Code letters: A D M O

7a The fool pulled the bull from the full pool.

10

Key

church

11 Your words: ■ fringe benefits
■ stock exchange
Your definitions:

Repayment of part of a sum paid.
Money owed to another person or company.

Role card—student 11

1 Your name is C. Lavender. Your interests are local history, cooking and gardening. You know J. Waller and M. Spencer very well. You have met D. Odling and B. Winfield briefly on a previous occasion.

6a The Argentinian's name was Fred.
6c You are working for the Americans.
Passwords: cheer   praise   sank
Code letters: C O P R S

7a Who knows the news about Howard's new nose?

10

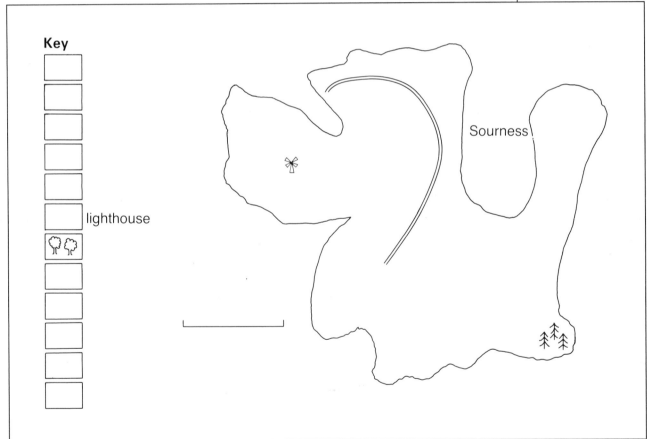

Key

lighthouse

Sourness

11 Your words: ■ income
　　　　　　　　■ subscription
Your definitions:
The sum charged for the use of borrowed money or the sum paid for the use of money invested.
A card or token that allows you to buy things at certain places without producing any money—normally you pay at a later date.

Role card—student 12

7b

1 Your name is S. Franks. Your interests are local history, gymnastics, and bird-watching. You know B. Winfield and A. Gardener very well. You have met M. Spencer and A. Watson briefly on a previous occasion.

6b The man with the pistol and the man whose motive was revenge were on adjoining floors.
6c You are working for the British.
Passwords: badge   beard   blouse
Code letters: A B D N O

7a Is this thick sack the thing that Smith sent?

10

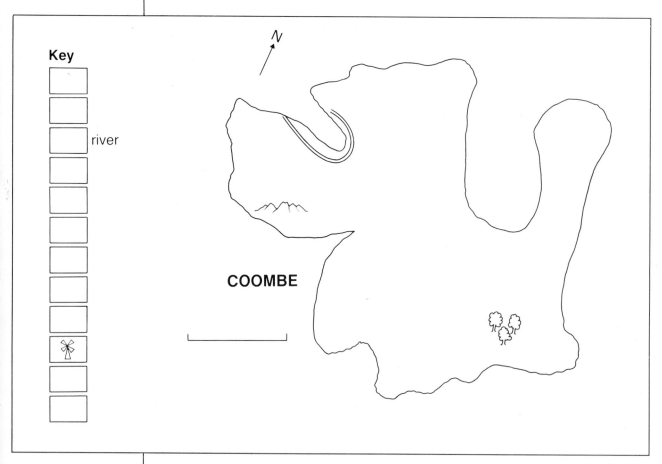

Key

river

COOMBE

11 Your words: ■ inflation
■ mortgage

Your definitions:
The place where shares in companies are bought and sold.
Financial gain.

Listening comprehension tapescript

UNIT **1**

HOMES

Doorbell rings.

Peter Hello, John. Nice to see you. Come in. How are you?

John Fine, thanks, Peter. And how are you? I expect your patients are keeping you busy at this time of year?

Peter Ah, well. I can't really complain. Let me take your coat. There we are. Well, now. I don't think you've met Ann Patterson, have you? Ann, this is John Middleton. He's the local schoolteacher.

Ann Oh! How do you do?

John How do you do?

Ann Well, that's very interesting. Perhaps you'll be looking after my son.

Peter Yes, that's right. Ann and her family have just moved into the old barn, up by the village hall. They're in the process of doing it up now.

Ann Yes, there's an awful lot needs doing, of course.

Doorbell rings.

Peter Er, please excuse me for a moment. I think that was the doorbell.

John Well, if I can give you a hand with anything ... I'm something of a handyman in my spare time, you know. I live just over the road.

Ann That's very kind of you. I'm an architect myself, so ... Oh, look! There's someone I know. Eileen!

Eileen Ann, fancy seeing you here! How's life?

Ann Oh, mustn't grumble. Moving's never much fun though, is it? Anyway, how are things with you? You're still at the same estate agent's, I suppose?

Eileen Oh yes, I can't see myself leaving, well, not in the foreseeable future.

Ann Oh, I quite forgot. Do you two know each other?

John Yes, actually, we've met on many an occasion. Hello, Eileen. You see, we play in the same orchestra.

Ann Oh, really? I didn't know anything about that.

Eileen Yes, actually, just amateur stuff, you know—once a week—I come down from London when I can get a baby-sitter for Joanna.

Paul Er ... excuse me, I hope you don't mind my butting in. My name's Paul Madison. I couldn't help overhearing what you said about an orchestra.

John Come and join the party. I'm John Middleton. This is Ann Patterson and Eileen ... er ... I'm terribly sorry, I don't think I know your surname?

Eileen Hawkes. Pleased to meet you, Paul. You play an instrument, do you?

Paul Yes, I'm over here on a scholarship to study the bassoon (*loud yawn from Ann*) at the Royal Academy of Music for a couple of years ...

Ann Oh, I *am* sorry. It must be all that hard work on the barn ...

Paul Well, anyway ...

UNIT **2**

TRAVEL

Travel agent Good morning. Can I help you?

Dad Yes. Good morning. We saw your ad about cheap package trips ...

Travel agent Yes, of course. Well, ... these are the ones that are left. How many of you . . . er . . . ?

Dad Just the four. My wife and I, and the two children.

Child Mum, can I sit over there and read my comic?

Mum No, you can't. You want to help us choose, don't you?

Travel agent We've just got . . . four family trips left. Er . . . ranging from £660 for this camping holiday on the French Riviera to . . . £1,499 for a week in Corfu—that's a first-class hotel with swimming-pool, night club, you know, everything included. So, you know, . . . something to suit all tastes and . . . pockets.

Child Dad, is it OK if I . . . ?

Dad No, it isn't. Well, I must say, that last one certainly doesn't suit my pocket. Do you think you could . . . tell us what you get for those prices?

Travel agent Certainly. Well, of course, there's the flight, and transport to and from the airport . . . Accommodation, of course. Otherwise, well, it varies a bit. In Copenhagen all your meals are included, you know, because it's a guest house, and . . . er . . . this chalet in Sardinia, for example, is basically self-catering, but there are certain activities like parties and . . . excursions, and . . . er . . . they're included in the price.

Dad That last one sounds very interesting.

Mum What d'you mean 'interesting'? Who's going to do all the cooking and cleaning? I must say, I rather like the sound of the guest house.

Child Mum, . . .

Mum No!

Travel agent Well, actually, madam, there are extra catering facilities provided for all our self-catering holidays, should you need them.

Child Dad, . . .

Dad Look, do us all a favour and go and sit over there and read your comic, will you?

Travel agent These are all-inclusive family budget prices—I assure you they represent a substantial reduction on our normal prices. Er . . . down here you can see your dates for departure

and return—18th to 25th of July on all trips except . . . Copenhagen, which is two days earlier, and, by the way, extremely good value for money—£300 off the normal price at . . . £899.

Mum Oh, really? You know, I've heard Copenhagen is such a beautiful city . . .

Dad Well, . . . I don't know. This camping one's obviously out—I mean, it says here that they've got a casino and cinema and all that, but it sounds too much like hard work for me. But what about Sardinia? You know, £975 isn't *too* expensive . . .

Mum Mmm . . . probably nicer for the kids, too—you know, warmer, and beaches and all that. Yes, let's take it.

Travel agent You won't regret it, madam, I can assure you. Now, I wonder if you'd mind just giving me a few particulars . . .

Mum Jimmy, what are you doing over there? I told you not to read your comic. Come and have a look at the place we're going to.

UNIT **3**

HEALTH AND FITNESS

In a department store.

Salesman Come along now, ladies. Oh, and gentlemen too . . . sorry, sir, didn't see you there at first . . . have to keep your wits about you in these days of equality, don't you? . . . Well now. Come on now, dears, a bit closer. I'm not going to eat you. That's better. Now, I'm not going to take up too much of your time, ladies (and gentlemen) . . . but I would just like to take this opportunity of demonstrating to you this marvellous little timesaver from Phillips Foods, the leading manufacturer of household appliances. We call it the Fruit Case Mark 1. Now I wonder, madam, if you'd care to come up here and take a piece of fruit, any fruit, from the basket there . . . let me give you a hand . . . there we are, that's right . . . a banana? Good . . . and put it in the cup here, please . . . thank you very much . . . and stand back, please, so everyone can see.

Thank you. Now, you'll see a little green light has come on here; that shows that the machine has found out absolutely everything there is to know about that banana—its weight, its width and length, the thickness of the skin, you name it. Now, we just put this lid over the cup and press this little button here and ... hey presto! What do you find inside the cup? The finest quality mashed banana! Incredible, isn't it? Would you like a spoonful, madam? There you are.

Woman Thank you ... Mmm ... delicious. Thank you very much.

Salesman Don't mention it. But what about the skin, you might ask? Well, if we just slide this tray out here ... there we are ... finely chopped banana skin! It's hard to believe, isn't it? And all done by lasers, so there are no moving parts to worry about, no maintenance worries, none of that awful noise that so many kitchen appliances drive you mad with. How does it work? Well, inside here there's a microprocessor that can recognise and analyse the 256 most common types of fruits and vegetables. You can set it to chop, grate, slice, or press. It's programmable, too, so that you can do all your household budgeting, finances, and so on, *and* it can be adapted very easily to connect up with your TV set to play a whole range of exciting games. Guaranteed for six months. Light as a feather. Fit in your handbag. Now, I expect you're thinking that all this must cost the earth. But! Well, you're not going to believe this, but the normal list price is an amazing £299; and just this week, as a special introductory offer, we are giving them away at the ridiculous price of £199, plus—to the first hundred purchasers—the chance of winning an all-expenses paid holiday for two in the Bahamas. Beat that if you can. Well now, let's see what happens with an apple or an orange. Sir, would you like to have a go? That trip to the Bahamas could be yours.

Man No, thank you. That's very kind of you, but I'm in a bit of a hurry.

Salesman Anyone else like to try it out?

UNIT **4**

THEATRE

Policeman What is the meaning of this?

Percival But ... but ...

Housekeeper Captain Percival, I find your behaviour quite unacceptable. You are a scoundrel. Pack your bags and go.

Gasps from the audience, followed by resounding applause.

*　　*　　*

Man Ah well. Would you rather stay here or ... go out and stretch your legs?

Woman I'd prefer to stay here—we can get some coffee in the next interval. Anyway, what do you think? Not as good as *Bats*, is it?

Man Goodness, no. Muller's—

Woman —awful? I can't stand the man. You know, there's nothing I like less than an actor who—

Man —can't act. Yes, I know. I mean, have you ever seen a policeman who looked less like a policeman? He's 38, you know—funny age to take up acting.

Woman Yes. Give me John Hodsworth anytime. I mean, he may be 70-odd, or whatever he is, but you really can't beat him when it comes to, er—

Man —acting. Yes. But don't exaggerate. The programme says he's only 67. I agree with you, though. He does make a splendid Captain Percival, doesn't he?

Woman Remember him in *The Diplomat*?

Man I think I missed that one, actually. But I saw him in *Three's Company*, as ...

Woman ... the aging tycoon. Yes, I remember ... Er ... What about the housekeeper, eh?

Man Julia Donaldson? Funny, isn't it? She always seems to be a housekeeper. I saw her play a housekeeper in—

Woman —*The Revolving Staircase.*
Yes, I did too. A bit—
Man —disappointing, wasn't she? I
mean, not *bad*, but, well, I suppose
she's getting a bit past it.
Woman Rubbish! She's in her mid-
forties. The prime of life ... When I
was in *Molotov and the Spare Part*, I
was only 45, you know, ...
(*Bell rings.*)
Man Ah, those were the days. Well, at
least Act II can't be any worse.

UNIT 5
GAMES

Commentator It's Carter to serve—
he needs just one more point. He
serves, AND SMITH MISSES! WHAT
A GREAT SERVE! ... So the
championship goes to 19-year-old Harry
Carter. Who'd've believed it a week
ago? Poor old Smith just shakes his
head in bewilderment. Well, well! What
a way to finish it off! ... And now I'll
hand you over to Peter Plumber, who's
on court waiting to interview the two
finalists.
Plumber Thank you, David. Well,
Harry, congratulations on a
marvellous victory. You were on
tremendous form.
Carter Thank you, Peter. Nice of you
to say so. You know, well, I think I
won because, well, I just knew all
along I was in with a good chance.
Plumber Yes, you certainly were
pretty convincing today, but what
about the earlier rounds? Any nervous
moments?
Carter Well, you know, I *was* a bit
nervous against Jones when he took
the lead in the second set, but then ...
er ...
Plumber Yes, that was in the quarter-
finals, wasn't it? And of course you met
Gardener in the next round, didn't
you? Er ... the score was ... er ...
6-4, 7-5, wasn't it?
Carter Yes, that was quite a tough
match, I suppose, but ... er ...
Plumber Anything else you'd like to
add?
Carter Well, I *would* like to say how

sorry I am for John Fairlight not
making it past the quarter-finals. He's
unbeatable, you know, on his day, and
... er ... I'd also like to say what a
terrific job the officials here have done,
you know, the ballboys and linesmen
and umpires and so on. You know ...
er ... lots of players have been
complaining, but ... er ...
Plumber Well, that's great, Harry.
Well done again. And now let's have a
quick word with the runner-up to the
title, Mark Smith. If you just stand
over here, Mark ... that's right ...
Well, bad luck, Mark. It wasn't really
your day, was it? I mean, what a
terrible final set! Anyway, the less said
about that the better, as I'm sure you'll
agree.
Smith Yeah, but you know, I did
pretty well to beat Hutchins in the
semis and ... er ... what's his name?
... Brown in the quarter-finals. And, I
mean, what a terrible umpire, eh? I
mean, half of Carter's points were on
... er ... doubtful decisions, weren't
they?
Plumber Well, that's probably a bit of
an exaggeration, but anyway, it's time
for us to leave the tournament now at
the end of a tremendously exciting
week, and I hand you back to the
studio in London.

UNIT 6

CRIME

Doorbell rings. Door opens.
Boss At long last! Why did it take you
so long?
1st villain Er ... I really am sorry
about this, boss ...
Boss Come on! What happened?
Where's the money?
1st villain Well, it's a long story. We
parked outside the bank OK, on South
Street, and I went in and got the
money—you know, no problems, they
just filled the bag like you said they
would. I went outside, jumped into the
car, and off we went.
Boss Yes, yes, yes. And then?
2nd villain We turned right up Forest
Road, and of course the traffic lights at

the High Street crossroads were against us. And when they went green the stupid car stalled, didn't it. I mean, it was dead—

1st villain —so I had to get out and push, all the way to the garage opposite the school. I don't know why Jim here couldn't fix it. I mean, the car was your responsibility, wasn't it?

2nd villain Yeah, but it was you that stole it, wasn't it? Why didn't you get a better one?

1st villain OK, it was my fault. I'm sorry.

2nd villain The mechanic said it would take at least two days to fix it— so we just had to leave it there and walk.

1st villain Well, we crossed over Church Lane, and you'll never believe what happened next, just outside the Police Station, too.

2nd villain Look, it wasn't *my* fault. You were responsible for providing the bag—I couldn't help it if the catch broke.

1st villain It took us five minutes to pick up all the notes again.

Boss Fine, fine, fine. But where *is* the money?

2nd villain We're getting there, boss. Anyway, we ran to where the second car was parked, outside the library in Ox Lane—you know, we were going to switch cars there,—and then—you know, this is just unbelievable—

1st villain —yeah. We drove up Church Lane, but they were digging up the road just by the church, so we had to take the left fork and go all the way round the north side of the park. And then, just before the London Road roundabout—

2nd villain —some idiot must have driven out from the railway station without looking, right into the side of a lorry. The road was completely blocked. There was nothing for it but to abandon the car and walk the rest of the way.

Boss All right, it's a very fascinating story. But I still want to have a look at the money.

1st villain Well, that's the thing, boss,

I mean. I'm terribly sorry, but this idiot must have left it somewhere.

2nd villain Who are you calling an idiot? I had nothing to do with it. *You* were carrying the bag.

1st villain No, I wasn't. I gave it to you . . .

UNIT **7**
THE SENSES

Interviewer Mr Davies, thank you for coming along. I'd like to ask you some questions about the phenomenon you observed last night.

Mr Davies Sure. Well, it probably sounds a bit odd, but it looked like a big white banana, with small red lights on. It flew across the sky at a tremendous speed, completely, er, soundless.

Interviewer What time was this?

Mr Davies About two in the morning, so it was pitch black. I think it must have been about a couple of hundred feet above the ground, and I should say it was about twenty feet long and three or four feet across. It seemed to have a dull, metallic surface.

Interviewer Do you have an explanation, Mr Davies? What do you think it was?

Mr Davies Haven't a clue. I've never seen anything like it before.

Interviewer Well, thank you very much, Mr Davies. Mrs Evans, then. I wonder if you could tell me exactly what happened last night.

Mrs Evans Well, I was woken up by a sort of low murmuring noise. I thought it must be the fridge at first, but then I realised it was coming from outside. When I looked out, I saw this huge spherical thing in mid-air.

Interviewer I'm sorry—what sort of thing did you say it was?

Mrs Evans Oh, er, spherical.

Interviewer Can you tell me exactly how large it was?

Mrs Evans Er, it's hard to say, you know, since I don't know how far away it was—but it was, er, really big—I suppose, maybe, twice as big as my house.

Interviewer And did it move at all?

Mrs Evans No, it just sort of hung there, and then suddenly vanished.

Interviewer Are you sure it wasn't a cloud or something like that?

Mrs Evans Oh, I'm absolutely certain. It was a golden red colour, smooth and shiny like glass.

Interviewer Thank you, Mrs Evans. And what about you, Patrick? Can you tell me what you saw last night, please?

Patrick Yeah, it was a cigar-shaped sort of thing that sort of danced about in the sky, you know, up and down, backwards and forwards, sort of not knowing where it was going.

Interviewer Did it make a noise of any kind?

Patrick Yeah, it sort of whistled, like the wind, you know, a sort of whining noise.

Interviewer What about its colour?

Patrick Oh, all sorts of colours, changing all the time, with lights flashing all over the place.

Interviewer Can you say how big it was, or what it seemed to be made of?

Patrick I can't say for sure, because the flashing lights sort of made it hard to see exactly. It seemed to get bigger and smaller all the time.

Interviewer All right then. Thank you very much, Patrick. You've been very helpful.

UNIT **8**

LEARNING

Judy Close the door, will you, please, John? Well then, let's see. What do you think about the idea of spending the morning at the local museum? It's, er, what we've done before, very often, and, er, it's always been very popular, hasn't it, John?

Maria But don't you think it might be a bit boring for some people?

John (*laughs*) I see what you mean, but in fact, you know, it isn't one of those stuffy old places with bits of old vases and coins and so on. It's really presented in a very interesting way. Above all, I think students find they really *learn* a lot about Britain and the British way of life. I'd do a bit of preparation in class, you know, so you know what to expect.

Maria Well, I can go along with that, then. Er, one of my fellow students has suggested that we spend a couple of hours on the beach, if the weather's nice.

Judy Oh, that can't be meant seriously, can it?

John Quite. You don't have to have a special outing to go to the beach, do you? You do it every day anyway.

Maria Okay, we'll skip that, then. Er, some people want to go and see the castle. How do you feel about that?

John Oh yes. It's a most impressive place, and you get a really marvellous view of the surrounding countryside and coastline.

Judy Let's put that down for the early afternoon, then, shall we, and then, er, what about a cricket match?

Maria Oh, no! If you ask me, cricket's the most boring activity ever invented.

John Oh, it is, is it? Well, I don't agree. But I suppose in a way you're right—most of the students would find it a bit slow and difficult to follow. Er, we could go to the cinema instead— what do you think about that, Maria?

Maria That's something else we can do any time, isn't it?

Judy I couldn't agree more. And anyway, the budget won't run to twenty-five cinema tickets, not if you're going to be able to do anything else during the day. But we could ask the brewery to give us a guided tour— it went down very well last year.

Maria That sounds good. Do we get free beer, too?

John 'Fraid not. But I agree—a very good idea.

Judy Well, that's that, then. I'll see to all the arrangements, if you two make sure that everyone's outside the school at 9 o'clock. Thank you for coming along.

Maria Thank you.

John Bye.

UNIT 9
WORK

Interviewer Hello. My name's Hudson. Dick Hudson.

Applicant I'm Pamela Gable.

Interviewer Well, take a seat, please, Miss Gable—it is Miss, isn't it? Thought so. Well, let me just check that I've got these particulars right. Your surname is Gable, spelt G–A–B–L–E, and your first names are Pamela Ann ... Fine. You live at 147 Collingdon Road, Croydon ... your telephone number is 246 8008 ... you were born on July the eighth 1965, and ... that's about it ... OK? Fine ... Let's see ... what are you working with at the moment?

Applicant I'm the personal assistant to the manager of a modelling agency.

Interviewer Oh, really? And what does that involve?

Applicant A bit of everything, really. I have to keep the accounts, write a few letters, answer the telephone, look after bookings and engagements and that sort of thing.

Interviewer You work with people a lot, do you?

Applicant Oh yes. I have to look after all the models who work for us, you know, keep them happy, lend an understanding ear to their heartaches, you know.

Interviewer Have you ever done anything to do with hotels or conferences—hotel management, for instance?

Applicant No, not really. I did work for a short time as a courier for a tour operator, taking foreigners on guided tours of London. Perhaps that's the sort of thing you mean?

Interviewer Yes, I think it is. Do you speak any languages?

Applicant Yes, I do. I speak French and Italian—you see, I spent several years abroad when I was younger.

Interviewer Oh, did you? That's very interesting. And what about any exams you've taken?

Applicant Well, I left school at 16. You know, there didn't seem to be any point in staying on somehow; I was sure I could learn much more by getting a job and a bit of experience and independence.

Interviewer So you have no formal qualifications at all? I see ... Well, I don't suppose it matters.

Applicant Um ... I was wondering if perhaps you could tell me a bit more about the job? You know, it said in the ad that you wanted a go-ahead girl with car and imagination, but that's not very much to go on.

Interviewer No, it isn't. Well, we run conferences, and your job as conference co-ordinator would be, well, much the same as the one you have now, I suppose. Meeting people, transporting them from one place to another, making sure they're comfortable, a bit of telephoning, and so on.

Applicant It sounds like just the sort of thing I want to do.

Interviewer There is the question of salary, of course.

Applicant Well, my present salary is £8,000, so I couldn't accept any less than that. Especially if I have to use my car.

Interviewer Ah! We have something like £7,500 in mind, plus of course a generous allowance for the car. But look, if I were you, I'd take some time to think about this. Perhaps you'd care to have a quick look round the office here, see if you like the look of the people who work here.

Applicant What do you think I should do then ...? Should I ...?

UNIT 10
THE ENVIRONMENT

Couple in car. Sounds of heavy rain.

Man This is awful. I can't see a thing.

Woman Isn't that a light there? Yes, stop ... it's a policeman. (*winds down window*)

Policeman 'Fraid you'll have to pull over and abandon your car, sir, for the time being. The roads are nearly all blocked.

Man Oh, no. Do we really have to?

We're looking for the B6103 to Canterbury. It's very important.
Policeman Well, you might have a chance, I suppose. If you turn on your radio, they'll be broadcasting the latest information on which roads are open. There's a chance you might be able to go south to Garth, and then east from there.
Woman Thanks, I'll try it. (*tunes radio to the right wavelength*)
Radio announcer . . . and since Garth is 50 feet above sea-level, it's likely to remain unaffected by the flooding. Motorists in the area are advised to make for Garth, though do proceed with caution, because visibility is low and driving conditions are altogether extremely tricky. Er, motorists in Pennington are warned that roads south and east of Pennington are impassable. Do not, repeat, do not attempt to reach Garth by the direct A626 route. Take the B6105 towards Baldeswell instead, and . . . after two miles turn south on to the B6110 which will take you into Garth after about three miles. Compton is now completely cut off . . . er, the B6110 about a mile south of Compton is reported to be under three feet of water. The route south out of Baldeswell is also under water, so motorists in Baldeswell should take the Pennington road, the B6105, and turn right towards Garth after about five miles. Let me just repeat that for those who may have . . . (*radio turned off*)
Woman It looks as though we can make it then, doesn't it?
Policeman Well, it's up to you. Do you see that white car over there? Turn right just the other side of it, and you'll be on the right road. Drive carefully.
Man I will. Thanks very much for your help. Bye.

UNIT **11**
MONEY

Customer Good morning.
Assistant Good morning, sir. Can I help you?
Customer I hope so. I'd like to make a complaint. I bought a cardigan, a rather expensive cardigan, from you last week . . .
Assistant And has there been any trouble with it?
Customer Any trouble! My goodness! Not only is the cardigan completely ruined, but it's also managed to ruin a large number of other very expensive clothes.
Assistant Oh, dear. That doesn't sound too good.
Customer No, it certainly doesn't. First of all, I was out in the garden, and it started to rain. The colour ran. I could *see* the dye dripping from it—absolutely ruined my trousers, shirt, vest, and even my skin was a sort of blotchy purple colour for several days.
Assistant Oh, how awful. But if you'd looked at the label, sir . . .
Customer We'll get to the label in a minute, my good woman. What happened next was that I hung the wretched thing up to dry, and the following morning it was about half its original size.
Assistant Well, I hope you don't mind my saying so, sir, but with all garments of this kind you have to stretch them carefully before drying.
Customer Look here. If you continue to make excuses for this miserable piece of clothing, I shall get extremely annoyed. Anyway, I tried to stretch it, of course, when I saw what had happened, and all the buttons fell off.
Assistant Well, sir, if you use excessive force—
Customer —Excessive force, woman? I shall be obliged to speak to the manager if you continue to insult me in this manner.
Assistant Perhaps you could show me the garment in question, sir?
Customer Yes, of course. Here it is.
Assistant I'm afraid, sir, I don't think you can have bought this here. You see, the label—
Customer —You'd be very unwise to provoke me any further, you know. That label . . . yes, I was going to tell

you about that. The original just came off in my hands, revealing this one, ... er ... made in Hong Kong. I mean, obviously you've been trying to cheat me by putting one of your fancy labels on a cheap mass-produced article.

Assistant I can assure you, sir, that we have the highest reputation for both quality and honesty. I really think you'd do well to put an end to this farce. You're not going to get away with it.

Customer What do you mean? I've never been so insulted in all my life. I shall phone the police. Better still, I shall withdraw my custom. Good day to you.

Assistant Goodbye, sir.

■ **Activity**

1 Here is the Stock Report for Monday, December 12th. The market remained steady last Friday, and at the end of the day prices for all metals were exactly £1.

Our market expert predicts that there will be only small fluctuations, though there may be increased interest in gold. In the long term, it looks as though silver and tin are very good buys. And that's all from today's Stock Report.

2 Here is the Stock Report for Tuesday, December 13th. Yesterday was quite a busy day at the Stock Exchange. Gold was very much in demand, and closed at £1.40. The price of tin increased to £1.05, but there were falls in the prices of silver (to 83p), platinum (95p), and nickel (92p). Copper remained firm at £1.

Our market expert predicts continued increases in gold and tin, and it is thought that the decline in the price of silver is only temporary. And that's it from Stock Report.

3 Here is the Stock Report for Wednesday, December 14th. Prices of all metals except nickel and tin fell yesterday. Closing prices were gold £1.35, silver 79p, platinum 91p, copper 98p, nickel 99p, and tin £1.10.

Our expert predicts a good future for

silver, and it looks as though nickel is on the way up, too. That's all from Stock Report today.

4 Here is the Stock Report for Thursday, December 15th. The market does seem to be strengthening somewhat. Silver recovered yesterday to £1.02, and there were rapid increases in nickel (£1.10) and tin (£1.18). Gold, platinum and copper all fell slightly, to £1.30, 87p, and 95p respectively.

Our market expert predicts considerable fluctuations in the prices of many metals, though it seems that silver and gold are the safest investments at present. And that's all from Stock Report.

5 Here is the Stock Report for Friday, December 16th. As predicted in yesterday's report, there were many dramatic changes in prices. Nickel soared to £1.60, while at the other end of the scale gold plummeted to a record low of 81p. Copper also fell sharply to 65p, while tin ended the day at £1.15. Platinum and silver remained steady at 87p and £1.02 respectively.

Our market expert predicts improved long-term performance for all metals, though there may be a temporary decline in the price of tin. That's all from Stock Report.

6 Here is the Stock Report for Monday, December 19th. Prices dropped last Friday for all metals except copper, which finished at 90p. Tin and nickel were the worst sufferers, with prices falling to 82p and £1.25 respectively. Gold dropped a further 5p to 76p, silver fell to £1, and platinum ended at 82p.

Our market expert predicts further decreases in the price of tin and platinum, though all other metals are expected to improve. That's all from today's Stock Report.

7 Here is the Stock Report for Tuesday, December 20th. Tin plummeted yesterday to a new all-time low, at a price of only 20p a share. Platinum also declined slightly to 80p, while all other prices rose. Gold recovered slightly to 81p, while silver, copper and nickel all rose sharply, to £1.30, £1.20 and £1.50 respectively.

Our market expert predicts that all metals except silver and copper will rise. That's all from Stock Report.

8 Here is the Stock Report for Wednesday, December 21st. There was a sudden surge of interest in platinum yesterday, and it closed at 92p. Improvements were also shown by gold (94p), nickel (£1.60) and tin (30p). Silver and copper fell to 99p and 98p respectively.

Our expert predicts increases for all metals except platinum. And that's it from Stock Report.

9 Here is the Stock Report for Thursday, December 22nd. As predicted in our report yesterday, all metals showed sharp increases, except for platinum, which dropped 20p to 72p. Gold finished at £1.07, silver at £1.15, copper at £1, nickel at £1.80, and tin at 75p.

Our market expert predicts continued increases, especially in gold and silver, though it seems unlikely that nickel will maintain its high price, and platinum is still weak. That's all for today from Stock Report.

10 Here is the Stock Report for Friday, December 23rd. Yesterday was a day of extremely dramatic price fluctuations. Tin soared to a record price of £1.80, gold and silver continued their steady rises of the last few days, ending at £1.55 and £1.52 respectively, copper improved marginally to £1.03, while platinum fell slightly to 68p. As predicted, the price of nickel dropped to £1.10.

And that's all from the Stock Exchange for this season. We hope you've all managed to make a fortune.

UNIT **12**

THE NEWS

A busy street.
Interviewer Excuse me, madam, sir, I wonder if you'd spare a moment to answer a few questions.
Woman Well ... I don't know ... Er, what's it about?
Interviewer I work for a company called M.R., er, Market Research, and we're doing a survey on behalf of a well-known daily newspaper to find out what sort of news people are interested in, er, how people react to different types of news.
Man Which paper's that?
Interviewer I'm afraid I can't tell you. You see, it might influence the way you, er, react.
Woman Well, why not, George? We're not in any particular hurry.
Interviewer Oh, good. Well, I'm going to read a few brief news items and I want you to react to them in as normal a way as possible, as if you were reading the paper at breakfast, or watching the telly. OK? Well, here's the first item. *Buckingham Palace announced today that the Princess of Wales is expecting a baby.*
Man Oh, I think that's great. She's such a lovely girl, isn't she? I'm very keen on the royal family, you know.
Woman Well, so what, I say. To be quite honest, that sort of thing leaves me cold—there are thousands of babies being born every day.
Interviewer Fine. Thank you. Now for the next piece of news. *After only two days of talks, representatives of the Employers' Association and the trade unions have come to an agreement on wage levels for the coming year.*
Woman Well, I never! Someone must have given them a kick up the pants or something, because normally that lot do nothing but sit around and talk, as far as I can see.
Man Thank goodness for that, is what I say. I mean, it's not good for the country with all these strikes, and nobody knowing how much they're going to get, or if their job's safe.
Interviewer Right. Now the next one. *Rod McNeary, leader of the popular music group 'Soft Angels', is to make a personal appearance tomorrow night at the Town Hall in a charity performance*

on behalf of handicapped children.

Man Who is!? Rod McNeary!? Wow! That's sensational! I've been wanting to see him in the flesh ever since the great song he made—what was it called, Mabel?

Woman Haven't a clue. You're so childish, aren't you? I mean, it really makes me cross, I mean, it's all for publicity, isn't it? Just to make a few extra pounds. Charity! Huh!

Interviewer Very good, very good. And there's just one more news item. *Paul Coggan, the local centre forward and top goal-scorer of the season, will be unable to play in the match on Saturday, owing to an injury.*

Man What a shame! We really need to win that match, you know.

Woman Just our luck, isn't it, when an important cup match comes up. We haven't got much of a chance then, have we?

Interviewer Well, thank you very much indeed. You've been most helpful.

Woman Oh, not at all. Was it all true, those news items you read out ...?

UNIT 13
MACHINES

A board meeting.

Chairman Thank you all for coming along. I must stress the secrecy aspect of what we're about to hear. Any leaks to the press or general public could have catastrophic effects. Do I make myself clear?

The rest (*mumbled*) Sure/Quite clear/Fine/Yes, etc.

Chairman Good. Mr Jarvis is the director of the technical development team, and he will give you the overall picture. Mr Jarvis ..

Mr Jarvis Well, I'd like you all to imagine a pane of ordinary window glass. Light strikes one of the surfaces, travels through the glass, and is emitted from the other surface. At the same time, this other surface is receiving light signals from objects on its side, and passing them through the glass to be emitted from the first surface. Both surfaces act, in fact, as simultaneous receivers and transmitters. I hope that makes sense. (*Mumbles of 'Fine' etc.*) Now, suppose that you insert an object, say a sheet of paper, between the two surfaces; all that observers on either side can see now is the paper—the light from the opposite side is blocked out. Now we connect up the two surfaces so that the light that enters from one side is carried by, say, electronic means to the opposite surface and emitted there as if it were the original signal, if you follow my meaning. Let me put it another way. The observer can now see what is on the other side of the glass. He cannot see the sheet of paper. In other words, the paper has become ... invisible.

Chairman (*pause*) Get on with it, Jarvis.

Mr Jarvis Well now. Suppose we move the two surfaces slightly further apart and put a man in there, or a building, or a tank, or a whole army. I'm sure you can all see the possibilities.

Woman Do you really mean to say this can be done with ordinary glass?

Mr Jarvis No. Unfortunately, or perhaps fortunately, this is not possible. We have developed a new substance which we call Phloxitron.

Man Pardon? How do you spell that, please?

Mr Jarvis Phloxitron. P–H–L–O–X–I–T–R–O–N. I'm afraid I'm not at liberty to reveal how it is manufactured, or what it's made of, but I can say that it is extremely light-sensitive, and it also has the property that it can transmit (*background noise of coughing*) light signals that are passed to it electronically.

Man I'm sorry, I didn't quite catch that last part.

Mr Jarvis Well, I think the best thing for me to do would be to hand out a brief description of the process, and then we'll see if anyone has any questions. I would just like to point out something as a demonstration of what Phloxitron can achieve: if you look carefully down towards that end of the room, you'll see that there's a sort of shimmering effect, with a slight mistiness near the walls. That is Phloxitron. There are in fact three men sitting there with a mass of electronic equipment, tape recorders, computers and so on, between you and the sofa that you can see there. If I just throw this switch, the Phloxitron will become neutral, and the men will become visible. There.

(*Gasps of astonishment from everybody.*)

Chairman Thank you, Mr Jarvis. Well? What do we do with it?

UNIT **14**
POLITICS

A party political meeting.

Candidate Well, that's all I have to say. Thank you very much for your attention, ladies and gentlemen. It's always stimulating to talk to such an appreciative audience. (*Laughter, boos, rubbish, etc.*) If anyone has any questions, I'll do my best to answer them.

1st questioner What are you going to do about all of us that haven't got jobs? (*Yeah! Boo! Sit down! etc.*) I've been out of work for three years, and . . .

Candidate Thank you very much. This is, of course, one of our top priorities. I have every intention of making sure that when we get into power every possible step is taken, first of all to halt the increase in the unemployment figures, and secondly to provide a meaningful and worthwhile job for every man and woman in the country. (*Hear! Hear! Rubbish! etc.*) And I feel quite confident that our policies will bring this about within the foreseeable future. Now are there any more questions?

2nd questioner What about the traffic congestion in the centre of town? All that heavy through traffic is ruining business for small traders like myself.

Candidate I'm glad you brought that up. As you may know, my own father is a grocer, and so this is a topic that is very important to me personally. I think that in these days of falling oil prices and increased technology, and when so many people are concerned with the problems of the environment, it's essential that each one of us realises the responsibility we all have in the fight against pollution and in the preservation of our cultural and social heritage. We must hope for better times. And, more importantly, we must do everything in our power to achieve those better times.

3rd questioner Are you going to do anything for the old age pensioners?

Candidate Of course we are. The retired people of today are the people who built this country, who made it what it is. And to be quite honest, I have my doubts about the present government's ability or willingness to tackle this problem. Vote for me, and a better deal for all old age pensioners.

4th questioner What do you intend to do about the hooligans, then, the kids that go around smashing things up because they haven't been educated to do anything better with their time?

Candidate This is obviously a very serious and difficult problem. Now I don't want you to get the wrong idea— there are thousands of well-meaning, respectable teenagers, and it is my firm conviction that they are in the majority. The trouble is caused by a handful of violent and well-organised louts, and we have no intention of letting them get away with it. (*Cheers, hisses, boos, etc.*) Well, thank you very much again for coming along. Vote for me, and a better future for old and young alike. Thank you. (*Cheers, boos, etc.*)

UNIT **15**
THE FUTURE

At the crystal ball.

Fortune-teller Come in, dear. Come in and sit down. Don't be nervous. There's nothing to worry about.

Client Thank you. No . . . er . . . shall I sit here?

Fortune-teller That's right, dear. Now then. Oh, you *are* nervous, aren't you? Is there any particular problem you have, anything in particular you want me to find out about?

Client It's my ... girlfriend. I'm worried sick ...

Fortune-teller Left you, has she? Gone off with someone else?

Client How did you know? Yes, she just ... left. Without a word. I'm terrified that she's found ... someone else.

Fortune-teller There, there! It's not the end of the world. Let's turn the lights down a bit, and see what the crystal ball has to say. Three toads in a hole of mud, mixed with a pint of lizard's blood. Ah! now it's coming ... Your girlfriend—she's fair-haired?

Client Yes, can you see her?

Fortune-teller And is she ... er ... medium height?

Client Well, quite tall, actually.

Fortune-teller Ah, yes. She is sitting down. She's waiting for you.

Client Where is she? Let me see her.

Fortune-teller Calm yourself. There's no reason to be alarmed. She's beckoning to you ... she wants you ... she longs for you. But wait! There is a cloud, a dark cloud on her brow. You are approaching. Her hand goes up in horror. You have another girl.

Client What? Me? Another girl? I don't know any ... other ...

Fortune-teller With dark hair. A young, pretty girl.

Client Oh, my goodness. Is she wearing glasses?

Fortune-teller Yes, she is.

Client It must be June. But she's not my ... I've never ...

Fortune-teller Ah, but you will. Very soon.

Client But how ...? I don't ...

Fortune-teller Now the picture is changing ... I see children on your knee—one, two, three, four, five, six.

Client How many? When is this ...? When ...?

Fortune-teller It takes time, my dear. You are the happiest family in the world; you are rich and famous ...

Client But who is the mother?

Fortune-teller She is hidden in the shadows.

Client I don't want to get married to June. I want my girlfriend back. Oh, if only I'd been nicer to her ...

Fortune-teller A few extra pieces of silver will persuade her to come out of the shadows, I'm sure.

Client Pardon? Oh, I see, yes. Here you are. Is that enough?

Fortune-teller Ah, now her face is becoming clearer. Is she dark-haired?

Client No, she can't be. Here—more silver ... please ...

Fortune-teller No, it was a trick of the light. She is a tall girl with fair hair ... it is your girlfriend ...

Client Oh, what a relief! How can I ever thank you?

Fortune-teller The pleasure is all mine, my dear. Goodbye and good luck. Next!

ACKNOWLEDGEMENTS

Many thanks to the teachers of Key English Language Services, Stockholm, for ideas and support.

The publishers are grateful to the following for permission to reproduce copyright material:

Barratt Ltd for their advertisement; Parkway Publications Ltd for an extract from *Buying your Home* Vol. 1, no. 7, August 1983; Times Newspapers Ltd for an extract from 'Warning: holidays can damage your health' by Julie Davidson published in *The Times* of 6 August 1983, an extract from 'Critics' choice' by Anthony Masters and Irving Wardle published in *The Times* of 27 August 1983, the list of contents from *The Times* of 14, 21 and 28 September 1983, a selection of short front page articles published in *The Times* of March – September 1983 and an extract from 'Living space' by Tony Osman from *The Sunday Times Colour Magazine* of 31 July 1983; the Controller of Her Majesty's Stationery Office for specimen pages from a British passport; P & O Cruises Ltd for an extract from their 1983 travel brochure; Humberside and South Yorkshire Executive for an extract from 'Fitter ... but not much thinner (yet)' from *The Humberside and South Yorkshire Executive* of July 1983; Skandia Insurance Company Ltd and Professor Per-Olof Astrand for an extract from *Health and Fitness* by Professor Astrand; Faber & Faber Ltd for an extract reprinted by permission of Faber & Faber Ltd from *The Real Thing* by Tom Stoppard; Andre Deutsch Ltd for an extract from *The Senses of Animals and Men* by Lorus and Margery Milne; Penguin Books Ltd for Table 114 from *Facts in Focus* compiled by the Central Statistical Office (p. 136, Penguin Books, Fifth edition 1980) Crown copyright © 1972, 1974, 1975, 1978, 1980, reprinted by permission of Penguin Books Ltd; Equinox (Oxford) Ltd for an extract from *Manwatching* by Desmond Morris; W.H. Allen & Co plc for the back cover and an extract from *The Train Robbers* by Piers Paul Read (1978); Ladybird Books Ltd for an extract from *Your Body* by David Scott Daniel, illustrated by Robert Ayton; Wildwood House Ltd for an extract from *An Index of Possibilities – Energy and Power*; Martin Secker & Warburg Ltd for an extract from *Vintage Stuff* by Tom Sharpe; The Observer News Service for an extract from *The Observer* of 28 August 1983; Hobsons Ltd for an extract from *Your Choice at 17+* by Michael Smith and Peter March; Thames & Hudson Ltd for an extract from *The Doomsday Book* (1970); Collins Publishers for an extract from *TSB Money Guide* by Marie Jennings; Guardian Newspapers Ltd for an extract from the programme guide by Sandy Smithies from *The Guardian* of 28 June 1984; The Foley Agency for an extract from *The Handbook of Psychic Discoveries* by Sheila Ostrander and Lynn Schroeder; Pavilion Books Ltd for an extract © Not the Nine O'clock News Ltd (BBC), taken from *Not the Royal Wedding*, published by Sphere Books; The Labour Party for an extract from an election leaflet 'Programme of emergency action' (1983); Deborah Rogers Ltd, International Creative Management Inc and the authors for an extract from *The 80's – a Look Back* by Tony Hendra, Christopher Cerf and Peter Elbling.

Every effort has been made to trace owners of copyright, but if any omissions can be rectified the publishers will be pleased to make the necessary arrangements.

The publishers wish to thank the following for permission to reproduce photographs:

Barnaby's Picture Library: 130; Camera Press: 44, 105, 117, 166; Format Photographers: 142; Mike Hinton: 91; Jane Munroe: 70, 81; Photobank: 193, 196; The Photo Source: 33, 155, 202; Sporting Pictures: 57; Chris Schwarz: 6; John Topham Picture Library: 20.

Book design by Small Back Room

Illustration by Gecko Ltd